The Voice of the Rural

The Voice of the Rural

MUSIC, POETRY, AND MASCULINITY AMONG MIGRANT MOROCCAN MEN IN UMBRIA

Alessandra Ciucci

THE UNIVERSITY OF CHICAGO PRESS

CHICAGO AND LONDON

The University of Chicago Press, Chicago 60637
The University of Chicago Press, Ltd., London
© 2022 by The University of Chicago
All rights reserved. No part of this book may be used or reproduced
in any manner whatsoever without written permission, except in
the case of brief quotations in critical articles and reviews.
For more information, contact the University of Chicago Press,
1427 E. 60th St., Chicago, IL 60637.
Published 2022
Printed in the United States of America

31 30 29 28 27 26 25 24 23 22   1 2 3 4 5

ISBN-13: 978-0-226-81676-0   (cloth)
ISBN-13: 978-0-226-81869-6   (paper)
ISBN-13: 978-0-226-81868-9   (e-book)
DOI: https://doi.org/10.7208/chicago/9780226818689.001.0001

Library of Congress Cataloging-in-Publication Data

Names: Ciucci, Alessandra, author.
Title: The voice of the rural : music, poetry, and masculinity among
migrant Moroccan men in Umbria / Alessandra Ciucci.
Other titles: Chicago studies in ethnomusicology.
Description: Chicago : University of Chicago Press, 2022. |
Series: Chicago studies in ethnomusicology |
Includes bibliographical references and index.
Identifiers: LCCN 2021047959 | ISBN 9780226816760 (cloth) |
ISBN 9780226818696 (paperback) | ISBN 9780226818689 (ebook)
Subjects: LCSH: Music—Morocco—History and criticism. |
Moroccans—Italy—Umbria—Music—History and criticism. |
Foreign workers, Moroccan—Italy—Umbria. | Masculinity in music.
Classification: LCC ML355.M8 C58 2022 | DDC 782.00964—dc23
LC record available at https://lccn.loc.gov/2021047959

♾ This paper meets the requirements of ANSI/NISO Z39.48-1992
(Permanence of Paper).

For Francesco and Rosa

Blue-eyed Alì,
one of many sons of sons,
shall descend [...]
on sailboats and rowboats. With him
shall be thousands of men
with tiny bodies and the eyes
of wretched dogs of the fathers
on boats launched in the Realms of Hunger. With them they shall bring little children,
[...].
They shall bring their grandmothers and donkeys, on triremes stolen in colonial ports.

PIER PAOLO PASOLINI, *Prophecy*

Contents

Contents

Figures and Tables

Audio and Video Examples

All examples may be accessed on the accompanying website, https://press
.uchicago.edu/sites/ciucci/index.html.

INTRODUCTION

Video example 0.1. Television interview with Abdelaziz Stati

CHAPTER 1

Audio example 1.1. Excerpt from an interview with Mohamed Atir

CHAPTER 2

Audio example 2.1. "L-ḥərraga" performed by Abidat Rma Khouribga
Audio example 2.2. "Mgabəl l-bḥər u tbki" performed by the Ouled Brahim

CHAPTER 3

Audio example 3.1. "Rjal mshat ḥərga" performed by Abdelaziz Stati

CHAPTER 4

Audio example 4.1. "L-ghaba" performed by Shikh l-Bachir
Audio example 4.2. "L-ghaba" performed by Fatna Bent l-Houcine
Audio example 4.3. "L-ghaba" performed by Abidat Rma Khouribga
Audio example 4.4. *Shaʿbi* version of "L-ghaba"

CONCLUSION

Video example 5.1. "L'Couple"

Notes on Names, Transliteration, and Accompanying Website

The conversations on which this book is based were mostly conducted in Moroccan Arabic punctuated by Italian, and other times in Italian punctuated by Moroccan Arabic. In the transliteration of the narratives and of the songs I have tried to follow as much as possible the pronunciation of the words, in an attempt to convey the distinctive character of the vernacular in question. I have also consulted Richard Harrell's *A Dictionary of Moroccan Arabic* (1962), Dominique Caubet's *L'arabe marocain* (1993), and A.-L. de Prémare's *Dictionnaire arabe-français* (1993).

For consonants, I have followed the system used by the *International Journal of Middle Eastern Studies*. For vowels I have diverged from this system, since Moroccan Arabic does not employ long vowels as in standard Arabic. To meet the Moroccan pronunciation, I have used full vowels to represent the phonemic rendering of the Moroccan vowel system. For short vowels, instead, I have introduced the schwa (*ə*) in the transcription, which should be pronounced as a shorter *a*. In addition, *o* should be pronounced as a shorter *u*, and *e* as a shorter *i*.

Hyphens signal the articulation between nouns and their affixes such articles, prepositions, and so on:

- Definite articles before nouns: *l-bit*, the room.
- Prepositions when they are not followed by a vowel: *f-l-bit*, in the room.
- Definite articles as prefixed for proper names: *l-Houcine*.

When the definite article is attached to a consonant made with the front part of the tongue, it is assimilated, repeating the first consonant of the word it accompanies, such as in *ḍ-ḍar*, home. The consonant involved are *t*, *d*, *r*, *z*, *s*, *sh*, *ṣ*, *ḍ*, *ṭ*, and *n*.

When the definite article is a prefixed to a personal name and pronounced as a part of the name, I have capitalized the first letter of the name in the transcription to highlight the name as *l-Houcine*.

When quoting directly from a written Arabic text I have transliterated from standard Arabic. Spellings used by other authors are retained when I reference or quote their publications. The same is true for names and terms that are commonly used in English writing. Finally, because so many French transliterations have become standard, I have chosen to employ these transliterations for place-names and personal names as they more commonly appear in writing.

Throughout the book I present most of my interlocutors by their first names. When I need to distinguish between people with the same name, I include the first letters of their last names and, rarely, their full last names. I do so always with their permission.

All audio and video examples are available on this book's companion website, https://press.uchicago.edu/sites/ciucci/index.html.

Introduction

19 November 2019, Ponte San Giovanni-Umbertide

"They would arrive with few things of their own; but almost always with the plates and hubcaps of the car they bought in Italy and sold back in Morocco in the suq *of the town of Khouribga, and audiocassettes. By the time they made it to the Alta Valle del Tevere, they did not even have a place to sleep. There was an abandoned farm in the village of Montecastelli that housed between forty and forty-five men at a time. They lived there the best they could; that is, without a bathroom, electricity, or running water. They would come and go between Morocco and Italy every three months or so before the* Schengen *[agreement] came into place; afterward they would come with all sorts of visas and permits, and when all else failed, they would clandestinely cross the Mediterranean. Once their visas or permits expired, they would remain in Italy as undocumented, and if they were caught and taken to the frontier at Ventimiglia, they would take the mountain route and walk all the way back to Umbria. They would lie about their lives back home, make up stories that their families were hoping to hear, ashamed to admit to their own conditions. Some of them did well, went back to Morocco, bought land, built a home for themselves and their families; but the majority continued to struggle. The Italians were suspicious—they did not trust them. Around here there is nothing but villages and small towns. People have been living here for generations. They all know one another. Can you imagine? You know what Italians think of Moroccans. It was not the same thing for immigrants from other countries. Nobody would rent them an apartment; it was only in the '90s, after a number of amnesties were put into place to regularize migration, that Moroccans began to settle, and sometime after that Italians started renting them stables but not apartments. It took me a while to get my own studio. The first time I walked in there I thought it was a castle," Abdelilah Am. reveals as "they"*

1

turns into "I." It might be the way he is used to speaking and advocating for "them"; he is the head representative of one of the largest trade unions in Umbria.

"They were coming to Italy to work as itinerant vendors, and in this region, there were two or three people affiliated with the Beni Meskine and the Mzab tribes who managed everything. Moroccans would come looking for them in Umbria; they made everything happen, they took care of everything, helped them get to Italy, provided them with the merchandise they needed, got permits, and even managed to get the local police off their backs. They were well organized: a car would drop itinerant vendors off in different areas and come back to pick them up at the end of the day. It was a sort of caporalato [illegal labor recruitment system often associated with the mafia where intermediaries receive a bribe for their service] but was run in accordance with tribal affiliations. You should have seen the vendors; they would carry all the stuff on their backs like mules. You probably do not know this, but while the Mzabi use the term ḥəmmal—that is a porter, but also a donkey that transports goods—the Beni Meskine use the term ḥlas—a blanket used on the back of a mule, a horse, or other working animal—to refer to these vendors; it is as if they were no longer men." "I remember them, you know?" I tell Abdelilah. "They would walk the beaches in the summer under the scorching sun for hours and hours selling all sorts of goods. They would stop at every beach umbrella, unload their goods onto the sand and talk us into buying anything. We all remember them, but we never got to know them; they are a ghostly presence for us."

"It was only afterward, after regularizing their status, that they began working in the tobacco fields and in construction," Abdelilah continues, "and yet, they made less money than before." "But what about those audiocassettes?" I ask. "They would always bring back songs about l-ghorba [the exile], songs about migrating to Europe. Most of the cassettes were by musicians like Abdelaziz Stati, Mustapha l-Mils, later on Daoudi and so on. All sha'bi *music, but the* sha'bi *from l-'arubiya [the rural, the countryside] of course!*[1] *And then, they had the music of the* shikhat *[professional female singer-dancers], and that is all they would listen to when they would go back at night." "But with no electricity? How could they do so?" "They would play the music on their car stereos. Blast the volume and enjoy the evening among themselves as if they were at the types of ḥəflat r-rajjala [intimate male gatherings] with* shikhat *back home. That was probably the only time that they felt like men once again. Everyone around here still listens to the same music."*

Figure 1. Map of Umbria

This ethnography argues for the significance and the endurance of a specific notion of the rural, the countryside, *l-'arubiya*, in music, poetry and the voice among migrant Moroccan men in the Alta Valle del Tevere in the Umbria region in Italy.[2] I had stumbled onto this local notion of the rural through the vicissitudes of fieldwork more than a decade ago in Morocco, but it was in the context of migration that the experience of the rural reemerged with unforeseen intensity in the compelling tropes used by the men I met in Umbria.

Entangled with a sense of place, longing and belonging, the idea of *l-'arubiya* becomes particularly meaningful in Italy because it also articulates a personhood rooted in a masculinity that is itself problematically perceived and ultimately denied to these men. This book posits that these migrants are able to recover such personhood through what it is commonly referred to as *ṣawt l-'arubiya* (the voice of the rural). It investigates *ṣawt l-'arubiya* as a means for these migrants to reclaim a way of being in the world: through music, poetry, and the voice, they claim a space in contemporary Italy and turn their ears away from an integrationist rhetoric that rejects their difference.

It is at this fraught intersection of words and sound, politics and place, that I attempt to explore the significance of *l-'arubiya* in the precarious lives of these migrants, to capture the emotions conjured by the rural and to recognize the possibilities that the voice offers during a time of profound transformations engendered by migration. It is at the borders of a dehumanizing present, memory, experience, and desire that *l-'arubiya* becomes the privileged medium through which migrant Moroccan men are able to preserve their rural ethos by drawing from the past, the heroic, the erotic and the familiar, to experience wholeness and, in turn, to respond to their invisibility and nonexistence.

The method used for this exploration has become clear to me only in retrospect, for these agricultural laborers and unskilled workers are not performers, nor are they able to experience *ṣawt l-'arubiya* in traditional performance contexts in Italy. Yet, if one listens attentively, music, poetry, and the voice of the rural are ubiquitous in their everyday life. This book therefore attempts to grapple with concepts that emerged during fieldwork through these migrants' tropes, narratives, expressions, humor, and everyday talk, as well as in that which is left unsaid; we have much to learn from listening to their silence and from their stoic postures.[3] Consequently, my writing is shaped by the way in which my interlocutors theorize *l-'arubiya* and the way in which they guided my listening during my fieldwork in Morocco (which began in 2000) and in Italy among migrant Moroccan men (which began in 2015). Grounded in local ways of knowing through sound (Feld 1984), I am interested in engaging with Moroccan terms as "decolonizing exercises" (Fellezs 2019, 7) to unsettle "the philosophical ground for the formation of concepts" (Ochoa Gautier 2014, 122).

This book aims to connect the listening practices of my interlocutors to the way in which *l-'arubiya* unfolds during moments of sociability in Italy and Morocco, that is, when *l-'arubiya* is sensed together at cafés, homes, streets, local markets, stores, restaurant, cars, weddings, and labor union meetings. It aims to disturb the assumption of linearity in migration, temporality, the here and there, and the then and now with an assemblage of moments, memories, and encounters through which it is possible to explore what it means for ṣawt l-ʿarubiya to be "the source of everything." I present fleeting images, narratives, and sounds in an attempt to reproduce the poetic fragments that are at the core of ṣawt l-ʿarubiya—fragments layered with history, allusions, and local knowledge used to strengthen the association with l-ʿarubiya.

> a l-mʿashi wa bti ra sidi sʿid ʿla mul zitunat
> a bti r-rathnani wa l-kafər a sidi ḥsin u rəgraga məjmuʿin
> ya bti l-ghlimi wa ʿauni ra sidi ḥməd l-ʿəṭfa ya bən ʿabbad
> a mul l-ʿlamat wa zin slamat mulay ʿəbdəllah bən ḥsin
> ya l-qadmiri wa bti ra sidi ʿomar ʿla mul ḥəmriya

> l-Mashi, my dear daughter, my lord Said,[4] the owner of the olive trees[5]
> My dear daughter, r-Rathnani, the ungrateful, my lord Hussein,[6] the
>   Regraga[7] have gathered
> My dear daughter, l-Ghlimi, help me, my lord Ahmed,[8] the benevolence
>   of Ben Abbad
> The owner of the banner-bearers, the one with the heartfelt greetings,
>   Mulay Abdellah Ben Hussein[9]
> l-Qadmiri, my dear daughter, my lord Omar,[10] owner of the red soil

. .
.

In contextualizing the deeply felt construction of the rural in the commercial recordings of two interrelated traditional musicopoetic genres—ʿaiṭa and ʿabidat r-rma—and their contemporary renditions, categorized as shaʿbi, I ask how and why the music, the poetry, and the voice of the rural matter when we examine the experiences of these laborers, migrant men reduced to working bodies whose intimate lives have been shamed, silenced, ignored, and analyzed in troubling discourses on sexuality. In this book I attend to how the notion of l-ʿarubiya is voiced, performed, listened to, understood, and experienced in reference to these genres. I follow David Coplan's work among Basotho's migrants, arguing that my purpose is not "simply to tell the story" of migrant Moroccan men in the Alta Valle del Tevere but rather to "articulate social forces and processes with cultural principles, practices, and forms" (1994, 87). Like him, I take seriously the role of consciousness and agency: if we are ever to understand what these migrants are saying, to recognize the content of their messages, it is crucial to explore how they choose to speak and act. For this reason, it is important to focus on the grain and texture of these musicopoetic genres.

'Aiṭa (lit. cry or call) is a musicopoetic genre interpreted first and foremost by professional female singer-dancers (*shikhat*, sing. *shikha*) accompanied by male instrumentalists who, according to regional styles, perform on some combination of *kamanja* (viola),[11] *'ud* (Arab lute), *lotar* or *loṭar* (a three- or four-stringed, semi-spiked plucked long-necked lute with a skin-covered pear-shaped body) (Schuyler 1979, 119–31), *swisdi* (a small two- or three-stringed pear-shaped lute), *məgrunat* (double clarinet), large circular frame drums (*bnader*, sing. *bendir*), small and medium single-headed goblet drums made of pottery (*ta'rij*, sing. *ta'rija*), and a large single-headed goblet drum (*darbuka*). If for practitioners and connoisseurs *'aiṭa* specifically refers to an old repertoire of vernacular *qaṣa'id* (odes, sing. *qaṣida*) that have been orally transmitted since at least the nineteenth century and, implicitly, to the manner of their melodic and rhythmic performance, in actuality *'aiṭa* may best understood as a "complex genre" that may also encompass primary or simple genres (Bakhtin 1981). *'Aiṭa*, in fact, refers to different forms of poetry sung in vernacular Arabic and performed in styles that are identified according to location, musical characteristics, and poetic repertoire. Because a text (*klam* or *naṣṣ*) of *'aiṭa* is essentially made up of independent poetic fragments or units (*ḥəbbat*, sing. *ḥəbba*), what actually distinguishes one type of poetry from another is the manner in which the *ḥəbbat* are organized. As a genre, therefore, *'aiṭa* may be best defined as a historically specific convention and ideal according to which the *shikhat* compose discourse and the audience receives it (cf. Hanks 2000, 135):

- simple exposition of the *ḥəbbat*, commonly indicated by the term *ḥsab* (quantity or calculation), where the poetic units are sung one after the other or with a *lazima* (vocal or instrumental refrain) connecting them;
- short poems (*brawəl*, sing. *bərwala*) consisting of a succession of lines that often share the same meter and rhyme; the poems always employ a *lazima*. Considered the "light" songs of the *'aiṭa* repertoire, these poems are associated with dancing and are usually performed with a rhythm that musicians describe as "light" (*khfif*) or that is suitable for dancing; often, a fast compound duple meter; and
- long poems (*qaṣa'id*), characterized structurally by a succession of *fuṣul* (sections, sing. *faṣl*) containing an irregular number of lines whose syllabic poetic meter and rhyme may vary from one section or line to the next. Each *faṣl* is customarily performed over a different rhythmic cycle and melody and is separated by what might be defined as a refrain (*qəṭib*, pl. *qoṭban*).

'Abidat r-rma (lit. servants of the hunters) is a term that designates an all-male ensemble that traditionally performed for wealthy male patrons during day-long hunting expeditions.[12] As servants and performers, the men of these ensembles played a double role. During the day they were *ḥaiḥaya* (beaters), driving prey toward the hunters while shouting *ḥay ḥay*, accompanied by their dogs; at night they entertained the hunters, recounting the events of the day, imitating the way in which prey ran away, and so forth (Nassiry 2013, 9–10). The ensemble's singing, dancing, acting, and acrobatics—indicated by the same term—are customarily accompanied by an array of percussion instruments: large circular frame drums, single-skin goblet-shaped hand drums, and a sawed-off pair of large scissors (*məqqəṣ*) beaten with a metal rod whose timbre can be modulated by opening and closing the shears, an instrument with a penetrating sound used as the main rhythmic organizing principle. The poetic form of the songs of *'abidat r-rma* is based on the vernacular *qaṣida*.

Although *'aiṭa* and *'abidat r-rma* are closely related, the key distinction between the two is in the voice. As the musicians unequivocally point out, while *'aiṭa* requires the voice of a woman (*ṣawt mra*), *'abidat r-rma* needs a man's (*ṣawt rəjal*). Consequently, if it is true that one should not overlook the presence of male singers in *'aiṭa*, it is also crucial to recognize that some of the most important male performers have embodied the feminine in their appearance and vocality; this was the case with the late Bouchaib Bidaoui, one of the most beloved male interpreters of *'aiṭa*, who sounded like and dressed as a *shikha* in performance.[13]

This book engages one additional genre in discussing *ṣawt l-'arubiya*: *sha'bi* (from *sha'b*, folk, people). Although commonly translated as "popular music," *sha'bi* is more aptly described as a category at the intersection of tradition (*taqalid*), heritage (*turath*), and a notion of the term "popular" as that which "is widely disseminated by the media and well-liked by many people" (Danielson 1988, 142). As a genre that questions Western ontological categories of tradition and modernity in music, *sha'bi* should not be understood as analogous to popular music in the West. As will become clear throughout these pages, *sha'bi* has the capacity to absorb a great variety of local music practices, making them sound contemporary through a variety of techniques (such as recording technologies, rhythms, instruments, as well as the vernaculars) while carefully retaining the aesthetic qualities that mark the tradition that is being reworked. In this sense, the contemporaneity of *sha'bi* appears to reflect the notion of modernity argued by the Moroccan philosopher Mohamed Abed Al-Jabri, for whom modernity means not refuting tradition or breaking with the past but rather "upgrad[ing] the manner in which we assume our relationship to tradition to the level of what we call contemporaneity" (1999, 2).

Because the term *sha'bi* is somewhat multivalent and even ambiguous in the Arab world (Puig 2006), my discussion focuses on *sha'bi* in Morocco where the term—as well as, to a lesser extent, the genre—has been discussed by a number of scholars. Jeff Callen, for example, understands *sha'bi* as "popular" in the sense "of the people" (2006, 31–32); Tarik Sabry posits that it refers to its working-class audience and, implicitly, their listening modes (2010, 54–57); Brian Karl defines it as a meta-genre, as a "highly absorbent and somewhat fluid category of cultural practice that subsumed or intertwined with a great number of other distinct genres or subgenres" (2012, 17); Ahmed Aydoun locates the genre among the urban lower classes, arguing that internal migration, urbanization, and technology have shaped its heterogeneous character (2014, 161–64); while Lhoussain Simour argues for the critical role of *sha'bi* in understanding the heterogeneous character of Moroccan identity (2016, 7–20). In this book, discussion will focus on a style of *sha'bi* that draws from *'aiṭa* and, as such, continues to give voice to *l-'arubiya*.

• •

25 July 2017, Ouled Ziane

One of the masters of Moroccan sha'bi, *Abdelaziz l-Arbaoui—known as "Stati" because of the sixth (sətta) finger on his left hand—lives in Ouled Ziane, a rural commune located about twenty-five kilometers (fifteen and a half miles) southeast of Casablanca. It is not easy to arrange a meeting with Stati, for he is always in demand, particularly in the summer, during the wedding season. But today we are invited to a couscous at his farm.*

Amezzane, a lotar *player from the Middle Atlas and friend of Stati, comes to greet us and escort us inside the huge open space on the ground floor of the recently built farmhouse. Low wall dividers and arched doorways separate each living section: the kitchen from a sitting area, the dining space—furnished with a square wooden table—from an entertainment area equipped with a billiard table, and, last but not least, a Moroccan-style salon. Although wide open, the space feels cluttered, perhaps because it is full of photos and portraits of Stati—reflecting his long and successful career and his authority in* sha'bi *and* 'aiṭa—*or perhaps because there are instruments lying around everywhere. This is the space where Stati practices and hangs out with musicians and friends.*

"Piacere come va? Tutto a posto? Benvenuta!" *[Pleasure to see you, how are you? Is everything OK? Welcome!], Stati says as he invites us to sit down. His salutations in Italian take me by surprise—but they shouldn't. Stati is among the most requested performers in Morocco and in European countries with a strong Moroccan presence. He often performs in Italy and is quick to inform me that he spent some time in Verona. "When?" I asked curiously. "Five, eight, or maybe ten years ago." "See, that is a real 'arubi [a person from the countryside]; look at how he answered!" Hassan Na. points out. "There is a different conception of time in the countryside . . . five, eight, ten years ago, it is all the same. It is not like in Europe." Stati agrees with this characterization of someone whose origins are also from the countryside but, as a public intellectual, is also acutely aware of the problematic construction of l-'arubiya and l-'arubi in Morocco.*

Unlike other musicians I have worked with, Stati is not only used to attention but actively seeks it. When we sit down, he asks me to pretend that I am interviewing him and asks the others to take pictures. I decide to play along, and he hands me a tape recorder that I will never be asked to turn on.

Stati has an interesting relationship with his own fame and status, most apparent in the dialectic between Abdelaziz (l-'arubi) and Stati (the star of Moroccan sha'bi). This dialectic is manifested not only in the way he refers to himself in the third person, but in his use of a third-person point of view in his narrative. If the use of the third person is characteristic of rural parlance, signaling modesty in the avoidance of using the first person, Stati's use adds a different layer. In a recent interview on Moroccan television, when asked what fame took away from Abdelaziz Stati, he commented that Stati took many things away from Abdelaziz. "Abdelaziz was a poor [məskin] and innocent [bari] man who kept away from noise [b'id mən ṣ-ṣda'], but Stati brought him into big problems [mashakil kəbira]. He started to stay up late and took him on planes even though Abdelaziz is scared to fly; Stati forces him on the plane and takes him away. Stati has behaved badly toward Abdelaziz [tkərfəs 'la Abdelaziz]," he concludes in front of a bewildered journalist who fails to understand how the narrative—why, that is, Abdelaziz has quarreled with Stati [kifash Abdelaziz mkhaṣm m'a Stati]—reflects the ways in which Stati experiences the split between a traditional and a contemporary sense of personhood (video ex. 0.1).

I seize the opportunity of the fake interview to ask Stati about the role of l-'arubiya in his music. "Music comes from nature [ṭəbi'a]; people have always sung about it. People sing about a sentiment [ḥsas] and then they put it into music. It is like the verse 'he has the beauty, he has the pigeon in his home' ['andu z-zin 'andu l-ḥmam dairu fi daru]." Stati cites the title to a traditional song performed by female groups entertaining all-women parties at family celebrations, a song that is now interpreted by many sha'bi *singers in Morocco. All present agree: "Now everyone sings it!" Stati continues, "We have taken everything from* l-'arubiya. *The voice of the rural [ṣawt l-'arubiya] is at the source of everything."*

∴

This book focuses on the multiple notions intertwined in the Arab concept of *ṣawt*. This term, which Arab grammarians use to describe the resonance emitted from the chest (as distinguished from *nafsa*, exhalation), is a fundamental concept used to designate sound, voice, and song. Despite the elasticity of the term, I will use "voice" in accordance with the way that my interlocutors do. There is a long-standing tradition in Arab theoretical writings on the aesthetic and the production of voice, for which there is a rich terminology used to classify and judge vocal qualities against specific ideas about beauty and perfection (see al-Fārābī 1934; d'Erlanger 1930–59; Shiloah 1963 and 1991; Al-Kātib 1972; Sawa 2004 and 2019; Reynolds 2020). With respect to more contemporary debates on the voice in the Arab world, Philip Schuyler has described how the beauty of a rough voice in Sana'ani song in Yemen is evaluated in reference to the "sincerity" of a performance and the respect for the text (1990–91, 59). Virginia Danielson has discussed how specific vocal colors of Umm Kulthum were closely linked to the sound and meaning of the text and the way in which they heightened its emotional impact, allowing listeners to feel the meaning of words (1997, 93 and 139). Similarly, Ali Jihad Racy (2003) and Jonathan Shannon (2006) have also noted the impact of timbre in conveying a text, in allowing audiences to "taste" the words.

Beyond the acoustic properties of voice, scholars have also commented on how a voice that is valued cannot be disentangled from a singer's ability to enunciate the text properly, linking this ability to those singers trained in Qur'anic recitation and other Islamic aural practices where sound and meaning converge (Nelson 1985; Hirschkind 2006). The sound of that which is considered a beautiful voice, therefore, is intrinsically connected to a good enunciation of texts and, in turn, to the value placed on pronouncing classical Arabic, the language of the Qur'an and of other Islamic aural practices.

Voice, as Ochoa Gautier argues, works on a double register: it refers to its acousticity and to an ideology of language (2014, 97), since language is always linked to power (Barthes 1978). This double register, in turn, allows voice to be "recognizable as a generalized figure of a certain type" (Keane 2011, quoted in Ochoa Gautier 2014, 97). In this book I am interested in investigating what *l-ʿarubiya* "is supposed to invoke, provoke, and incarnate," and, again following the work of Ochoa Gautier (2014), I explore how these migrants "acoustically embody" *l-ʿarubiya*. Understanding the significance of a vernacular Arabic rooted in place and a vocal timbre that is thought to be unaffected by urban influences allows us to explore how *l-ʿarubiya* is embedded in a set of aesthetics that is said to reflect rural life, the land, the environment, the peasants' hard work, and their verbal expressions (Ciucci 2012a).

Maria Sonevytsky argues that a performance of *avtentyka* in Ukraine is evaluated by how successfully a singer conveys rurality, sonically rendered through the unmistakable timbral quality of a voice that performs "wildness" (2019). In this book I explore how the use of a full-throated voice that Moroccans describe as rough or coarse (*ḥarsh*) performs a particular notion of the rural. I explore how Moroccans from the plains and plateaus conceive of the voice as a sonic phenomenon in which they perceive timbre as central because it acoustically embodies nature, the environment, and experiences of space, time, and memory. Moreover, I demonstrate how voice is used as a privileged medium to differentiate the rural and the often nonliterate population from the urban lettered elites; voice, as Amanda Weidman demonstrates, has "the capacity to be both iconic (able to embody particular qualities) and indexical (able to point to or index particular subjectivities or identities)" (2014, 40). It is in this context that I am especially interested in a detailed analysis of the poetic language of *ʿaiṭa* and *ʿabidat r-rma* anchored in the vernacular.

Drawing from the work of Amanda Weidman, I also explore the concept of "ideologies of voice" (2014, 45) to examine ideas concerning the practices of singing in relation to local gender narratives. Manhood is central to *ʿaiṭa* and *ʿabidat r-rma*—although differently invoked and expressed—and embedded in the performance of the rural. The sound, poetry, and gestures of these genres celebrate a sense of self, embedded in the countryside through codes and conventions that participants understand and share.

Just as the poetry conjures up local images, history, and tradition, the gestures evoke a personhood associated with the sensory and the erotic, with the land, nature, passion, and desire, and with the historic battles of Arab horsemen (Ciucci 2012a and 2017). I argue that performing *ʿaiṭa* and *ʿabidat r-rma* allows the imagination and creativity to arouse and reconstruct a sense of the rural and manhood that is muted in Italy. I engage with the work of Marc Schade-Poulsen (1999) on the role of songs and masculinity in the contexts of *raï* music in Algeria and, more particularly, with the work of Louise Meintjes on the production of masculinity in song and dance in South Africa (2017).

As a trope of social identity and cultural style, the rural marks *'aiṭa* and *'abidat r-rma*. The rural provides the link between verbal art, everyday language, aesthetics, and ideological and moral discourse, as well as distinctive forms of sociability that emerge in performances. As a trope of cultural, sonic, and musical essence, *l-'arubiya* refers to the historical ties of my interlocutors to rural values and ways of life. It is in this context that I engage with work on the relationship between music, voice, and the rural by Aaron Fox (1997), Alexander Dent (2009), and Alex Chávez (2017), although I recognize crucial differences. Unlike the *el rancho* trope in Mexico (Chávez 2017), *l-'arubiya* has never been the geographical landscape where nationalism situated its essence in music—rather, it is the landscape whose sound the nation has marginalized; unlike Brazilian rurality and its musicality (Dent 2009), *l-'arubiya* does not evoke an ideal country past over a debased urban present, nor is it associated with an actual revival.

Building on the work of Steven Feld and Keith Basso (1996) and on more recent anthropological literature on the senses (Porcello, Meintjes, Ochoa Gautier, and Samuels 2010), I describe a particular way in which *l-'arubiya* involves the senses. I look at how the rural is voiced, evoked, imagined, described, symbolized, employed, understood, listened to, and circulated through live and mediated performances, listening practices, and discourses. I register a full range of discursive and nondiscursive modes of expression through which the rural is articulated, and, in doing so I trace how *l-'arubiya* is connected to social imagination and practice, to memory and desire, and to dwelling and movement.

In this book I draw inspiration from Chávez's work on music and migration, which presents sound ideologies as "instructive in understanding how migrants live in and hear the world" (2017, 11). I sketch strategies that might orient the reader to the possibilities that these migrants enter when they listen and discuss the music, poetry, and voice of *l-'arubiya*. I understand *l-'arubiya* as a tradition whose "apt performance" (Asad 2009, 20) must be constantly debated. I draw from Talal Asad, who posits that tradition consists of discourses aiming to instruct practitioners about the correct form and purpose of a given practice attuned to "discourses [that] relate conceptually to a *past* [. . .] and a *future* [. . .], through *a present*" (2009, 20).

The people who appear in these pages, through poetic and sonorous fragments interpreted by a gendered voice and experienced as embodying *l-'arubiya*, claim an alternative sense of space in the Italian present, assert a creative force in the experience of movement and emplacement, and recover a personhood interrupted at the border. By grappling with a notion of the rural that is both intensely local and part of a transnational network, I aim to provide a different point of entry to explore critical questions about migration and belonging.

To place *l-'arubiya* at the center of an ethnomusicological analysis means examining how a particular migration responds and repositions itself in reference to the formation of twenty-first-century Europe through a construct of the rural whose resonances continue to be meaningful in the everyday lives of migrant Moroccan men in the Alta Valle del Tevere. The main questions driving this book concern not only how we can listen to *ṣawt l-'arubiya* or understand its significance for migrant Moroccan men, but also why it is important to do so. Ultimately, this book thinks critically about the centrality of *ṣawt l-'arubiya*, arguing about its role in shaping a different sense of geography, belonging, and self within the borders of Italy and Europe through migration.

∴

1 June 2019, Ponte San Giovanni-Umbertide

We always meet at the train station in Ponte San Giovanni, a suburb of Perugia built in the 1960s to accommodate the thousands of Italian peasants who were then migrating from the poverty of the Umbrian countryside. Ponte San Giovanni is now one Perugia's largest and most diverse neighborhoods, and it has a new class of migrants, a new class of stranieri (foreigners), that has little in common with the student population at the University for Foreigners in Perugia.

We stop by a butcher shop where a man in his early forties from the town of Ben Ahmed welcomes us from behind the counter. He is known to have fresh halal meat and other Moroccan products in his store. Today Nidal and Luisal have asked their father to buy Moroccan olives, which are not always easy to find.

The butcher comments on the cancellation of a weeklong event that was to celebrate Moroccan culture with horses and riders, music, food, a fashion show, and more. Organizing events like these is no easy task: there are issues with visas and permits, and bribes are expected on both sides. Such events used to take place more frequently, when there was money and an actual interest in promoting or a will to promote so-called interculturalism, but that moment seems to be gone, at least in this region. Abdelilah Am. worries about the lack of infrastructure for migrants, and I share his concerns.

Figure 2. Tobacco plantation in the Alta Valle del Tevere

Photo by Omino Rosso

The Tiberina is the longest freeway in Italy; it connects Terni to Ravenna, passing through the Alta Valle del Tevere. The view of villages and small towns emerging from the greenery of Umbria is breathtaking, even when looking from the window of a moving car: Ponte Felcino, Villa Pitignano, Civitella Benazzone, Solfagnano, Tavernacce, and so on. We are on our way to Umbertide, driving past a territory where there are more than 450 farms cultivating tobacco in about 6500 hectares that produce 20,000 tons of Virginia Bright for Philip Morris and Japan Tobacco. The fields are empty now, and the workers have gone home; from afar, where one might not know what one is actually seeing, the color of the leaves is stunning. Umbria's greenery is complicated.

In contrast to the popular image of Umbria as a hilly landscape, Umbertide is flat. As we enter the town's limits, family homes and low residential buildings begin to appear on one side of the road, train tracks on the other. As we drive toward the center of town, before the Tiberina turns into Via Garibaldi, houses, bars, stores, and restaurants begin to crowd the roadside, together with food cooperatives and small businesses turning out products considered to be typical of Umbria: ceramics, grain mill products, truffles, wine, and olive oil. But it is the other side of the

*Tiberina that catches my attention: the industrial zone of Madonna del Moro, where small and large industries of machinery manufacturing, carpentry, metal manufacturing, metal recycling, industrial pavement, and metalwork follow one another until we arrive at the Metalmeccanica Tiberina, an important group that manufactures car components for Italy and abroad. Like the rest of the Alta Valle del Tevere, Umbertide has been described as a "urbanized countryside" (*campagna urbanizzata*), where a network of small industries, or "light industrialization" (*industrializzazione leggera*), came into being as the countryside was increasingly abandoned by Italians (Grasselli, Musotto, and Sediari 2006).*

Umbertide is one of the largest towns in the region, with nearly seventeen thousand residents, and 15.4 percent of the population consists of migrants. Of these, 31.4 percent are Moroccans;[14] *they represent the largest community. These are big numbers for a town, numbers that signal an important demographic shift. It is hard to miss the presence of the people behind the numbers, and the invisible wall separating them from the Italians.*

The green of Umbertide is a different shade from that of *Umbria verde* (green Umbria), the image of the region created by sixteenth- and seventeenth-century European travelers, crystallized by Carducci in a nineteenth-century poem praising the landscape of the region, and turned into a stereotype by the Fascist regime in the twentieth century (Covino and Gallo 1989, 75). It is that bucolic green, rather than the green of Umbertide, with all its contradictions, that forms the basis of a successful tourist slogan *cuore verde d'Italia* (green heart of Italy).

Aaron Fox describes the countryside in rural Texas as a bizarre and paradoxical landscape where the "folkloric pastoral and the apocalyptic postindustrial" are confusingly intertwined (2004, 76), while Kevin Fellezs argues that the countryside in Hawai'i obscures the "apocalyptic postindustrial" (2019, 100). Umbria's greenery is likewise complex and historically problematic rather than idyllic and intact. This is especially true when it is used to emphasize a specific memory and sense of tradition as a means of obscuring the industrial reality—in addition to Umbertide, the city of Terni is an important site for the steel industry and Perugia is famous for its confectionery industry—to erase *mezzadria* (sharecropping) and antifascist struggles, and to romanticize a region historically marked by the backwardness of its agriculture, agrarian crises, economic stagnation, and marginalization, not to mention the changes that a mass exodus of rural Umbrians brought to the region beginning in the 1950s (Covino and Gallo

1989, 115–18). In this sense, the slogan "Umbria verde" has been quite consistent with the idea of insulating the region from modern contamination, even in the face of processes that have radically transformed Umbria over the course of the twentieth century.

> "Green heart of Italy" is chosen as a concise self-portrait, where "heart" alludes not only to the geographic center of the country, but also to the possession of most authentic traditional national characteristics, at least for what concerns central Italy, which, with Rome and Florence, constitutes the most representative area of the country; "green" evokes the natural environment as the dominant component of the landscape [. . .] substantially preserved from aggressive urbanization and therefore to be understood as still "intact." (Giacchè 1989, 502)[15]

As early as the 1960s Umbria was a rather urbanized society. As migrant peasants began congregating in the urban peripheries, those who remained in the countryside witnessed the end of the *mezzadria* and an unprecedented expansion in large-scale commercial farming. It was at this time that the major agribusiness activities with national and international distribution networks—wine, tobacco, and olive production—began (Covino and Gallo 1989, 118–19).

Umbria experienced a series of critical transformations over the next few decades. While throughout the 1970s it had raised the standard of living of its rural and semirural populations to an unprecedented level, surpassing the national averages, and had experienced a major industrialization and transformation of agriculture, from the 1980s until the end of the twentieth century the mixed economy and social welfare apparatus were challenged by the expansion of a global capitalism that caused a deindustrialization of the region and an overall decrease in the standard of living (Bracalente 1989, 451–94).

Since the global movement of capital and products went hand in hand with the movement of people, migrants from North Africa arrived in the 1980s and 1990s, causing an important demographic transformation and dramatic changes in the workforce. As these new migrants turned into a labor force that would work at a fraction of the pay asked by local workers, Umbria's large-scale commercial agriculture—particularly its olive and tobacco farms—became the almost exclusive domain of migrant workers. Construction, light industry, and restaurant work were also taken over by these underpaid migrants, who in turn became the new locus of an emerging racialized poverty in the region. This development marked an important break with that which was thought to be the cohesive social model of the previous decades: as Umbrian poverty acquired an increasingly foreign dimension, a particular sense of solidarity began dissipating, and the difficult plight of migrant workers drew little of the concern that had once been afforded to the locals employed in the fields. Racist and xenophobic attitudes soon emerged in a region whose economic growth, even now, is inferior to that of the rest of Italy (Papandreu 2005, 235–37).

Trapped by its greenery, Umbria has in recent decades reimagined itself through the staging of "tradition" at festivals and historical reenactments associated with the Middle Ages and Renaissance; this is a cultural and political decision that is particularly significant in the face of migration. Behind this problematic reinvention and its rhetoric,[16] an angry and disillusioned majority unequivocally comments on the mere presence of migrant bodies as threatening specific ideas about Umbria, Italy, citizenship, and belonging in the twenty-first century. The victory of a far-right coalition in the regional elections in 2019 has confirmed how "green Umbria" has outlasted even "red Umbria" (*Umbria rossa*), which, from the 1930s, had strongly supported left-wing parties, particularly the Communist Party.

It is at the dawn of the political changes that began in the first decade of the twenty-first century that I situate my research with migrant Moroccan men in the Alta Valle del Tevere, among the documented, the undocumented, the seasonal, the transient, and even the few who managed to obtain a "red" passport, that is, an Italian passport. I knew these men before coming to the Alta Valle del Tevere—or, to be more precise, I knew some of their families, friends, and relatives, as well the territory from which the overwhelming majority of these migrants came. In other words, I knew *l-'arubiya*, the territory of the Moroccan Atlantic plains and plateaus and, in particular, the regions of Casablanca-Settat and Beni Mellal-Khenifra, where I had conducted extensive fieldwork when studying the role(s) of a class of professional female singer-dancers (*shikhat*) at life-cycle celebrations in Morocco (Ciucci 2008, 2010, 2012a, 2012b, and 2017).

⁖

Like the rest of Italy,[17] Umbria became an important pole of migration owing to its low birthrate and, subsequently, the local population's inability to meet the needs of a labor market in which agriculture, construction, and manufacturing have always needed migrants; particularly as a labor force that would work at a fraction of the pay of local workers. It is in this context that tobacco has played a key role in attracting Moroccans to the Alta Valle del Tevere, particularly because this seasonal crop necessitates a large workforce (Duca 1997, 85–127). Scholars, however, have also indicated agnatic solidarity as a critical pull factor that marked the earlier stages of Moroccan migration in Umbria and beyond as predominantly masculine.

> At first, Moroccans came here for seasonal work, such as the tobacco harvest or the construction industry; this type of migration started in the eighties, and it was mostly "agnatic," that is to say, based on groups of brothers or cousins, at any rate masculine, and not [based] on families: when they found more stable work, they began bring over their wives and children. (Giacalone 2003)[18]

It was after the 1973 oil crisis that Moroccans began to arrive in greater numbers in Italy during the summer months to work as itinerant street vendors and agricultural laborers. The oil crisis prompted European governments to halt recruitment, and the ensuing economic recession led to rising unemployment among migrant workers (Berriane, de Haas, and Nattar 2015, 506). These men, almost all of whom were from the countryside of the Atlantic plains and plateaus (particularly from the Casablanca-Settat and Beni Mellal-Khenifra regions), tended to be in their thirties, forties, and fifties and to have little formal education. They were attracted by the prospect of earning what they perceived as good money in a short time before going back to Morocco, a trend that, through family-based migration, persisted well into the 1980s, as more Moroccan men continued to arrive in Italy, consolidating their presence in the territory (IDOS 2013, 9).

Together with Spain, Italy began to emerge as an alternative destination for Moroccans who could travel with relative ease to find informal work.[19] Unique to Italy, in fact, was that until the country joined the Schengen visa regime in 1990, there were practically no norms regulating the arrival or legal status of migrants. This situation facilitated fluxes of migrants employed overwhelmingly in sectors characterized by economic marginality, underdevelopment, and irregularity, as in the case of agriculture, construction, other low-skilled service work and informal commerce (Devitt 2013; de Haas 2014; Berriane, de Haas, and Nattar 2015). Unlike France, Germany, Belgium, or the Netherlands—countries with which Morocco had signed labor recruitment agreements—migration to Italy was never the consequence of a demand from the heavy-industry sector (Campani 2008, 182).

In the 1980s Moroccan migration grew considerably more diversified with the arrival of younger males with higher levels of formal education and skills. They came from the cities of the Atlantic plains and plateaus, ready to take jobs outside of agriculture. Among the new arrivals were students, who enrolled in Italian universities and began working as cultural mediators, educators, and social workers (IDOS 2013, 9–10).

Migration in the 1990s, however, was characterized by the arrival of an increasing number of women, leading to more (but not only) family reunifications, which in turn signaled a more stable population of Moroccans in Italy (IDOS 2013, 10). As the opportunities to enter Italy legally diminished owing to visa restrictions, annual quotas, and the requirement to obtain a contract and a residence permit, migrants were forced to find new ways of reaching their destination. They needed, that is, to acquire the type of know-how that David McMurray refers to as "migration lore" (2001) and Jeffrey Cohen as the "culture of migration" (2004). Part of this new know-how was to take advantage of amnesties (*sanatorie*, sing. *sanatoria*) for undocumented migrants that, until 2012, occurred with each new law or decree on migration.[20] In the 1990s Moroccans were recognized as the largest migrant community in Italy,[21] thanks in part to the 1995 *sanatoria*, of which Moroccans were the major beneficiaries (34,300 people) (Colucci 2018, 20).

Camilla Devitt has summarized the situation that migrants have been confronting in Italy:

> This system of *ex-post* regularization is a reflection of the general functioning of the Italian state and labour market. The state administration's difficulties in planning and enforcement have resulted in a reliance of regularizing *fait accompli* [. . .]. The main recruitment channels in the Italian labour market are informal (i.e., via personal and face-to-face contacts, rather than anonymous, meritocratic systems), and there is, moreover, a large informal economy by Western European standards, which provides employment for irregular migrants. The quota system is also the object of fraudulent applications; in the absence of a genuine job offer, employers request work permits for foreign workers, often following payment by an intermediary in Italy. (2013, 91)

Since 2000, despite Italy's economic troubles, Italians' problematic attitudes concerning the "integration" of Moroccans,[22] and the tightening of laws on migration, the number of Moroccans in Italy has continued to increase owing to the persistence of family reunification and family formation, which became a significant source of new migration from Morocco. Family reunification or family formation, in fact, has been one of the strategies through which Moroccans have continued migrating to Italy, in defiance of increasingly restrictive immigration policies (Gaffuri 2019, 126–29).

Moroccan migrants are distributed throughout the country, but with a larger incidence in the north, particularly in the regions of Lombardia (91,530 or 7.97 percent of the foreign population), Emilia-Romagna

(60,680, or 11.29 percent), Piemonte (53,013 or 12.87 percent), and Veneto (44,837 or 9.23 percent). Often statistically unremarked, Umbria is one of the regions with a comparable incidence of migrants in its territory, if we consider that the 9260 Moroccans legally residing in Umbria constitute 10.02 percent of its migrant population.[23]

If, as has been asserted, the stereotypical image of the economically marginalized, low-skilled Moroccan migrant worker has become less tenable (Berriane, de Haas, and Nattar 2015, 507), it must be considered that statistics of a considerably more heterogeneous character in the last two decades seem to hide a shameful presence, *l-ḥuthala* (the scum), the worst of Morocco, the lowly who migrated to Italy and from whom other Moroccans, at home and abroad, wish to be distinguished (Persichetti 2003a, 30–33). They are described in a popular saying that is unequivocally directed at *l-ʿarubi* (a rural person or someone whose origins cannot be disentangled from the territory of the Atlantic plains and plateaus): *min l-ḥamar ṭ-ṭyara*, from the donkey to the airplane.[24]

Although scholars have acknowledged that the migration of low-skilled workers to Italy and Spain continues to this day (Berriane, de Haas, and Nattar 2005, 506), discussions about "les Marocains du monde" (Moroccans of the world) have emphasized the feminization of Moroccan migration and the transformation of the Moroccan community abroad, of whom "migrant worker" is no longer considered to be an accurate description (Boussouf 2019, 91). In 2018, 34 percent of Moroccans worked in the industrial sector, 33 percent in commerce and restoration, 11 percent in public and social services, 17.3 percent in transportation, and 10 percent in agriculture. A closer look at these numbers, however, reveals that 45 percent of Moroccans continue to work as unskilled manual laborers in the industrial and agricultural sectors, and that, among the new jobs available to Moroccans in 2018, 46 percent were in the service sector, 36.5 percent in agriculture, and 17.8 percent in the industrial sector (ANPAL 2019, 19–25). These numbers highlight the prevalence of Moroccans, surpassed only by Romanians, among migrant agricultural laborers (Magrini 2019, 284).

Moreover, it is important to remember that in 2018 Morocco was ranked third among countries of origin for seasonal migrants; that only 45.2 percent of Moroccans are employed; that the rate of Moroccans who are not in the labor force is 41.7 percent; that 49 percent of the youth is excluded from the labor force; and that, of new contracts for Moroccan workers, 78.5 percent are temporary. In addition, the level of formal education among Moroccan migrants remains relatively low, with more than half of the laborers having at most a middle-school diploma (79.5 percent), 17 percent a secondary-school diploma, and only 3.5 percent a degree that goes beyond high school (ANPAL 2019, 20). In short, non-EU migrants continue to be employed as manual laborers, in low-skilled and unskilled positions, and to receive lower pay than Italians; for this reason, Moroccans are also among the top recipients of welfare among non–European Union migrants (Di Giacomo and Demaio 2019, 279).

These numbers illustrate how the job market operates according to both a functionalist principle (welcoming migrants while they are useful) and a segregationist criterion (welcoming them only if they do not compete for jobs with the locals), effectively excluding professional Moroccan men and severely limiting social mobility (Di Sciullo 2019, 329). Thus, although hidden, silenced, or in the worst case erased, the category of the migrant Moroccan worker continues to be relevant to contemporary Italy, and it is critical that it be considered.

Furthermore, old and new migrants share a similar cultural background because—despite some of the gradual changes I have mentioned—the different waves of Moroccan migrants hailed from the same regions (Casablanca-Settat and Beni Mellal-Khenifra). Alessandra Persichetti unequivocally posits that a certain homogeneity of the migrant population in the Alta Valle del Tevere has been maintained by *catene di richiamo* (chain migration), in which the choice of sponsoring close or distant relative(s) has been dictated by an agnatic solidarity that has allowed the maintenance of a sociocultural homogeneity and sense of personhood (2003a, 147–202), one that, I argue, is entrenched in *l-'arubiya*.

Scholars of Moroccan migration who anchor their work in multiple fieldwork sites in Italy and the Moroccan Atlantic plains and plateaus have acknowledged the importance that origins play in the lives of these migrants and have recognized the endurance of a problematic distinction in Morocco between rural and urban. Their work has analyzed the rural origins of migrants at the intersection with tribal affiliations (Jacquement 1996; Alzetta 2004; Bachis 2009), tribe and kinship (Giacalone 2003; Persichetti 2003a), transnational migration networks (Capello 2008), and socioeconomic marginality (Mescoli 2014; Bianco 2015; Vacchiano 2018). Abdelmalek Sayad's call to consider the migrant also as an *emigrant,* that is, to consider their conditions of origin in order to problematize the partial and ethnocentric trope of adaptation to the host society (2004, 29), has shaped much of this work as well as my own.

In Morocco, the question of origins in migration, and more particularly of Moroccan migration to Italy, has brought to the fore the crucial dilemma of *l-'arubiya* and *l-'arubi.* Thus, notwithstanding some insightful works (Kharaoufi 2004; Harrami and Mahdi 2006), the erasure of *l-'arubiya* from discussions about migration appears to reflect the way in which the rural population of the Atlantic plains and plateaus has historically been perceived.

The urban/rural divide is a powerful paradigm through which Moroccans from the plains and plateaus understand and approach their world. Their discursive division of the countryside and the city serves as commentary on the long history of the economic crisis and the profound economic disparities between rural and urban Morocco. The urban/rural divide has also been critical in the formation of an official national culture from which *l-ʿarubiya* has been historically excluded as backward and unrefined.

Although the division between rural and urban predates colonialism in Morocco, I am interested in how the French Protectorate widened the fissure, with lasting results: rural Moroccans came to be despised and exploited by the urbanites even after independence.[25] The ideological foundations of the Protectorate rested in part upon a representation of Morocco as divided between city and countryside, a representation that was particularly insidious because it was based on problematic French translations of fundamental texts by Ibn Khaldun, giving rise to what Abdellah Laroui came to define as "Khaldunism" (1992). The responsibility of French colonial historiography in the production of the "Arab-Bedouin stereotype" and, in turn, *l-ʿarubi* was aggravated by the devastating effects of colonial agricultural policy in the Atlantic plains and plateaus (Bouderbala, Chraïbi, and Pascon 1974; Daoud and Engler 1981; Swearingen 1987; Davis 2007; Davis and Burke 2011; Sebti 2013). As *l-ʿarubi* came increasingly to refer to the poor and dispossessed peasant, its construction inevitably became entangled with class. This imbrication became even more dramatic with internal rural-to-urban exoduses and the subsequent crystallization of *l-ʿarubi* into the antithesis of the town dweller (*l-mədini*), differentiated in terms of ethnicity, socioeconomic status, mentality, culture, and civilization.

It is this construction of *l-ʿarubiya* and, more particularly, of *l-ʿarubi* that migrant Moroccan men from the Atlantic plains and plateaus challenge at home and abroad. For my interlocutors, *l-ʿarubiya* encapsulates their sense of self and their knowledge of the world. It is a site where a particular expressive culture originates; a constellation of ideas, embodied dispositions, knowledge, experiences, and meanings; a notion grounded in the history of the Atlantic plains and plateaus, entangled with an Arab identity associated with a Bedouin past; an image that destabilizes the French colonial mirage of the "granary of Rome" on the Atlantic plains and plateaus; and an aesthetic that challenges those connected with *al-Andalus* (medieval Muslim Iberia). In short, it is a creative force that questions what has been erased in the image of a nation-state forged by the urban elites, and in an image of Italy increasingly forged by the Global North.

Katherine Hoffman argues that the characterization of Morocco as "mixed"—part Arab, part Mediterranean, part African, and part Amazigh—disregards the historically situated struggles around ethnicity, language, and economic differences, as well as the political factors that shaped them. It raises the question of what "mixed" and "pure" mean on the ground and in people's everyday lives, particularly since dominant discourses around mixing and hybridity claim that ethnicity is grounded in a distant past and shared by all Moroccans in an undifferentiated amalgam of cultural practices (2008, 16). Hoffman, whose analysis also draws from Bauman's "redintegration"—processes oriented toward "preserving, restoring or renewing [a] community's sense of wholeness, however it is locally defined (Bauman, quoted in Hoffman 2008, 17)—discusses the role of expressive culture in mediating constructions of place, personhood, and community in Amazigh rural communities in the Anti-Atlas Mountains of southwestern Morocco. She illustrates how the links between rurality, language, and land are constantly debated and actively nurtured by its residents (2008, 5).

Hassan Rachik, in his discussion of the importance of rurality in studies by Maghrebi scholars and specialists in the Maghreb, reflects on a critical preoccupation: when and under which conditions the fragments of an ancient language completely disappear. Rachik writes that, although "a Bedouin who leaves the plains continues to share his fellow Bedouins' ancient values, and their ancient perceptions of social relations and of space, as well as the knowledge of livestock and plants,"[26] once he becomes a city-dweller a Bedouin learns new values and new ways of perceiving space and social relations. He becomes part of a society in which different traits belonging to different groups can coexist (2019, 232–33). Rachik illustrates his argument through a compelling and moving statement collected during his fieldwork, recounting the way in which the death of Bedouin culture was revealed by an old nomad, whose twenty-year-old son had never seen a camel and whose small children thought that it was the same creature as the cow they saw in their (European-influenced) picture books.

In engaging with a notion of rurality associated with the Arab-speaking populations of the Atlantic plains and plateaus, I share Hoffman's attention to understanding the voicing and construction of a sense of place on the ground and in people's everyday lives in the context of migration. Having a sense of place, as Keith Basso reminds us, is an activity lived collectively, since "relationships to place are lived most often in the company of other people, and it is on these communal occasions—when places are sensed *together*—that native views of the physical world become accessible to strangers" (1996, 109). I also remain attuned to Rachik's important question about when and under which conditions one learns new values and new ways of perceiving space, as

I reflect on the resonances of *l-'arubiya* in these migrants' lives; resonances that continue to echo in music, in both live and mediated performances, although listened to in somewhat different circumstances.

In analyzing the role of *l-'arubiya* in the lives of migrant Moroccan men in the Alta Valle del Tevere, I draw upon these writings and upon David Harvey's concept of "geographical imagination" (1973), which I propose as a way of understanding how my Moroccan interlocutors (1) acknowledge the role of *l-'arubiya* in their biographies, (2) recognize the relationship that exists between them and *l-'arubiya*, and (3) fashion and use this space creatively as well as politically, even when they no longer inhabit it, through *ṣawt l-'arubiya*.

∴

27 July 2016, Spello

Bouchaib Bo. is originally from the countryside near the town of Ben Ahmed; he often sends me pictures of what he calls la mia 'arubiya *(my* 'arubiya*). He has lived in Italy for nearly thirty years now, for the last two decades in Assisi, his wife's hometown. He sells women's clothing at local markets in the region, driving his truck to a different market every day: Monday to Santa Maria degli Angeli; Tuesday, San Terenziano; Wednesday, Spello; Thursday, Petrignano; Friday, Spoleto; and Saturday, Assisi. These small local markets remind him of the itinerant ones found all over Morocco and usually indicated by the day of the week on which they take place:* suq l-hədd *(the Sunday market),* suq t-tnin *(the Monday market), and so forth. Hardworking, generous, and possessed of a sunny disposition, nothing seems to bother Bouchaib. In Assisi he has a small plot of land where he lovingly tends to Moroccan mint, tomatoes, hot peppers, potatoes, apricot and hazelnut trees, and a number of hens that, as he jokingly claims, always hide their eggs because they are ashamed* (si vergognano) *to be seen by him.*

Today we are in Spello, a small, sparsely populated medieval town in the province of Perugia with magnificent Renaissance frescos, Roman ruins, and narrow streets that in the warmer months are full of blooming flowers. Like other towns in the region, Spello emphasizes its medieval and Renaissance past and rustic quality to attract and welcome tourists, but not migrants.

Bouchaib's four daughters have taught him to be patient, but something about his female customers bothers him today. "See how they are?

Figure 3. Bouchaib Bo.

Photo by Omino Rosso

Just look behind you, but carefully." I slowly turn my head. In the im-
provised dressing room inside his truck, two Italian women are trying
clothes on with the curtain left practically open. I gasp, and quickly turn
my head back to Bouchaib. I am embarrassed. He laughs and tells me,
"You have no idea what I have to see, they do not care . . . and I have even
put up a curtain for them. It is as if I do not exist, as if I am one of them
and not a man!"

There are two reasons that I focus on male migrants to the exclusion of
female migrants. First, the voice of *l-ʿarubiya* is deeply entangled with a
construction of masculinity, of what it means to be a "real man" (*rajəl*), defined in relation to a man's courage, his stoicism, the sense of duty he shows
toward his family and his community, the respect he has earned in both the
private and the public sphere, his generosity, his physical as well as moral
strength, and, last but not least, his virility; manhood (*rujula* and *fḥula*) is a
critical dimension of *l-ʿarubi*. Second, because of the role that gender and
sexuality play in the relations between Moroccans and Italians, I aim to situate discourses about masculinity within the larger colonial and imperialist
context that portrays the West as advanced and modernized and the East
as backward and underdeveloped. Sexuality, as Joseph Massad reminds
us, is one of the many indices by which civilization and barbarism can be
classified in colonial projects, since sex was always an important feature of

Orientalist fantasy and scholarship (2007, 6–9). The perceived manhood of *l-'arubi*, in fact, was central to his characterization during the French Protectorate, but also after independence.

In asking how the weight of history presses on particular modes of characterization—that is to say, how contemporary transnational migration in Europe has not only reactivated colonial memories but has also shown how colonialism cannot be confined to a distant place and time—I explore how contemporary modes of proximity reopen prior histories of encounters (Ahmed 2000), tracing the production of difference concerning migrant Moroccan men through a traumatic encounter that has been problematically rearticulated in contemporary Italy.

In this context I examine the unfortunate term *marocchinate* (Moroccan deeds), used to refer to charges of murder, rape, theft, and other acts of violence committed against Italian civilians by the French Expeditionary Corps during World War II. Seventy percent of the Corps was composed of colonial solders from North Africa who fought in central and southern Italy late in the war. Aside from scholarly works on the subject, I also discuss how the nonscholarly treatment of this dramatic and complex wartime scenario has been quite problematic, particularly when contextualized with the rise of neofascist parties.

This is the context in which my interlocutors in the Alta Valle del Tevere are forced to negotiate a manhood that is considered to be an uninhabitable way of being in Italy. This kind of manhood is marked by *marocchinate* and, like that of the migrant Turkish men in Berlin described by Ewing (2008), is perceived as culturally backward, nonmodern, and embodying the manhood of a traditional village man whose honor and reputation are closely linked to those of his female relatives, leading to their oppression.

This book posits that these fetishized migrant men, who preoccupy public discourses and representations, are able to mark their presence and articulate another sense of self through their intimate relations with *l-'arubiya* and its music, poetry and distinctive voice. Drawing on their conception of manhood, on what it means to be a "real man" (*rajəl*), what it means to be "good at being a man" (Herzfeld 1985), in performing a particular but also necessary manhood in the face of migration whose danger is recognized in the loss of one's sense of self and in the risk of "becoming Italian" (Persichetti 2003b), I engage with the work of Flagg Miller (2005), Steve Caton (1990), and David Coplan (1994) and their discussions of poetry as an important tool emphasizing a masculine discourse, fundamental mores and values, and moral integrity and providing a "moral map" (Caton 1990) for its listeners. It is in this context that I echo Ayşe Parla's call for "thicker ethnographies of exactly where and how honour continues to matter" (2020, 101).

•.•

The title of this book reflects my purpose in writing it. The voice I discuss invokes places, historicities, and personhoods that are crucial to the migrants in this book, to the people who are listening and experiencing the voice of *l-'arubiya* across borders. In doing so I argue that people carry a particular location with them, a specific sense of the rural that can be invoked in Morocco and abroad in Italy, one that does not need to be read in the context of nostalgia and loss but can be seen as nestled in a personhood that nowadays is also part of a transnational experience.

In the end, these pages are about the resilience of creativity and imagination among migrant Moroccan men. Shameful figures marginal to the nation, whose lands were rendered unusable and taken away. Men who were forced to migrate first internally and then transnationally. Migrants who have drowned at sea and who continue to drown on land. It is about those who no longer make the news. The ghosts of the *sbarchi fantasma* (ghost landings) and of alternative routes. Those who are unaccounted for in the endless reportage about the so-called European migration crisis and the problematic mass mediatization of migration. Men who are simultaneously ignored and fetishized. The ready-to-use labor force that Europe is as quick to attract as to erase and expel. The "foreign" residents whose citizenship continues to be denied. The seasonal migrants and the undocumented. Agricultural laborers, unskilled workers, masons, water-well drillers, itinerant vendors, and those who simply get by. Migrants that the Italian *buonismo* does not welcome. Those who are perceived with profound hostility as they incarnate a historical trauma. Those who are criminalized rather than embraced. Shadows whose utterances are ignored. Thus, what is at stake here is "attention to people's own theorizing of their conditions" (Chávez 2017, 33) and the ways in which the rural may open up the possibility to aurally remap twenty-first-century Italy. In this sense, this book hopes to provide a different point of entry, showing how *sawt l-'arubiya* becomes a locus of memory for a class of migrants and as such, a critical source through which it is possible to reconstruct and understand a different history from the inside and look into the contemporary experiences of migrant Moroccan men in relation to burning political questions about migration and belonging not just in Italy, but in Europe as a whole.

•.•

This book is organized in four chapters. All except the first center on the mediated performance of particular songs available on YouTube and other

Internet sites. In mobilizing these "ubiquitous objects of internet public culture," I aim to connect them to "the thickness of situated ethnographic research" (Sonevytsky 2019, 22) and to resound the theme of each chapter. The "silence" of chapter 1, "The Engendering and the Othering of *l-ʿarubi* and *l-ʿarubiya* in Morocco," reflects the marginalization and, to a certain extent, the silencing of the rural during the French Protectorate and postcolonial Morocco. The chapter traces the construction of *l-ʿarubi* from different perspectives, beginning with an analysis of the way in which the terms appeared in a multivolume dictionary of Moroccan Arabic and French compiled by French Orientalists and Arabists who held important administrative positions during the Protectorate. Second, it analyzes how French colonial historiography produced the "Arab Bedouin type" and, in turn, *l-ʿarubi*. Third, because *l-ʿarubi* cannot be disentangled from *l-ʿarubiya*, it focuses on the effects that colonial agricultural policy had on the territory and its population. As *l-ʿarubi* incarnated the poor and dispossessed peasant from the Atlantic plains and plateaus, its construction became inevitably entangled with class. Fourth, with the rural-to-urban exoduses that began in the 1920s, *l-ʿarubi* was crystallized as the antithesis of the town dweller (*l-mədini*) and discriminated against on the ground of ethnicity, socioeconomic status, intelligence, and level of "civilization." It is from this complex interaction that converged during the French Protectorate (1912–56)—and which continued after independence—that I analyze how a particularly negative connotation of *l-ʿarubi* emerged in sound. The chapter lays the foundation for the central argument of the book, which posits *l-ʿarubiya* as key to understanding how migrant Moroccan men from the Atlantic plains and plateaus engage questions of selfhood, manhood, and belonging through *ṣawt l-ʿarubiya*.

Chapter 2, "The Voyage: Voicing *l-ʿarubiya* in the Crossing," focuses on the voyage and particularly on the sonorous account of a hazardous crossing from Morocco to Italy. Because death is "a reality that migrants face" (Chávez 2017, 233), I analyze "L-ḥərraga," a song that narrates the experience of undocumented migration and ends with the tragic death of a young Moroccan man crossing the Mediterranean. The chapter reflects critically upon the song's ability to convey the emotions and the state of mind of those who cross, and contextualizes it within a musicopoetic genre, *ʿabidat r-rma*, embedded in *l-ʿarubiya* and whose sonic nexus of music and poetry is particularly meaningful to these migrants. The chapter introduces a discussion about what role *l-ʿarubiya* plays in this testimony about a journey across the Mediterranean, and how it allows men whose rural sense of self has historically been excluded from other sonorous formations of the Mediterranean to respond to such exclusion by experiencing the rural at both a local and a transnational level. The chapter provides a basis for reflecting on the complex and asymmetrical connections among regions, broader modalities of power, and the critical undercurrent transforming the contemporary Mediterranean. It traces the voice of those who travel in search of a different life, making it audible, turning it into a testimony of those who cross, allowing migrants to generate and share knowledge about their voyage.

Chapter 3, "Spectral Guests, *Marocchini* and 'Real Men,'" begins with a discussion of terms that incarnate "difference," terms that, directly or indirectly, my interlocutors acknowledge, engage with, and react to. From there I trace how a collective trauma, caused by an earlier colonial encounter between the French Expeditionary Corps and the Italian population at the end of World War II, has profoundly influenced the image and perception of migrant Moroccan men in Italy. This historical discussion is aimed at locating their difference in reference to how the manhood of these migrants has been problematically constructed and fetishized. The chapter concludes by juxtaposing my interlocutors' conception of manhood, their own notion of what it means to be a "real man" (*rajəl*), which, as we shall see, is indivisible from the notion of *l-ʿarubi*. This final discussion centers on a contextual analysis of a *shaʿbi* song by Abdelaziz Stati, which is understood as providing a "moral map" for its listeners on what it means to be a "real man" and how to enact it.

Chapter 4, "Longing (*ḥnin*), Intimacy (*rasi rasək*), and Belonging (*intima*): Voicing *l-ʿarubiya*," analyzes two commercial recordings, "L-ghaba" (The Forest) and "Ḥajti fi grini" (I Long for My Male Companion), which exemplify the everyday listening practices of my interlocutors in reference to *ʿaiṭa* and *ʿabidat rma*. The discussion focuses on a detailed poetic analysis that examines the role of poetry and vernacular language in the construction and the articulation of *l-ʿarubiya*. It also examines sonic characteristics of the genres in question, particularly those concerning the voice, and investigates how the voice is conceived of as a sonic phenomenon in which timbre becomes central because it acoustically embodies nature, the environment, and particular experiences of space, time, memory, intimacy, and male desire. This final chapter attempts to convey how migrant Moroccan men draw from sonic practices that index a concatenation of rurality and masculinity, allowing them to reconstruct a sense of the rural and of the masculine self that is silenced because of stigmatization, racialization, and the fear of, alienation of, and othering of Moroccan men.

CHAPTER 1

The Engendering and the Othering
of *l-ʿarubi* and *l-ʿarubiya* in Morocco

Any study of migratory phenomena that overlooks the emigrant's conditions of origin is bound only to give a view that is at once *partial* and *ethnocentric*. On the one hand, it is only the *immigrant*—and not the *emigrant*—who is taken into consideration, rather as though his life began the moment he came to France. On the other hand, the problematic, both explicit and implicit, is always that of adaptation to the "host" society. (Sayad 2004, 29)

5 December 2018, Umbertide

It is a cold day, and Hassan Ja. is waiting inside a café in Umbertide. It is the first time we are meeting, but the awkwardness of this first mo-ment quickly disappears behind a smile that reveals a playful attitude and more: the dərghmus—*the mottled enamel of his teeth, caused by a high concentration of fluoride in tap water—is unmistakable. Hassan is forty-two years old and comes from Boujniba, a small town in the province of Khouribga. This area is renowned as the world's largest cen-ter of phosphate mining, and that industry is what is at the root of the* dərghmus *endemic in the region, of the catastrophic changes that mining and extraction have inflicted upon the land, and of a number of diseases affecting the population. One can tell many things from a simple smile.*

Hassan is quick to tell me that he is a Beni Meskine; "We are all here in Italy," he tells me half-jokingly. Tribal affiliations continue to be an important marker of identity for Moroccans from the countryside or for those tracing their origins to the countryside, whether at home or abroad. This is particularly true for the Beni Meskine, traditionally shepherds, who were among the first to arrive in Italy in the 1970s and '80s after a series of droughts brought famine to the region (Kharoufi 1983 and 2004; Alzetta 2004). Hassan arrived in Italy in 1990 with his father, who then went to work in the tobacco plantations in the Alta Valle del Tevere.

Figure 4. Hassan Ja.

Photo by the author

Hassan also worked on the same plantation before finding a job in a nearby factory, but when it shut down he was left with having to take small jobs to make ends meet. If it were not for his wife and their three children in Italy, he would have moved back to Morocco by now. "I miss the smell [r-riḥa] of the bread baked in the fərran [traditional earth oven used in homes in the countryside], I love that smell! You know, when I go back to Morocco I can stay in the city for a couple of days, but after that I need to get back to the countryside, to l-'arubiya; I need to look out and see empty fields and not buildings in front of me."

As we continue to talk, his longing for l-'arubiya turns to the animal world. "When I go back home, to the countryside, I go back to the fields and to the animals I love: sheep, goats . . . do you know that I used to be in love with a donkey when I was little? I was so happy to ride that donkey, it was as if I were riding a Ferrari!" We burst out laughing, though it is not the first time I have heard such an expression of affection. Donkeys are not only an essential means of transport in the countryside—they are also central characters in Moroccan folklore (Légey 1926; Ouachene 2020) and literature (Chraïbi 1956), and in street performances where storytellers, jesters, acrobats, and other itinerant artists and entertainers combine fantastic, mythical, and historical narratives with political and social commentary, often in the form of parody. Music has always been intrinsic to these performances.

Hassan's reminiscing, however, comes suddenly to a halt as he claims: "I am proud of being an 'arubi . . . *you know? People think that an* 'arubi *is someone who does not go to school, who does not know how to act, who is poor and who has nothing.*[1] *But this is not true! Nowadays* l-'arubiya *is better than the city, there is everything we need there, it is just like Italy!"*

L-'ARUBI AND L-'ARUBIYA

L-'arubiya that Hassan evokes is familiar to me. I have been recording tropes about *l-'arubiya* for years, trying to recognize the ways in which people relate to an affective place that is central in their biography and in their very definition of personhood. The multiple meanings of *l-'arubiya*— the emotions it conjures, the ways in which it is experienced, remembered, imagined, and constructed—are integral to an ethnography that strives to understand how *ṣawt l-'arubiya* mediates a sense of place, personhood, and belonging among migrant Moroccan men in Italy. In what follows I propose to listen to and explore the difference in Hassan's statement. That is to say, the tension one perceives between the affective and the historical dimensions of *l-'arubiya* that inscribe *l-'arubi*—a rural person or someone whose origins can be traced to the territory of the Atlantic plains and plateaus; rural places, in fact, "are as much historically shaped as are towns and cities" (Hoffman 2008, 5). Similarly, because "the Middle East is second to no other region in the diversity of actors frequently clustered under the label 'peasant'" (Waterbury 1991, 2), it is critical to discuss *l-'arubi* through its relationship with *l-'arubiya* and, in this context, to recognize the weight of history in tropes that reclaim and attempt to refashion a rural sense of self among migrant Moroccan men in Italy; that is the discursive construction of *t'arubit* (rurality) as a concept and a place. I ask, what does it mean to be proud to be an 'arubi? To which experience(s) does this statement respond? What difference does Hassan articulate? And what does the dichotomy between rural and urban mean for my interlocutors in Morocco and, subsequently, in Italy?

In tracing the historical production and reproduction of the country and the city, Raymond Williams argues that the distinction between rural and urban served to hide the replacement of a feudal structure by a capitalist structure in which the rural was just as critical as the urban. Williams also adds that labor and migration accompanied capitalism from the start, determining "the unequal interaction between the country and the city" (1973, 147). It is not my intention to uncritically reproduce or fetishize the rural-urban dichotomy; rather, I am interested in exploring the persistence and, to a certain extent, the historicity of this division by being particularly mindful of the role of colonialism in engendering and othering *l-'arubi* and *l-'arubiya*. Although the economic ties between the country and the city kept them quite reliant on one another, colonialism emphasized the cleavage between the two, forging the idea of the rural space as inhabited by "savages," with *l-'arubi* who came to represent a "savage without culture, without faith," despised by the urbanites who exploited him just as the Europeans did (Bentahar 1988, 59–60). This is the image that became part of the ideological underpinnings of the Protectorate, an image difficult to erase even in contemporary Morocco.

Historians warn us that "merely disregarding the colonial literature on the history of the Maghrib does not prevent it from exerting a profound influence" (Laroui 1977, 4), and that colonial knowledge and the colonial archive continue to structure the ways in which Moroccans understand and engage with their own history and society (Burke 2014). Although attentive to history, I remain cautious about the political use of the past, including the counter-vulgate that Moroccan historians produced in the effort to oppose the colonial vulgate (Sebti 2001), and am aware that some of the colonial tropes may have derived from existing tropes and patterns.[2] One of the musicians I have worked with eloquently illustrated the perils of the past when it came to the music tradition he performs.

I have a funny story to tell you about the past; it's the story of a man who, after losing his wife, found himself all alone with his kids. One day he went to see a friend of his, a merchant who sold herbs and spices, to complain about his solitude and about all the problems he had had since he was left alone. His friend suggested that he remarry and told him about a family he knew where there was a woman who had just lost her husband. The widower went to propose marriage, and the family accepted without the two ever meeting. The first time the husband went to the weekly market he bought something that he thought his new bride would like. Once home, however, the bride was not happy about the gift. The second time he went to the market he bought her something different, but she was still dissatisfied and even complained that he was not capable of buying things she liked. The poor husband went back to his friend to tell him what was going on, and while he was sitting in his friend's shop a water vendor came by. The friend offered to buy everything the water vendor carried in his basket, and the vendor gladly accepted. The poor husband could not understand what was going on, but his friend told him to take everything to his wife so as to solve his problem. Although hesitant, the

husband went back home and gave the basket to his wife. When she
emptied it and saw what was in there—small utensils, candies, legumes,
pieces of dried mutton, and so forth—she became so happy that even her
husband was taken by surprise. Do you know why? That's because the
woman's dead husband was a water vendor! Somehow, the bride was
always a bit melancholic, and that is why whatever the dead husband
used to bring she thought of as the best, whether it was or not! This is why
people say that ʿaiṭa was at its peak in the past.

My attention to the ways in which colonialism engaged with *l-ʿarubiya*
as a territory—that of the Atlantic plains and plateaus—and with its population is twofold. First, it is critical to recognize which notion of the rural my
interlocutors reject and, in turn, how they rearticulate *l-ʿarubiya* in their
tropes. This understanding is fundamental for analyzing the silencing and
marginalization of *ṣawt l-ʿarubiya* in Morocco, and how *ʿaiṭa* and *ʿabidat*
r-rma were reclaimed at the turn of the twenty-first century by a number
of Moroccan intellectuals. Second, we need to acknowledge the peculiarly
Arab dimension of *l-ʿarubiya* and, in turn, how my interlocutors rearticulate
l-ʿarubi in response to the colonial Arab Bedouin stereotype.[3] The rural of
l-ʿarubiya, in fact, cannot be conflated with *tamazirt*, the term used by the
Amazigh population to refer to the rural or the countryside (Hoffman 2008).

This chapter begins with a concise exploration of how the term *ʿarubi*
appears in a multivolume Moroccan Arabic–French dictionary compiled
by French Orientalists and Arabists who held important administrative
positions during the Protectorate. It then outlines how French colonial
historiography reinforced the negative connotations of the Arab Bedouin
stereotype and, in turn, *l-ʿarubi*. Because *l-ʿarubi* cannot be disentangled
from *l-ʿarubiya*, I focus on the devastating effects that colonial agricultural
policy had on the territory and its population. As *l-ʿarubi* came to embody
the poor and dispossessed peasant from the Atlantic plains and plateaus, it
inevitably became entangled with class. During the rural-to-urban exoduses
that began in the 1920s, *l-ʿarubi* became crystallized as the antithesis of the
town dweller (*l-mədini*) and differentiated in terms of race, ethnicity, socioeconomic status, mentality, culture, and, inevitably, the degree of civilization. It is from this complex mutual interplay, which converged during the
French Protectorate (1912–56), that a particularly negative connotation of
l-ʿarubiya and *l-ʿarubi* emerged in sound as well.

LEXICONS AND DICTIONARIES

ɛrəb / ɛrăb 1. lă-ɛrəb / lə-ɛrăb the Bedouins—f lă-ɛrəb at the Bedouins,
in the countryside [. . .] *plur. pej.* ɛrəbbān Bedouins who are rough;

pl. poetic ɛorbān / ɛăṛbān Bedouins, country people [. . .].—2. lă-ɛṛəb
the race / of Arab language in general, the Arabs; the arabophones. (de
Prémare 1993, 9:58)[4]

āɛṛāb / ɛṛāb 1. l-āɛṛāb the Arab Bedouins [. . .]. (de Prémare 1993, 9:58)[5]

ɛăṛbi 1. Arab [. . .].—2. Arab type [. . .].—3. Bedouin; countryman; peasant; *pej.* yokel, crisp, unpolished (*like a Bedouin*). (de Prémare 1993, 9:59)[6]

ɛṛōbi 1. [. . .] Bedouin; countryman, peasant [*cont.* mdīni]; particular
to the Bedouins [. . .]—ɛṛōbīya Bedouin woman.—2. lā-ɛṛōbīya the
Bedouins [considered as a whole]; the Bedouin milieu, the Bedouin
population.—3. *ext.* the rural population. (de Prémare 1993, 9:59–60)[7]

As part of the "scientific" inventory of Morocco—a systematic French effort
to gather information about Morocco—lexicons were an important tool for
the governance of colonial peoples (Burke 2014, 6 and 61). Dialectology,
a field that emerged over the course of the nineteenth and early twentieth
centuries, became critical for understanding the native population through
dialects, which were thought of as disclosing much about the nature of
Moroccan culture, the structure of society, and the evolutionary level of
the culture. Dialects, in fact, "were intimately connected with differentiated populations whose very identity might be so determined in linguistic terms" (Kosansky 2016, 6). It was against this background that Georges
Séraphin Colin (1893–1977)—a French Orientalist and Arabist who came
to Morocco in an official capacity in 1921 and remained there for the rest of
his life conducting research—began to compile a multivolume Moroccan
Arabic–French dictionary published, although unfinished, in 1994. Colin's
work was one of the principal sources of the most comprehensive Moroccan
Arabic–French dictionary, compiled by Alfred-Louis de Prémare (1930–
2006). Enriched by de Prémare's own work on Moroccan language and
culture, as well as by the work of other dialectologists who, like Colin, held
important positions during the Protectorate, the dictionary mostly draws
from the vernacular of traditional cities such as Tangiers, Rabat, Fes, and
Marrakech, emphasizing a colonial and urban perspective.

In the dictionary, which adopted a system of transliteration to capture
the phonetics of the vernacular (*darija*),[8] de Prémare makes two critical
moves: he does not maintain the traditional distinction between *'arab*
(Arabs) and *a'rāb* (nomads, Bedouins) (ɛṛab/ɛṛāb and āɛṛāb/ɛṛāb, as
they respectively appear in the dictionary entries), dehistoricizing the
two categories; and he transforms the Arab Bedouin category from des-
ert dwellers to inhabitants of the countryside. While the merger of *'arab*

with *a'rāb* had already been conceptualized from the late eighth to eleventh centuries by philologists aiming to codify the Arabic language via a process that transformed a negative picture of the Bedouin to the idealization of the Bedouins as archetypes of "the original Arabs" (Webb 2016, 294–340), in de Prémare's dictionary the Arab Bedouin residing in the countryside continued to embody negative connotations. As the Arab Bedouin turned into *l-'arubi*, the same negative qualities also set him apart from potential and less problematic synonyms such as *bədwi* (Bedouin), *fəllaḥ* (peasant, farmer), and *qarawi* (peasant).

In their analysis of ethnic stereotypes and lexical semantics in Moroccan Arabic, Ech-Charfi and Azzouzi posit that the concept of the rural or the countryside may have arisen from contacts with Western language and Western colonization, citing how in French there is a clear contrast between the city and the countryside in the vocabulary and in the social attitudes communicated through the use of these terms. This is the case for *paysan* (peasant), which in French can carry the same negative connotations one encounters in the definition of *l-'arubi*. These authors also argue that the North African elite probably became sensitive to the contrast between rural and urban through their familiarity with French culture and that, in addition, urbanization and rural-to-urban migration may have justified the development of negative attitudes toward new rural migrants (2017, 149).

In the attempt to unearth the discourses behind the emergence of the term *'arubi*, I now turn to how French colonial historiography engendered *l-'arubi* in opposition to *l-mədini*—the urbanite, the sedentary, the non-Bedouin, and the civilized. This dichotomy made particular use of the writings of Ibn Khaldun.

KHALDUNISM

Negative stereotypes about *l-'arubi* have been circulating and continue to circulate in caricatures (HuffPost Maroc 2014), jokes and proverbs (Sbihi 1932), and everyday talk, as well as in political conversations. In these discourses *l-'arubi* is portrayed through a series of well-known tropes bearing an indexical relation to what Bakhtin defines as a "prior discourse," where an "authoritative word is located in a distanced zone, organically connected with a past that is felt to be hierarchically higher" (1981, 342).

I have already analyzed the negative connotations entangled with the emergence and the characterization of *l-'arubi* in lexicons and dictionaries; in what follows, however, I am interested in outlining the engendering of *l-'arubi* from a different angle, locating a prior discourse in the writings of the Arab historian, sociologist, and philosopher Ibn Khaldun (d. 1406)—or, more precisely, highlighting how the French Protectorate made use of his writings (i.e., the French translations of his work) concerning the Arab Bedouins as part of a colonial historiography that Abdellah Laroui came to define as "Khaldunism" (1977).

> When the Banû Hilâl and the Banû Sulaym pushed through (from their homeland) to Ifrîqiyah and the Maghrib in (the beginning of) the fifth [C.E. eleventh] century and struggled there for three hundred and fifty years, they attached themselves to [the country], and the flat territory in [the Maghreb] was completely ruined. (Ibn Khaldun 1958, 1:305)

Although Ibn Khaldun has been criticized for his problematic views of the Arab Bedouins, Maghrebi historians and historians of the Maghreb have attempted to rehabilitate him, arguing for his writings to be understood in relation to the contradictory nature of the texts themselves and for their need to be historicized. While this intellectual effort has generated complex and nuanced readings of Ibn Khaldun in the Maghreb and beyond,[9] the translations and the subsequent use of Khaldun's texts by the colonial administration left an indelible mark on Moroccan society. This is particularly true concerning the introduction of images and categories that have outlived colonialism and shaped postcolonial subjectivities, as the stereotype of the Arab Bedouin and, in turn, l-'arubi demonstrates.

Translation was an essential part of the colonial administration in North Africa; in fact, while the "present was believed to be 'out there,' to be apprehended by observation[,] the past was assumed to be recorded in documents, to be grasped only by a work of translation either direct or indirect" (Hannoum 2003, 61). It is in this context that colonialism "discovered" Ibn Khaldun, extricating him from the civilization whence he came, detemporalizing his work, and turning him into a "solitary genius" (Hannoum 2003, 68). From the 1840s on, the supposed Orientalist discovery of Ibn Khaldun allowed French historiographers to construct the history of the Maghreb as an unending struggle between various tribes and dynasties, legitimizing French colonial presence and the efforts of its mission civilisatrice to guide the Maghreb into modernity.

Michael Brett has posited that the (in)famous invasion of the Beni Hilal and the Beni Sulaym erected by Ibn Khaldun were in reality a legend, based on a wealth of metaphor used to convey the impression of a disastrous flood, that French colonial scholarship turned into the cause of North Africa's ruin (1999, 67). Colonial historians, in fact, drew from what Ibn Khaldun had to say about the role of Arab Bedouins in the history of Morocco and the Maghreb and structured their works from a point of view influenced by a dichotomy in power between the Andalusian refugees—like Ibn Khaldun himself—and the Arab Bedouin tribes (Laroui 1977, 213).

In translated texts and in histories written on the basis of paraphrasing Ibn Khaldun, historians such as de Sacy, Mercier, Gautier, Carette, Marçais, and Terrasse, among others, injected nineteenth-century racial prejudices into Ibn Khaldun's reflections on modes of livelihood and civilization—*'umrān badawī* (Bedouin but also rural civilization) and *'umrān ḥaḍarī* (sedentary, urban civilization)—stripping his concepts of all their subtlety and reducing a complex historical situation to a dichotomy between nomadic and sedentary people, rural and urban. It is in this context that the figure of the Arab Bedouin was transformed into a "deus ex machina" (Laroui 1977, 220), as the one figure around which all the historians based their accounts about the arrival of the Bedouin tribes in the Maghreb.

This widespread interpretation of the coming of the Beni Hilal came to be associated with the country's impoverishment, its political instability, its economic and cultural regression, its overall decline and dissolution, and the destruction of civilization, understood first and foremost as sedentary and urban. Such an interpretation allowed colonial historians to give free rein to their prejudice against the figure of the Arab Bedouin and, in turn, to emphasize the dichotomy between Moroccan cities—the centers of government, trade, and religion, with a cultivated elite of Andalusian descent concentrated in the cities of Tangier, Tetouan, Salé, and Fez—and *l-'arubiya* (Ayache 1979).

As a cause of the supposed precolonial backwardness of North Africa, the Beni Hilal and the Beni Sulaym tribes entered systematically into French literature in order to validate the French presence. Building on precolonial differences, the history of Morocco came to be described as an unending conflict between the forces of regionalism (i.e., *siba*) and those of central power (i.e., *makhzan*), creating a dramatic rift between the countryside and the city, and between nomadic and sedentary peoples; in fact, it was not until after the coming of the French that Moroccan cities came to represent powerful centers of Arabism, high Islam, and modern values (Burke 1976, 2–5).

The so-called Arabization of North Africa was related from the eleventh century onward to the spread of the Arab Bedouins in the countryside, and their growing settlement as peasants rather than nomads on the territory of the Atlantic plains and plateaus. As "the way of the nomad turned very easily into the way of the peasant" (Brett 1995, 265), the category of *l-'arubi* emerged.

THE GRANARY OF ROME

Part of the narrative about the destruction of civilization also included the devastating effects that the Arab Bedouin invasion was said to have had on the environment. This is how the mirage of the Atlantic plains and plateaus as the so-called Granary of Rome came into being (Swearingen 1987; Davis 2007), a vision that drove much of Morocco's colonial agricultural policy and that, together with other agricultural and nonagricultural development formulas pioneered during the Protectorate, had devastating effects on the population of the Atlantic plains and plateaus.

The expression "le Maroc utile" (useful Morocco) was coined by the Protectorate after a series of reports generated by French study missions to Morocco in 1900, identifying the lands of the Atlantic plains and plateaus as among the richest in the world (Swearingen 1987, 16). At the beginning of the French Protectorate in 1912, it was believed that the Morocco's fortune lay in its agriculture, and that the cultivation of wheat was suited to colonization purposes. As early as 1915 a "wheat policy"—which predominated until the 1930 crisis and whose impact has continued to the present—began to be formulated, with the goal of converting Morocco into a breadbasket for France (Swearingen 1987, 9).

Based on an idealized image of Morocco as the former fertile Granary of Rome, the increase in the production of wheat was paraded as a good outcome of the Protectorate, able to restore an ancient land after centuries of Arab neglect. The policy, which encouraged mechanized wheat production for France, also allowed the creation of colonial wheat farms, where European settlers expropriated the best land and crowded Moroccan peasants onto less productive land. This is how the country's agricultural sector came to be divided into two zones: "a European zone, in which the best lands were cultivated with modern methods that required a substantial capital investment, and a Moroccan zone, in which marginal lands were cultivated with traditional methods because of lack of expertise and lack of access to the capital investments for modern methods" (Wyrtzen 2015, 89).

It is crucial to point out that in the nineteenth and early twentieth centuries the territory of the Atlantic plains and plateaus required cheap wage labor or share-tenant labor and was owned by *sharifian* families, *murabitun*,[10] and people who rendered services to the sultan and to French settlers. Beyond the uncertainty and lack of security in bad harvest years, taxation constituted a heavy burden for the populations of the countryside. This situation was exacerbated by the fact that local *pashas* and *caids*—city and provincial governors whose main task was to collect taxes—tended to squeeze out as much in taxes and extraordinary levies as the population under their control would put up with. Because popular revolt was the principal check on these abuses, a system of continuous violence, of "squeeze," "revolt," and "repress," often resulted (Zartman 1963; Burke 1976).

Although the Protectorate transformed the system described above and reduced the role of the central elements of the traditional system, the general effects that its policy, geared toward the exploitation of the agricultural wealth of these regions, had on these populations were basically the same (Waterbury 1970). Colonial agriculture, in fact, was capitalist, with a private system attracting European investors, and an official or public system favoring firms and large landowners. Land was thus obtained by a combination of force and legal subterfuge (Sebti 2013, 46). By the end of the Protectorate, in fact, over one million hectares of the best agricultural land were controlled by a relatively small number of French settlers, only 40 percent of the arable land was owned by Moroccan smallholders, and 3.6 million rural Moroccans were landless (Davis 2007, 138). These lands were never redistributed to peasants even after independence, when they passed into the hands of the Moroccan elite and foreign investors (Mahdi 2014).

Concomitantly with the wheat crisis of 1929, which demonstrated the failure of the policy, a California-inspired agriculture based on irrigation and the export of citrus fruit and market vegetables emerged, together with the implementation of an irrigation plan with the building of dams and the promotion of modern farming (Sebti 2013, 47). However, because they were embedded within colonial development and plans, the political and economic biases remained; thus, as intensive improvements continued, it was the French settlers who benefited, while the Moroccan peasantry suffered further distress (see Tenzon 2019 for the Gharb region). After a series of droughts leading to famine and widespread starvation, much of the rural population was forced into cities because the countryside could no longer support them.

These general lines of development continued after independence, and even though there were attempts made to change the rural social structures and move toward a general reorganization of the rural economy along more egalitarian lines, the government's hesitation to dispose of the land, together with opposition from both traditional rural elites and French settlers and distrust from the peasants, caused these initiatives to fail and the social conditions in the countryside to worsen (Bouderbala, Chraïbi, and Pascon 1974; Hammoudi 1997). It is this process of land concentration and privileges, during and since the Protectorate, that is thought to lie at the root of the contemporary rural crisis in Morocco.[11]

The history and uneven development of rural Morocco—weighed down by a political and administrative structure characterized by corruption, economic instability, and inadequate infrastructure—fostered further tension and disparities between the city and the country, a tension that deepened with a series of rural migrations and that gave birth to the compact formation of what came to be defined as a proletariat of rural origins in the cities of Morocco. During the forty-five years of colonial rule, one million Moroccans left the countryside for the cities (Daoud and Engler 1981, 29), and rural out-migration remains a problem in the postcolonial period (Davis 2007, 138).

THE RURAL EXODUS

The entire history of Morocco has been marked by the movement of people over time, and rural-to-urban migration occurred long before the Protectorate. In the 1920s, however, a flood of rural migrants began pouring into cities, driven by taxation, loss of water rights, land concentration, and dispossession. This movement was particularly pronounced in the Atlantic plains and plateaus, regions characterized as "areas of repulsion" because of too little land and too many people (Awad 1964, 51).

If, on the one hand, this vast rural-to-urban migration did challenge a strict dichotomy between the city and the countryside, in actuality it also heightened the same opposition now particularly noticeable in the spatial segregation rooted in a colonial urbanism based on ethnic and class divisions. Rural migrants began to move into the old, overcrowded, traditional cities (*medinas*) and shantytowns (known as *bidonvilles* in French and as *qaryat* in Moroccan Arabic) around the peripheries of the *ville nouvelle* (the European city built next to the *medina*) (Rabinow 1995). Relegated to the outside of the urban perimeter—often close to the new industrial zones created by French colonialism—these illegal settlements were later incorporated within the growing cities as new settlements kept appearing and the urban borders expanded (Zika 2008, 16).

Morocco's rapid urbanization went hand in hand with a housing crisis, with the impossibility of managing a massive migration that transferred rural unemployment to the city. *Bidonvilles* became the emblems of what came to be viewed as the "ruralization" of urban centers, a term that referred to the sheer number of rural migrants moving to the city, but also to the belief that by maintaining a rural mentality and way of life, these migrants would not adapt to city life and would thus be excluded from progress and modernity.[12] The rural exodus, in other words, came to be perceived not dissimilarly to yet another Bedouin invasion threatening urban civilization.

French colonial accounts now contrasted the Arab Bedouin from the countryside residing in the city with the Arab urbanite, in terms not only of ethnicity but particularly of their socioeconomic status, mentality, and level of "civilization" (Brunot 2013), reinforcing a problematic dichotomy that, as Hassan Rachik argues, aims to systematize the mindset of the different types of Moroccans and to unravel their essential characteristics (2016a).

Casablanca—a city that grew from about twenty thousand residents at the beginning of the twentieth century to well over three million today—provides an excellent example through which to understand both the relocation of rural migrants into low-income peripheral and unregulated quarters and their transformation into urban masses. The stigmatized and stigmatizing marginal spaces inhabited by rural migrants—spaces that, although they did not belong to the "real" or "legitimate" city, provided cheap labor, which played a large role in the industrial and economic growth of the city—became a symbol of deviance (Zika 2008, 116) and of a savage demographic aggression menacing urban order and civilization (Cattedra 2017).

Each quarter was characterized by the high concentration of a population of the same origin, as in the case of Carrières Centrales, the largest *bidonville*, where in 1952 roughly fifty thousand people resided (Adam 1968). Built near a power plant whose construction began in 1920, about 80 percent of the population of Carrières Centrales were Arabic-speaking people from the Atlantic plains and plateaus (Adam 1968). Despite the inevitable mixing that took place because of different peoples living in proximity to one another and the role of neighborhoods in shaping a new sense of belonging, regionalism continued to be a critical marker of identity.

It is in this context that the process of the transformation of rural migrants from the Atlantic plains and plateaus to proletarians and sub-proletarians occurred, and that the marginalization of the *'arubi*—now relegated to the lower urban social strata, lacking the necessary tools for integration, confined to the margins of urban life, and characterized by poverty and economic precariousness—continued (Rachik 1995). As the process of "othering" shifted from the rural to the urban milieu,[13] the Bedouin from the Atlantic plains, the *'arubi*, continued to be entangled with degradation.

The endurance of colonial stereotypes and of a "prior discourse" went hand in hand with a series of economic crises that, in the decades following independence in 1956, affected a population already denigrated and marginalized. Whether residing in the countryside, in small towns, or in the urban peripheries, by the mid-twentieth century a specific construction of *l-'arubi* and *l-'arubiya* had been put in place, and it proved difficult to dismantle. This is particularly true when difference was also marked by the erotic.

Sexuality is one of the main axes by which civilization and barbarism can be classified in colonial projects, since sex was always an important feature of Orientalist fantasy and scholarship (Massad 2007, 6–9). The perceived manhood of *l-'arubi*, in fact, became central to his characterization during the French Protectorate, but also after independence, when Moroccan urban elites, in the effort to forge a modern nation, marginalized *l-'arubi* and stereotyped him.

Christelle Taraud describes how a well-structured and normative discourse on manhood was put into place by the French in the Maghreb, whereby the stigmatized image of "the Arab man" alternated between the more or less effeminate pederast and the sexual predator. The sexuality of the latter often referred to the morphology of his genitalia. The hypertrophic penis of the Arabs was in fact regularly commented upon, just as Arab "sensuality" was commonly employed to explain the existence of harems and polygamy, as well as perverse sexual practices such as bestiality, necrophilia, sodomy, acts of violence, and rape. Pederasty, on the other hand, was presented as a common practice associated with the passive role and classified with the feminized. Thus, either "too virile" or "not virile enough," but never "normal" or "civilized," Arab men were relegated to the domain of sexuality, to the "bestiality" and "perversity" of their practices and the "savagery" and "primitivism" of their manners (Taraud 2016, 338–39).

Nadia Tazi posits how the tension between the masculinity (*dkura*) of the urbanites and the manhood (*rujula* and *fḥula*) of the Bedouins, in which virility is central, is intrinsic to Ibn Khaldun's modes of civilization (2018, 31–35). In Moroccan Arabic, the noun *dkər* can be translated as "masculine," "penis," "brave," "courageous," or "capable man," while the verb *dəkkər* means "to make something masculine." The verb *rəjjəl*, on the other hand, means "to encourage someone to be a man," "to be virile," or "to be courageous," since the noun *rajəl* indicates "a man," "a 'real man,'" "a man who is virile, courageous, and trustworthy and has a noble heart"; while *fḥəl*, aside from indicating a large male animal such as a stallion, a bull, a camel, an animal who has not been castrated and thus can reproduce, also indicates a courageous, intrepid, and brave individual.

SONIC DIFFERENCE

16 July 2016, Casablanca

I am sitting across from the Moroccan comedian Mohamed Atir at a hotel in Casablanca. I am there to interview him about his hit radio show Riḥt d-duwwar" (The Scent of the Village). *Born and raised in Hay Mohammedi—as Carrières Centrales was renamed after independence in honor of the returning King Mohammed V—Atir defines himself as a real* 'arubi: "My parents were members of the Mramer tribe from Chiadma who moved to Casablanca during the rural exodus."

In preparation for his show, Atir visits people in the countryside of the Atlantic plains and plateaus to collect songs, proverbs, jokes, and idioms, and he spends time with his sources to perfect the voice, the gestures, and the overall mannerism of an 'arubi. In his broadcasts Atir always plays the character of an 'arubi, setting his sketches in a rural milieu. Comic sketches are extremely popular in Morocco, originating with the ḥalqa, a gathering in the form of a circle around performers (ḥlaiqiya) in a public setting, usually in a marketplace or at the city gate of a medina (Schuyler 1984; Kapchan 1996; Amine and Carlson 2012). The ḥalqa, which is first and foremost associated with the rural, cannot be separated from the vernacular and the voice of l-'arubiya.

Atir explains that the success of the show is due to that fact that, for the first time, the tone or inflection (nəbra) of l-'arubiya can be heard on the radio without having to negotiate about what to say and how to say it; the voice of l-'arubiya, he reminds me, was not always welcome in the Moroccan mediascape. Atir uses a low gravelly voice whose timbre is thought to sonically capture the essence of the rural, giving authority and authenticity to the oral narratives he collects and that form the basis of the broadcast.

Atir believes that it is thanks to this voice that people can listen to and experience the scent of l-'arubiya. "Listen," he tells me, as he begins to narrate with a low soothing voice: "A father from Ain Kaichar—a rural province between Oued Zem and Fquih Ben Salah, you know . . . the area famous for its figs [l-karmuṣa]—has paid all the expenses for his son's wedding. The next morning, after the son was married, the father enters the room to find his son and his new bride sitting next to one another. The father, looking at them, tells his son. . . ." Atir pauses to build up momentum before the punch line. "Listen to this one . . . it's wicked [wa'əra]!" After clearing his throat, Atir changes to a gravelly voice thought to embody the timbre of an 'arubi and continues narrating a story that is meant to comment on the tough character of the 'arubi. "Aren't you ashamed?" the father asks his son. "The one whom you are sitting next to . . . did you even pay a dime to have her?" (audio ex. 1.1).

In her work on the relation between the voice and the ear in nineteenth-century Colombia, Ana María Ochoa Gautier posits that when sonic perceptions are troubling or perceived as unwanted, sound becomes unbearable, making it difficult to overcome an "acoustic disgust in order to undertake the project of epistemologically mapping sonic difference as scientific observation" (2014, 33). One can encounter the sonic difference Ochoa Gautier refers to in passages where the Arab Bedouin, and later l-'arubi, were described through sound and especially through a voice thought to embody excess and perceived as harsh, rough, coarse, loud, and deeply entangled with nonhumans.

At first the uncertain calls and the hesitating steps of people between sleeping and walking, soon to be succeeded by shouts and fierce disputes. The harshness and the deep-drawn aspirates of the Arab tongue, moreover, as it is used by the common people, might induce one to believe that they were overwhelming each other with abuse. All the usual morning sounds, such as the crowing of cocks, the neighing of horses, the braying of mules and the grunting of camels in the nearby caravansary are drowned in this grand concert of disturbance, which increases continually in volume. Before sunrise it has reached an infernal height; shrill cries, such as we hear from monkeys, a wild pandemonium fit to curdle one's blood [. . .] all is an inextricable confusion of men and beasts, all giving tongue at the very top of their voice. (Loti 1890, 20–21)

Once described and inscribed into writing, the vocal qualities of the Arab Bedouin and l-'arubi turned into a discourse that influenced the way in which the musical traditions of l-'arubiya were perceived and consequently integrated into or excluded from the Moroccan canon and the writings about Moroccan music. I now turn to the writings of Alexis Chottin—the head of the National Conservatory in Rabat (1929–39 and 1956–60)—whose publications on the music of Morocco under the aegis of the colonial administration's Service des Arts Indigènes had a profound influence on the treatment of 'aiṭa and 'abidat r-rma.

Jann Pasler writes that music was an "audible representation" of colonial differences, "the performance of intelligence, character, and even soul," and that studying indigenous music was a "mode for contemplating racial distinction, helping the French reflect on the ideology of Western superiority" (2012–13, 22). In discussing Guillaume André Villoteau's musical accounts from Napoleon's Egyptian campaign of 1798–1801, Ruth Rosenberg also discusses the significance accorded to music within the French imperialist venture (2015, 21–71), while James Mokhiber maintains that General Hubert Lyautey—France's first resident-general in Morocco—"clearly saw a propaganda opportunity in the arts" (2013, 265). In 1967 Abdellatif Laabi published an incisive analysis of the role of the arts in Morocco's colonial agenda, focusing on the Institut des Hautes Études Marocaines, established in 1920, particularly on its role in the "scientific exploration of Morocco," a project that touched every aspect of Moroccan life, including music.

[S]cientific exploration occurred long before direct colonization. [. . .] Yet it was only after the establishment of the Protectorate that a colonial ideology at a socio-cultural level, that is according to "indigenous realities," was articulated and became one of the pillars of colonialism.

This would occur primarily within the context of the Institut des Hautes Études Marocaines, established in 1920, and in its publication Hespéris, where a frenzy for research took hold, yielding one of the most spectacular cultural speleologies of all time. The I.H.E.M., sponsored by Lyautey, the supreme theoretician of the Moroccan Protectorate, chose for its first task "the scientific exploration of Morocco" [. . .]. A number of specializations developed within this organization and academics established themselves: in the domains of literature (Basset, Laoust, Justinard), geography (Célerier, P. de Cénival, Raynal), history (Michaux-Bellaire, de Castries, Terrasse), music (Chottin), linguistics (Biarnay, Lévi-Provençal, Laoust), and the arts (P. Ricard, Herber, Marçais, Terrasse). (1967, 4)[14]

When Prosper Ricard, the director of the Service des Arts Indigènes in Rabat, turned to music, he argued for the need to make an inventory, to study, and to revive its past, just as he had done for other indigenous arts. It is with this vision in mind that Chottin—who was brought to Morocco to direct the Conservatory of Moroccan Music in Rabat—focused his research on Moroccan music according to two categories, emphasizing the contrast between two civilizations identifiable in music through a "rhythmic phase" and a "melodic phase" (Pasler 2015, 35–37). In what could be understood as a colonial sonic interpretation of Khaldunism, rhythm sounded the nomadic, the rural, and the uncivilized; melody the sedentary, the urban, and the civilized.

A dual influence is discernible in the musical forms of this country, that of two ways of life which are juxtaposed, nomadism and sedentarism, as well as two civilizations—rural and urban:
1. *The rhythmic phase*, which subjugates the primitive or uncultivated being, who is always prey to nature, with its periodic necessities, with all its changes, of days and nights, of seasons, of works and of migrations;
2. *The melodic phase*, which is the prerogative of the civilized and sophisticated beings, crouched in the midst of pillows, lulled by the indistinct murmur of the water flowing in the basins, imperceptibly, which is how time flows for them, moments which dissolve in the unchanging twilight and warmth of the courtyards. (Chottin 1931, 20:218)[15]

While Pasler has suggested that these categories could be read as a "response to General Lyautey's need to see urban Arabs and rural Berbers as distinct in his strategy to divide and conquer Morocco" (2015, 37), Hassan Najmi posits that Chottin was particularly invested in *al-ala*—the term used in Morocco to refer to the Andalusian music tradition—and the music of the Amazigh because of the colonial interest in pre-Islamic Morocco, an investment that is also evident in the two conferences on Moroccan music held in Rabat in 1928 and Fez in 1939 (2007, 2:27–37).

Rather than focusing on such a division, I am interested in probing the description of *ʿaiṭa*—being that *ʿabidat r-rma* was effectively silenced—in the writings about the music of Morocco during the French Protectorate and, to a certain extent, their influences in postcolonial Morocco. It is critical to remember that the entanglement of *ʿaiṭa* with *l-ʿarubiya* is omnipresent, even in contemporary caricatures.

> Among the Aroubis, Mi Lalla retrieves the Taârija from the bottom of her closet and turns on some chaâbi: a real jam session of aïta, whether haouzia jeblia, gharbaouia, marsaoui or even mellalia. (HuffPost Maroc 2014)[16]

I begin the discussion looking at Chottin's most celebrated work, *Tableau de la musique marocaine* (1939), whose overall organization and treatment of the subject shaped much of the colonial and postcolonial writing about music in Morocco.

While part 1 of *Tableau de la musique marocaine* is devoted to what Chottin defines as Berber music, part 2—the section on which my analysis focuses—centers on Arab art music and, in turn, Andalusian music. Part 2 opens with an overview of the history of Arab art music, drawing from the works of Orientalists, Arabists, European specialists, and seminal medieval works by Arab, Persian, and Turkish philosophers, thinkers, theorists, and polymaths.[17] The aim of this section is to introduce the Andalusian branch and analyze its preservation in the Maghreb. Preservation (*conservation*), here but also in other writings, is a problematic term that continues to foster important debates among Maghrebi scholars who view the qualifier "Andalusian" as not acknowledging the historical contribution of the Maghreb to this musical tradition (Davila 2013). Preservation also suggests the need for this urban art tradition—Chottin's use of the term *hadariya* derives from Ibn Khaldun's *ʿumrān ḥaḍarī* (sedentary, urban civilization)—to be protected from the rural and the Bedouins.

> This is the state of preservation of the music that came from Spain, representative of a refined culture through which the civilization of the cities, called *hadariya*, that is to say of urban formation, developed in opposition to agglomerates of a rural nature. To a certain extent, the latter are more representatives of the national element of the country, the one

which expresses itself in the Bedouin speech which we could call the average Moroccan dialect. (Chottin 1939, 103)[18]

In the chapter titled "État actuel," Chottin subdivides Arab music into classical and folk (*populaire*), describing the former as a cultivated tradition from the Andalusian courts and the urban elites, and the latter as influenced by a number of traditions where those of the Bedouins, are conspicuously absent.

1. *Classical music*, of Andalusian origin, art of the court and art of the bourgeoisie, complex, learned and sophisticated;
2. *Folk music*, generally permeated by Andalusian singing, sometimes influenced by Berber singing, at other times of foreign origin: Turkish in music for processions, Negro in certain confraternities. (1939, 107)[19]

Chottin's distinction between art and folk music draws from the writings of Ibn Khaldun—who described art music as based on well-established rules and conventions that required the practitioner to be trained in order to acquire the necessary skills, and folk music as simple and spontaneously created and requiring no special instruction (1958, 2:395–405)—and from theories of performance and voice production of earlier Arab treatises concerned, first and foremost, with urban art music.

There is a long-standing tradition in Arab writings on the aesthetic and the vocal production, one that is accompanied by a rich vocabulary for classifying and judging vocal qualities relative to specific ideas about beauty and perfection. In his *Book of Songs*, Al-Iṣfahānī discusses an impressive number of terms as they relate to the positive and negative attributes of a voice through compelling anecdotes that reflect the rich debates about vocal production and the craft of singing. In one of these anecdotes, a voice classified as hoarse, rough, harsh, and low (*ṣaḥila*) is considered to be a poor voice (Sawa 2019, 190–91), while, in another anecdote that illustrates the negative quality of a coarse voice, the art of weaving is linked with music in order to compare a weak vocal performance with a coarse (*jāff*), inferior cloth (Sawa 2019, 263).

Al-Fārābī—for whom the tonal qualities of vocal ornaments derive their names from sensations peculiar to senses other than that of hearing—also includes roughness (*khushūnah*) among the palette of timbres that enable the voice to express diverse moods and emotions (Sawa 2004, 99). Al-Kātib, instead, describes the undesirable quality of a rough or gravely (*mutaqaʻqi*) voice, as a voice in which one can hear a sort of *qaʻqaʻa* (rattle), which resembles the way in which the Bedouins speak (1972, 175).[20]

Voice—which in the writings of Chottin is now divorced from the rich and complex debates at the intersection of singing, poetry, language, performance and a number of other disciplines—becomes a crucial arena where taste and morality converge. This is particularly true in his discussion on the category of Arab folk music, where Chottin now integrates his own perception about genres he considers to be a significant decline from the Andalusian arts, using street and vulgar language, syllabic verse, and full of irregularities and barbarism (1939, 153–54).

In the comparatively few pages he devotes to folk music—a category comprising a multiplicity of music ranging from Bedouin songs to the music associated with Sufi orders—Chottin emphasizes two modes of listening and writing about 'aiṭa. On the one hand, he focuses on vocality, describing 'aiṭa as a cry, a sonic utterance with no identifiable pitch and scale, a voice implicitly or explicitly associated with the Arab Bedouin, his vernacular, and his rough or coarse vocal timbre. On the other hand, Chottin focuses on the association between 'aiṭa and professional female singer-dancers (*shikhat*), describing and inscribing this musicopoetic genre with the type of sensual excess characteristic of colonial writings.

> The 'aïta [...] was originally a cry shouted across the countryside to let everyone know an important piece of news. Whence the long vocalises on a high note whose wavelike motions are like the subtle signs of a secret language. The 'aïta [...] is mostly cultivated by women, the singers [known as] shikhat, who combine it with their dances. [...] When the singing stops, the melody is played by the violin over a fast 6/8 rhythm and the belly dancing, stylized and coldly suggestive, begins. (1939, 163)[21]

The following "ethnographic" excerpt, which describes the performance of a group of *shikhat*, illustrates how Chottin's perception of sound is enmeshed in Orientalist tropes in which attraction and desire are juxtaposed with fear and disgust for a phantasmagorical Oriental woman,[22] whose sonic difference is problematically mapped onto scientific observation.

> [W]e will meet the libertine and sensual Morocco. This "face" is pleasant enough, there is a bit too much rouge on the cheeks and kohl under the eyes as well as jewelry—real or false—sparkling around it. What a profusion of bright colors and what an excess of adornment among the anesthetizing perfumes that waft out! And I rather fear that, alas! underneath there is nothing but a poor, thin face, a pallid and wrinkled pleasure-seeker, that wears itself out in the pursuit of impossible sensual bliss. [...] This, therefore, is that music which is so attractive and yet so deceptive; onto a line of melody that could be charming is applied the rouge of "grupetti," along with the glass beads of the "vibrati," enveloped in a sighing expression that too often is affected. [...] This laughter and

this joy blend and burst in the rhythm, dizzying rhythm, enchanting rhythm that lulls worries and sorrows; a vampire rhythm, whose wings flutter to anesthetize the pain caused by its fatal bite. This resembles the *tar*, which seems to want to bite the soul secretly, with each beat that veils the sweet jingling of its small cymbals. An orchestra of shiukh and shikhat consists essentially of male and female singers with their *tar* or tambourine. A single violin accompanies and supports their singing. The female apprentices who do not know how to play the tar merely mark the strong beats by clapping their hands. (1931, 21: 231)[23]

Chottin's "ethnographic" observation had also been shaped by the diaries of European travelers associated, directly or indirectly, with the French administration even before the Protectorate was established in Morocco. This is the case of Eugène Aubin, a member of the French foreign service, who had traveled extensively in the Middle East and central Asia before being appointed First Secretary of the French Legation in Tangier. In 1903, while spending six months on an official mission in Fez, he wrote about his traveling accounts in pre-Protectorate Morocco, collected in his book, *Morocco of Today* (1906). The excerpt below illustrates the similarities between Aubin and Chottin's acoustic perception and description, where vocality is linked to morality.

This music is of two kinds—the lighter music, *griha*, composed of easier airs and popular ballads with a vague sort of instrumental accompaniment; and serious music, *ala*, in which the airs are complicated, the song artistic, and the performance of real musicians on difficult instruments is required. [...] The other [music] is regarded as a frivolous pastime, suitable for foolish women or a man's debauch. [...] Today [Shikha Brika] is the darling of the city, although she is very coarse, and has a grating voice. (Aubin 1906, 270–75)

If it is true that the interest in Morocco's musical heritage formed part of the larger colonial cultural policies that attempted to support and preserve Moroccan traditions (Shannon 2015, 95), it is also true that the French shaped the music history of Morocco and the tastes of its elites with important historical ramifications (Najmi 2007, 2:15–30; Pasler 2012–13, 28).

Najmi cites the example of a contemporary of Chottin, Idris Ibn Abd al-Ali al-Idrisi, who described ʿaiṭa as a rural art practiced by those dwelling in the countryside, emphasizing the need to restore it (*liʾiṣlaḥih*) in order to help its progress (*taqaddumih*) and, consequently, the refinement (*tahdhīb*) of those who practiced and listened to ʿaiṭa. In this context, changes in the poetic language—from vernacular to classical Arabic—and the substitution of disgusting words (*alfaz shanī'a*) and foolish and ugly (*sufahā wa qabḥā*) expressions became paramount for reforming the genre (Najmi 2007, 2:27–37).

Following Najmi, I draw from a couple of contemporary passages that are representative of contemporary discourses, to illustrate the long-lasting effect that colonial writings had on the music traditions associated with *l-'arubiya*. While first statement erases an Arab Bedouin influence in the history and the panorama of Moroccan music, in the excerpts that follow, the acoustic perceptions and descriptions of *'aiṭa* continue to be permeated by Chottin's writings on the problematic entanglements between voice and morality, and roughness or coarseness—as negative qualities—and rurality.

> [T]he position of Morocco at the crossroads, at the western point of the *ancient world*, "grafted" on to the Berber substrate, made it predisposed to assimilate multiple influences: the African Saharan and sub-Saharan rhythms, the survival of Greco-Roman, Phoenician and African rituals, Arab modalism and the Andalusian sophistication. (Aydoun 2014, 10)[24]

> The younger *chikhât* perform their sensual dances (movements of the belly and hips, the body undulating and quivering, the hair swaying [. . .]), in front of the audience. [. . .] Nowadays, this entertaining and at times erotic side takes over the real meaning of 'aïṭa. (Ibid., 124–26)[25]

> Bouch'aïb's violin makes a rasping sound, emanating melancholy. [. . .] First, Fatna intones a cry full of suffering, "*houahhaaaa . . .*," a hoarse cry, nearly a sob. [. . .] It is great moment for the *'ayta*. This version of *Kharbusha* is soaked with raw rural emotion. (Aguila and Zagzoule 2000, 175)[26]

> The more guttural voices of Safi seek tragedy and tension, which have been transformed in the Casablanca version: this more plaintive, even sentimental version (which can also be called "glamorous"), puts the social effects of the migration of rural populations toward the city in a musical form: there is less roughness, with more sentimentality. (Ibid., 177)[27]

Ochoa Gautier argues that what it is possible "to hear through the pages of history is the contrasting perception of those who produced the sounds and those who listened to them, as mediated by potentially radically different interpretations of the same sounds" and that, she continues, "once sound is described and inscribed into verbal description and into writing it

becomes a discursive formation that has the potential of creating and mobilizing an acoustic regime of truths, a power-knowledge nexus in which
some modes of perception, description, and inscription of sound are more
valid than others in the context of unequal power relations" (2015, 33). As
colonial historiography magnified the Arab Bedouin stereotype and, consequently, l-'arubi, the colonial "acoustic regime" shaped their sonic difference in the history and the panorama of Moroccan music. Reclaiming ṣawt
l-'arubiya, has proved to be just as problematic.

Through the efforts of a number of Moroccan intellectuals from the
Atlantic plains and plateaus, it became possible to read and to hear a different perception of ṣawt l-'arubiya at the turn of the twentieth-first century
(Rakuk 2000a; Bahrawi 2002; Najmi 2007). The efforts of these intellectuals culminated in the creation of national festivals dedicated to 'aiṭa
and 'abidat r-rma, in the inclusion of both genres in a collection of CDs
produced by the Ministry of Culture, in television specials and mediated
performances broadcast on national television, in academic and nonaca-
demic publications, without counting the availability of performances on
the internet. However, a critical component of that which I have described
elsewhere as the process of "revalorization" (Ciucci 2010) meant shaping a
counternarrative turning both genres, particularly in the case of 'aiṭa, into
honorable artistic expressions and, consequently, anchoring them into a
specific past. In this context, three crucial points were reiterated:

1. The Protectorate was blamed for the degradation of both genres, by the
   way in which 'aiṭa and 'abidat r-rma were utilized and heard by the
   colonizers.
2. Critical debates focused on the poetic text, which, in the case of the
   qaṣida, is said to derive from the oral epics of the Beni Hilal as a war-
   rant of authority and authenticity (Bauman and Briggs 2003, 145–50).
   Turning the poetic text into an enduring historical object whose significance rests on a perceived unchangeability also motivated a form of tex-
   tual scrutiny meant to reshape the perception of the linguistic dimension
   of l-'arubiya.
3. The shikhat were presented as unsung heroes, so as to dispel any notion
   of impropriety associated with the voice of the rural.

The process of revalorization meant that ṣawt l-'arubiya came to embody a political, cultural, and moral struggle. Through the voice of the rural,
Moroccan intellectuals with origins in l-'arubiya attempted to validate their
moral worth and their authority at an important moment that coincided
with the ascension of the USFP (Socialist Union of Popular Forces) to the

head of the government; an ascension that marked a crucial change in the political and cultural life of Morocco. As members of a party whose support was historically most significant among the rural population and the urban lower classes, the intellectuals and the politicians of the USFP were no longer associated with the urban elites but instead anchored in the rural. It was this change that prompted ṣawt l-ʿarubiya to emerge at the center of a political and a cultural debate, for the new class of intellectuals were eager to prove that culture was not just an urban or an elitist phenomenon. However, and despite the mediated presence of ʿaiṭa and ʿabidat r-rma in Morocco, the voice of the rural continues to be a problematic presence, as much as the place of l-ʿarubiya in Morocco.

[T]he "coronavirus" is one of the manifestations of those changes which are happening in the world at this time. The Moroccan character, first and foremost, needs to be built on trusting personal capacities, local abilities in managing scarcity, and in the characteristics of beduinity (badawa), as Ibn Khaldun says, but not in the sense of "l-ʿarubiya." Beduinity in the sense of dealing with the hardships of life, with scarcity, and with daily challenges. These are the strengths of society and this is the strength on which we need to invest in the construction of a new Morocco. (Tozy 2020)[28]

CHAPTER 2

The Voyage

Voicing l-'arubiya *in the Crossing*

To consider the migrant from the shore [. . .] is equivalent to reinforcing the barrier between "us" and "them," the frontier between residents and foreigners. Above all, it means not taking the side of the migrant, not wearing his clothes, not assuming his point of view. (Di Cesare 2017, 34).[1]

23 February 2019, Citerna

Abdelilah Ab. is a forty-seven-year-old mason who arrived in Italy in 1997. Originally from El Borouj, a town and a rural commune in the Casablanca-Settat region, he is a proud Beni Meskine who asserts, albeit humorously, that El Borouj is the capital of Italy and that the Italian soccer team is that of the Beni Meskine. I was taken by Abdelilah on our very first meeting. Unlike other migrant men I met—tired, broken down, and understandably hesitant to speak—Abdelilah seemed unafraid and had a grin that kept me guessing. He is a wonderful raconteur who effortlessly commands attention with a narrative that often blurs, or perhaps challenges, the boundaries between reality and imagination.

Today we are invited to his home in Citerna, a small town in the Alta Valle del Tevere with a population of 3514 and where thirty-eight Moroccans are said to reside. Official numbers do not take into account seasonal workers and "visitors" who are known to overstay their visas, all of whom inevitably inflate the numbers of the undocumented. Governments have failed to take into consideration the daily "ghost" landings (sbarchi fantasma) of men, women, and children arriving at Lampedusa in small boats that go undetected. This flow has never stopped, even as the Italian ports were declared closed to the more mediatized arrivals of nongovernmental organizations' ships rescuing migrants at sea, or during the first wave of the COVID-19 pandemic.

Nobody seems to be able to account for these small boats and their "invisible" passengers.

It is a windy day, and Abdelilah quickly ushers us inside his home, where Bouchra, his wife, greets us with a warm embrace. They have been waiting for us. The living room is furnished Moroccan-style; two low wall-to-wall sofas (sdader) with a round low table on top of a modern carpet. With the exception of a large rectangular black and silver-like plaque inscribed with a verse of the Qur'an, the walls are unadorned. The table is covered by the type of generous spread that guests can expect to find in Moroccan homes, where hospitality is paramount. Bouchra's offerings are an interesting mix. She tells me that the olive oil and the honey come from Umbria; there are homemade Moroccan pancakes (msǝmmǝn), cookies, almonds, dates, warm Moroccan-style homemade bread, and olives that she gets from Morocco or from local stores with Moroccan products—food that Ruba Salih identifies as reflecting a double belonging (2000, 29). "Do you like tea?" she asks as she enters the room with a large teapot, which she places on a shiny metal tray of traditional Moroccan tea glasses.

We begin to converse, and I ask Abdelilah how he came to Italy. I am interested to learn more about how migrants remember and narrate their journeys, particularly their first. The media tends to focus on snippets of tragic accounts in which migrants can be heard for only a few seconds before being drowned out by long commentaries and discussions, silenced by more authoritative voices, anonymous images, and a soundtrack that, at best, may be described as a sonic misrepresentation of these migrants and their experiences. This is the type of fiction that seems to dominate the passage from the South to the North that undocumented migrants undertake these days (Álvarez 2013, 48).

I hand Abdelilah my notebook for him to draw and talk about his journey (see map below). He begins by drawing a line, tilted slightly downward, on top of which he indicates Morocco—his point of departure—in Arabic before switching to write entire names, or just the initials of places where he transited, in Latin characters: B for El Borouj, CS for Casablanca, and so on. Abdelilah is semiliterate; for the most part he writes what he hears, transcribing and interpreting sounds; this is how Caserta turns into Cazrta. I am familiar with his writing technique; it is the same one my mother uses.

"Ibn Battuta," someone comments, humorously comparing Abdelilah to the renowned twelfth-century Moroccan traveler. We start laughing as Bouchra—who received some formal education while growing up in

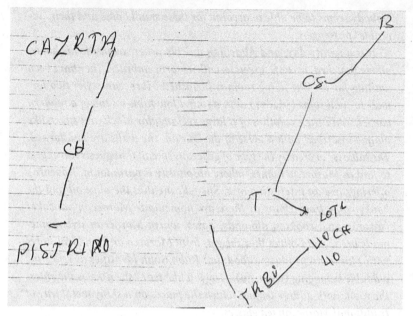

Figure 5. Map of Abdelilah

Casablanca—unsuccessfully tries to grab the pen and paper out of her husband's hands. Her voyage was quite different from those of Abdelilah and the other men: like most Moroccan women in Italy, she traveled legally through the 1998 family reunification law, which allows migrants who have a residency permit of at least one year, living in a suitable home, with a lease in their names, and with a verified annual income, to bring their spouses, children, and relatives to Italy. It was this law that marked the feminization of Moroccan migration to Italy, which until then had been predominantly male.

It is unclear how Abdelilah was able to be listed as an undocumented migrant in Italy while living in Morocco and, subsequently, how he managed to obtain legal status with the 1995 sanatoria. This is a complicated procedure in which undocumented migrants must pass a series of interviews in person before normalizing their status. We are all curious to know how much Abdelilah paid for such an elaborate arrangement to work, but our question goes unanswered. Instead, he begins narrating his journey.

"I was afraid to be interrogated at the European borders; that is what they do to find out if you are a fraud. I was afraid because I did not speak a word of Italian. I did not want to raise suspicions; how could I have

lived in Italy for two years as an undocumented person without speaking a word of Italian? I would have been caught and sent back . . . and this is why I decided to travel through Tunis. I left El Borouj for Casablanca by a karwila *[a cart pulled by horses or donkeys] and once in Casablanca I took a plane to Tunis.*[2] *It was the first time I had ever left Morocco. From the airport in Tunis I took a taxi and asked the driver to take me to a nice hotel. The taxi was expensive, about $40. And the hotel that the driver took me to, a five-star hotel, was also expensive—another $40. I was penniless after that!"* We look at him incredulously. *"But the hotel was really nice,"* Abdelilah continues, *"the best night I have ever spent! From Tunis I left for Trapani on a ferry. The one for Palermo was full."*

"Wait! Wait! First right and then left," someone tells Abdelilah. He stops drawing. He hesitates about the direction of the line between Tunis and Trapani, the line across the Mediterranean Sea. *"But you did not indicate the Mediterranean!"* I comment once he has made up his mind, aware that he prefers to keep a distance from the sea, to look at it from afar.[3]

As he once told me, the sea is nice when you look at it from a distance. *"It's right there! But it is best to leave it unmarked! Anyhow, as I was saying, once on the ferry I would not talk to anyone; I did not want other migrants to find out I had never been to Italy, so I remained silent and alone most of the time. When we finally arrived at Trapani, I was terrified. We were all waiting to cross the border and get off the ferry. Each time the policeman stamped a passport I felt sick. I felt a wave of heat going all the way up to my head, and as soon as I heard the sound of the stamp [he thumps his fist loudly on the table to mimic the sound], it felt as if I were coming down from something, and my legs would start to tremble. It was terrible! I was so afraid of being caught."* Abdelilah has run out of space on the first page of the notebook and ponders where he can continue to draw the map of his voyage. He looks at me to make sure that I do not mind and turns to a new blank page, at the top of which he writes *"Cazrta."* *"When I finally made it to land, I traveled to Caserta [at the time it was easier for migrants to get their residence permits since the Camorra would facilitate the process] and then to Naples, where I stayed at the train station for three days."* *"What do you mean?"* we all asked; *"why?"* *"I was going to travel to Rome, and so I was there waiting. I remember that when I first arrived in Naples and saw all those street beggars, I was shocked and asked myself, are they Italians? Impossible, I thought. In my mind everything was perfect in Italy. I thought that the country was protected by an invisible glass bulb* [bola, lit., light bulb] *and that nothing could happen."* *"Do you mean like a snow globe* [palla di cristallo*]*?" I ask. "Yes, yes, exactly!" Abdelilah continues "I ended up staying in the Naples train station for three days, and because I was afraid of being robbed while sleeping—I had noticed how people would steal the wallets of those who slept at the station—I remained awake for three whole days!" "Are you serious? Three whole days?" we all ask incredulously.

Train stations must have had a tremendous impact on the imagination of these migrants, who attributed to Italy an almost mythical character, and who thought of it as the land of fabulous adventures. with a "seductive halo of a mythical and golden elsewhere" (Jacquement 1996, 378), an El Dorado with wealth and abundance—a colonial vision shaped by Europe, which continues to think of and present itself as the object of infinite desire and envy on the part of the peoples of the South with regard to its civilization, its progress, and its wealth (Antonelli 2010, 90). Always places of ill repute, train stations are where many of these migrants first experience Italy outside of the "glass globe." "The train station of Catania was deserted when I arrived in the 1990s," someone else says. "I was scared because I was all alone and nobody was there. There is the Mafia in Sicily . . . I could feel it. The police would walk around the station kicking those of us sitting on the floor in the station. All I remember was them screaming: fuori, via, fuori, via di qui *[get out, leave, get out of here]*! I was all alone and terrified. Thank God someone took me to a hotel nearby so that I could close my eyes and sleep."

Abdelilah resumes his narrative, breaking through a silence permeated by memories of fear, solitude, and shame. "From Naples I finally took a train to Rome, and from there I went back to Caserta." "What? Why?" Once again we are astounded by such a trajectory. Wasn't he supposed to join his brother in Umbria? But here, as elsewhere, his narrative becomes unclear, puzzling, and fragmented, like his map—many of the details of the journey remain unmarked, unknown to me and to the others. "Yes, I was trying to join my brother, who was working for a family in Umbria, in Pistrino, and I needed to get in touch with him but had no idea where I was or how to get there! The family for whom my brother worked did not have a phone at the time, and so he had given me the number of an old lady who lived nearby." "Yes, remember how difficult and how expensive it used to be to make a call in the '90s?" someone else says. "One had to find a public phone and get a lot of change to be able to make a call. Other times, if one was lucky, one could find a phone store where it was possible to make calls and pay at the end. But there was usually a long wait. We would line up early in the morning to call home . . . particularly on Sunday. One could send postcards or, better yet, send *cassette tapes on which we could record messages for family members and friends at home." "Anyhow," Abdelilah continues, "I kept calling the number I was given—God bless her, the poor woman died—and she used to curse me out every time I called because she had no idea who I was or what I was saying. She would pick up the phone and say* pronto . . . pronto . . . pronto . . . chi è? *[hello . . . hello . . . hello . . . who is this?]. I was desperate. Then one day someone from the family with whom my brother was staying asked the old lady if anyone had called; it was then that she told them that someone would call her every day and bother her. That is when they understood that it was me, and the next time I called my brother was finally there. After that I went to Cerbara and finally to Pistrino. Thank God I made it."*

Abdelmalek Sayad argues that when someone is asked to account for his experience of migration and, in particular, for the contradiction one discovers between the reality of his migrant condition and the enchanted image that he previously held, "it is the traditional form of discourse, with its phrasing, saying, manner of speech and all of the colloquial expressions suited to the traditional ways of thinking, which is used to convey new contents" (2000, 166). Migrants recount their experience according to a self-narration that allows those who have traversed and continue traversing the same space in similar conditions to engage and to resocialize after the journey. Abdelilah's nonlinear narrative, with its fragmented geography, the details about some facts and the silence of others, as well as some of its bewildering itineraries, can be understood as the subjective reappropriation of the experience of migration, a resistance performed through techniques of an autobiographical reconquest (Makaremi 2011, 80–81), a way to undermine the assumed linearity of migration (Chávez 2017, 233), a way to recapture a voice that is critical for societies that Abdelkebir Khatibi defines as silent because "even as they speak, they are not heard in their difference" (2019, 28). But what about when a voyage is sung, set to music, mediated, and transnationally circulated? Is it then possible to recapture a meaningful voice and for migrant men from the Atlantic plains and plateaus to become audible? And if so, what might their account of an undocumented journey sound like?

This chapter focuses on the sonorous account of a hazardous crossing. In it, I analyze a song that narrates the voyage and the experience of undocumented migration and ends with the tragic death of a young Moroccan man crossing the Mediterranean Sea. My analysis argues for the song's critical reflection, for its ability to convey the emotions and state of mind of those who cross. The song allows different generations of Moroccan men from these regions who are engaged in the practice and the imagination of migration across the Mediterranean to be heard, and although commercially produced and in circulation beyond borders, it is steeped in its locality. Its rough or coarse quality marks and differentiates migrants whose intimate and enduring ties to *l-'arubiya* respond to the colonial construction and subsequent denigration of *l-'arubi* discussed in chapter 1. Through it we are able to reflect on critical questions concerning migration in a geocultural zone where the historically determined differences between North and South are increasingly acute. This song focuses on a critical passage that Abdelilah, in his account, left conspicuously unmarked: the Mediterranean.

Here I am asking, what would it mean to conceive of this song as a sonorous travelogue? What role does *l-'arubiya* play in this account, this testimony about a journey across the Mediterranean? How could the humiliating experience of clandestine crossing be reworked if we were to frame it in reference to a theological and moral dimension of "departing" (Pandolfo 2018, 194)? How does the song attempt to restore dignity and personhood in circumstances in which these migrants are normally portrayed as utterly undignified and desperate? And in this context, how does the song reveal a vocabulary that stresses not only the moral but also the physical qualities of what it means to be a "real man" (*rajal*)?

MIGRATION, COLONIALISM, AND PHOSPHATE: THE CASE OF KHOURIBGA

20 August 2014, Khouribga

On Sunday mornings the streets of Khouribga are relatively quiet except for the weekly market, located in a large, open, unpaved area; it is one of the largest in the region. The entrance is marked by constant traffic— cars, buses, food carts, and men and women carrying bags full of food and other items, as well as vendors who approach potential customers in the effort to sell loose cigarettes, tissues, lighters, and so forth. The market is also the site where most Moroccans come to buy used cars imported by migrants from Italy; Khouribga is, after all, located in one of the most significant regions of origin of Moroccan migrants to Italy.

The layout of this sizable market resembles that of the commercial neighborhoods of old cities in Morocco; the tentlike stands are organized in accordance with the products they sell. The butchers display their meat on counters; close by are the herbalists, who lay a selection of local herbs and spices on a piece of cloth on the ground; in a crowded stand one finds Italian soap and traditional black olive-based soap used by women

in their weekly visits to the hammam; *while on another stand* jellabas
*(traditional long, loose-fitting outer robes with a hood and long sleeves,
worn by both women and men) are sold next to T-shirts sporting the
names of Italian soccer teams and designers.*

*Ahmed and I are sitting behind one of the roasted-meat vendors, un-
der the tent of an open-air café where plastic stools and chairs are arranged around a few plastic tables. A group of young Moroccan men
wearing jeans, sneakers, and T-shirts sit and chat among themselves as
they wait for their orders to arrive. The vernacular Arabic of the region is
easy to recognize, but here in Khouribga it is peppered with Italian terms.
They are talking about Italy; one of them has returned to Morocco for his
summer vacation, just like the family sitting at a table next to us, eager to
tell me that they reside in Brescia.*

*Among the smoke of the roasted meat, the chaotic back-and-forth of
people, and the destitute women and children who wait for customers to
finish their meals so that they can scavenge the leftovers, an old man with
a beat-up viola moves from one table to the next. He performs short excerpts of a genre that the customers of the café grew up with. I recognize
the rough quality of the viola—an iconic marker of a sound embedded in
the countryside. This is the music that the group of young men sitting next
to us have requested; they begin to clap their hands and sing a few lines.*

Khouribga is a town of about 200,000 residents located in the Beni
Mellal-Khenifra region of the Atlantic plains and plateaus, whose history
cannot be disentangled from that of the Office Chèrifien des Phosphates
(OCP), a state-owned company with obvious colonial interests that has
been described as an "instrument of exploitation and domination par excellence" (Lenhardh 1921, in Bianco 2015, 69). Founded in 1920, during the
French Protectorate, the OCP became the driving force of the urbanization of this phosphate-rich region, establishing Khouribga as a mining town
in 1924 after a massive expropriation of collective lands belonging to local
tribes. The OCP kept the economic, social, and cultural life of Khouribga
under its control; the company was responsible for employment, housing,
health care, education, and services. The development of Khouribga, in
fact, went hand in hand with that of the OCP (Bleuchot 1969; Duchac 1970;
Adidi 2000; Bianco 2015).

In the 1950s Khouribga became an important site for the rural-to-
urban exodus triggered by the profound changes taking place during the
Protectorate in rural areas, by droughts that grew more intense with the es-
calation of phosphate extraction, and by the overcrowding of the available
cultivated land, which could no longer satisfy people's needs. Until the 1950s

local employment in Khouribga depended largely on the phosphate industry. But with the increasing mechanization of mining and the world phosphate crisis in the 1970s, the town faced economic difficulties. Unable to
go back to lands expropriated for laughably small sums of money and now
polluted by open-pit mining, it was impossible to restore the region's traditional agropastoral system, a situation that led to a level of unemployment
that continues to exceed the national average (Adidi 2000; Bianco 2015).[4]

Today Khouribga is an occasional stop for tourists heading elsewhere in
Morocco. Unlike Casablanca, the town never developed into a full-blown
urban center. Its dysfunctional job market, which led to the development
of an informal economy and an economy of survival, forces an exceptionally
high number of people—particularly the youth who were once attracted to
work in the mines—to migrate to Europe (Adidi 2000; Bianco 2015).[5] The
exploitation of phosphate—designed to benefit the agricultural industry of
the Global North—has transformed these men into migrants forced to flee
a devastated and unhealthy region that offers them neither viable employment, economic opportunity, nor, more importantly, a horizon.

> Just as armies of young people waited for a long time for the OCP to save
> them from the clutches of grinding poverty, they also threw themselves
> headlong into boats of death. Some of them were lucky and made it to the
> other side. Others, unfortunately, lost their lives, drowning in the sea. For
> example, the youth of the neighborhood of "Labrique" and those of the
> rural village of "Foqra" have experienced collective death off the coast be-
> cause of the clandestine immigration toward the Italian El Dorado: Italy, the
> preferred country for unemployed young Khouribgis. (Sahnoun 2012)[6]

VOICING THE CROSSING: "L-ḤƏRRAGA"

13 August 2015, Casablanca

*We are discussing "L-ḥərraga,"[7] a song that has haunted me since I first
heard a recording of it, a song about undocumented migration, clandestine crossing, loss, and death, since, as Alex Chávez reminds us, death "is
a reality that migrants face" (2017, 233). The song's fast-paced rhythm,
close call-and-response, and seemingly festive atmosphere might be heard
as being in stark contrast with its text and as having some other connotation. But it is not so, at least not for those whose listening has been shaped
by a musicopoetic genre that is thought to embody l-ʿarubiya.*

*"The subject of undocumented migration is a very sensitive one in our
region," Redouane El Aibed, the leader of a well-known music group and*

a native of Khouribga,[8] *tells me. "Do you know how they refer to our region?*
To Khouribga, Oued Zem, Tadla, Fquih Ben Salah, and Beni Mellal? As
*the triangle of death [*mutallat al-mut*]?*[9] *This is because of the great num-*
ber of youths who lost their lives attempting to cross the Mediterranean."
"Is that why you wrote 'L-ḥərraga'?" I ask Redouane. "Yes," he replies,
*"we wanted to tackle the idea of undocumented migration [*l-ḥərg*] in a*
song; we wanted people to be aware of the crossing. We all have friends
who died in the Mediterranean. To think that in our neighborhood of
Labrik alone, we lost twelve young men in one day . . . ! We needed to
send a message to those who want to make the crossing and go to Italy."

The title of "L-ḥərraga" (video ex. 2.1) refers to those attempting undocumented migration (*l-ḥərg*), which is metaphorically described as "the
burning" (from the verb to burn, *ḥaraqa*).[10] The title also refers to the figure
of "the burned life," a life without a name and without legitimacy, since undocumented migrants who successfully cross the Mediterranean have been
known to burn their papers in order to erase their legal identity, making
their repatriation challenging.

It is a song that belongs to the repertory of *'abidat r-rma*, a genre that has
been described as "an extension of the peasant's natural environment and
nomadic life ideally performed during harvest time" (Amine and Carlson
2012, 36) in the territory of the Atlantic plains and plateaus. Performances
of *'abidat r-rma* are embedded in *l-'arubiya*, as Shikh Sharqi explains.

Our songs are from the countryside . . . *'abidat r-rma* follows the harvest-
ers [*tab'in ḥaṣṣada*], follows the rural [*tab'in l-'arubiya*], dwells in the
countryside . . . we sing about the countryside and live in the countryside,
the countryside is who we are, it is our origin [*aṣəl dyalna*], and this is why
'abidat r-rma sings and praises this rural space, the plants, the trees. . . .
(Shikh Sharqi, personal communication, 7 August 2015, Ben Slimane)

Critical to a discussion about the ways in which Moroccans from the Atlantic plains and plateaus experience the rural are ideas about a voice coming from the throat, whose timbre or tonal quality is described as rough or
coarse (*ḥərsh*), in a metamusical discourse that disrupts the colonial "acoustic regime" discussed in chapter 1, revealing a local aesthetic that is said to
reflect the everyday life of the countryside and signaling an embodied sound
with collectively recognized meaning. In the process of reclaiming and re-
signifying the sonic difference of *l-'arubi*, this rough vocal timbre is central,
since it is thought to embody nature and the environment, as well as experiences of space, time, and memory.

Amanda Weidman reminds us that the materiality of the voice is also a feature of spoken language (2015, 235). Understanding the significance of a vernacular Arabic rooted in place and a vocal timbre that is thought to be unaffected by urban influences allows an exploration of how *l-ʿarubiya* is embedded in a set of aesthetics said to reflect the roughness of rural life, the land, the environment, the hard work of the peasants, and their verbal expressions.

The voice of the rural marks the musicopoetic genre to which "L-ḥərraga" belongs and from which it cannot be dissociated. It provides the linkage between verbal art, everyday language, aesthetics, and ideological and moral discourse; it also refers to the historical conditions that tie my interlocutors to rural values and ways of living.

Since the late 1990s *ʿabidat r-rma* has gone from being a musical tradition performed by older men to a thriving genre of popular music performed by young men at private and public celebrations, festivals,[11] and on television.[12] Produced and disseminated through cassettes, CDs, VCDs, DVDs, MP3s, and the Internet, nowadays *ʿabidat r-rma* circulates in Morocco and abroad. These changes have inevitably affected the poetic themes of *ʿabidat r-rma*, such as that of undocumented migration, as well as changes in technology and instrumentation.

Paul Greene (2005) has argued that Western sound technologies are drawn into music making around the world, and that their hard-wiring begins to structure local musical practices in certain ways, imposing their own musical logics onto the societies that adopt them. He has also argued that sound technologies are used to achieve local aims, and that the emergence of distinct studio sounds may reflect the drive toward difference and distinction in technological music production. "L-ḥərraga" exemplifies this argument. In the recording, the poetic lines are punctuated by the *kamanja*, an instrument that is not present in the tradition and that affects the genre in two important ways. On the one hand, its amplified sound is a reminder of the viola-saturated sound of Moroccan *shaʿbi*; on the other hand, the viola introduces melodic modes (*maqamat*) that are usually absent from the more traditional examples of the genre, and whose presence inevitably emphasizes the act of singing in a tradition otherwise characterized by the intertwining of speech, cries, and singing. In the recording, furthermore, it is also critical to take notice of the addition of an electric bass—used to reinforce the low-pitched strokes of the percussion instruments that traditionally signal the strong accents of a rhythmic cycle; the use of a glass soda bottle beaten with a wooden stick—to support the *məqqəṣ* and thus allow better clarity of sound in the recording; and the use of frame drums with

Figure 6. CD cover

plastic heads, rather than goatskin, which have a brighter sound and do not lose tension with changes in temperature.

The recording, therefore, continues to articulate an ideal sound, but it is adapted to the style of *shaʿbi* also entrenched in *l-ʿarubiya*. "L-ḥərraga" therefore still appeals to its local audience—those of the Atlantic plains and plateaus in Morocco—while simultaneously repositioning itself in a popular and transnational context in which the population of these very regions has migrated, is trying to migrate or is imagining migrating: in this case, to Italy. This repositioning is also evident in a CD cover reproduced above, where on one side the group wears a contemporary version of traditional Moroccan attire, while on the other side they wear what the group perceives to be an Italian attire, which is clearly inspired by how Hollywood has largely characterized Italians in the United States. It is also worth noticing the language of the CD cover—a mix of Arabic and French.[13]

In my discussion of a commercial recording of "L-ḥərraga," I will analyze some of the iconic sounds and poetic characteristics associated with *l-ʿarubiya* and at the same time draw attention to changes and adaptations to support my argument that rather than being a static identity formation, the notion of *l-ʿarubiya* I present is also necessarily forged against the backdrop of migration and, in particular, the crossing of the Mediterranean to Italy.

"L-ḥərraga" is a vernacular *qaṣida* (ode) characterized by a succession of verses, each divided into two hemistichs ending on the same or a similar rhyme, with rhyming understood more in terms of similarity of sound rather than as following set rules. Like other vernacular *qaṣaʾid*, it has no single rhyme or poetic meter. The poem is divided into two large sections, each followed by a refrain marked by a change in the poetic and musical structure (see lines 23–25 and 39–40). "L-ḥərraga," which recounts the experiences of the undocumented crossing from the point of view of a migrant and his mother, consists of three main narratives: the imagination of and preparation for the voyage, the actual experience of the voyage, and the death of the migrant, as experienced in the first person and as experienced by his mother.

In this commercial recording the first line of "L-ḥərraga" is preceded by an instrumental introduction that presents the basic compound duple meter that, aside from changes in rhythmic accents, accompanies the song throughout, and the *bayati maqam* on which the melodic material of the song is based.[14] All the lines are sung antiphonally: the first hemistich is sung by the lead vocalist and the second by the ensemble. The intimate dialogue between mother and son,[15] as well as their different perspectives, is effectively introduced in the first two lines. Particularly haunting is the mother, whose plea, *wa fin ghadi* (where are you going?), resonates throughout the first section of the song. This is a sonic presence that is particularly meaningful for my Moroccan interlocutors; it is the mother whom these migrants constantly invoke, as in the case of l-Bachir, a quiet and melancholic man from Khouribga, who lives alone and goes back to Morocco once a year to be with his family.

> L-Bachir works long and poorly compensated hours on a tobacco plantation in the Alta Valle del Tevere. It is not the life he had envisioned when he first arrived. Sitting outside a bar in Pistrino, he used a few verses of a song to convey his own experience through the experience of the protagonist, using a third-person narrative to veil his own sense of failure, the shame he carries around, the burden of not having achieved the better life he had hoped for.

> *mmwimti, mmwimti ash jabni hna*
> *ḥatta ana bghit ndir kif daru jirani*
> *kif daru jirani . . .*

> Mother, mother, what took me here?
> I too want to be like my neighbors
> To be like my neighbors . . .

> *"People saw what it is like here, what it is like [kifash]." There is no interruption between poetry and prose here. L-Bachir is now explaining*

the verses to me, echoing the final part of his comment, "what it is like,"
just as he did with the second verse of the song. "When he arrived, he
saw this view [məndər]. What did he think at first? He thought that one
arrives here and is at ease [kətriḥ], works, builds a home, is free of wor-
ries [tranquillo], and that everything is fine. But he saw something else
[shkəl akhor]! He still does not have his documents, and he tells her . . .

> *mmwimti bghit ghir nṣaib l-uraq*
> *wa nji ʿəndek*
> *wa nji ʿəndek . . .*

> Mother, I only want to get the documents ready
> And come see you
> And come see you . . .

it is a long time, six or seven years since he has returned to Morocco."

L-Bachir's shame is multilayered. One the one hand it is associated with
the fact that migration is "intimately intertwined with local ideas of masculinity and manhood" (Menin 2016, 27), since only a successful migrant is
referred to as a "real man" (Sabry 2005, 15); on the other, because migrants
who do not return home are considered to be cut off (*qaṭiʿin*) from their
families, they are scorned and considered not to have honor (Persichetti
2004, 96). Being away or cut off from one's mother, therefore, is not only
painful but also a source of humiliation with respect to the community
at large.

Another significant metaphor in "L-ḥərraga" is found in the second
hemistich of line 1, where the son describes his exile, *l-ghorba*, as fire, as
the burning desire to which the young man falls victim, a desire from which
he cannot escape. Similar to metaphors used to portray love in *ʿaiṭa* but
also common throughout Arabic poetry, it effectively describes the image
of an elsewhere that becomes an obsession, the sickness of the individual
affected by it and, consequently, the rift it produces in his own community.

> *wa mmwimti basləma rani ghadi / wa mmwimti nar l-ghorba ḥrəqtini*
> Farewell, my mother, I am leaving / My mother, the fire of the exile, you
> burned me

The use of a well-known poetic metaphor allows new meanings to be
juxtaposed with old ones and thus permits a listener who knows the poetic
codes to be intimately affected. In this line, however, it is the verb *ḥaraqa* (to

burn)—which refers to "the burning"—that is used in place of *kwa* (to burn with a branding iron, to cauterize), which is more commonly employed to express the pain of love, as in the verse *a kwitini 'la qalbi wa 'əshnu 'aibi* (you burned me, you burned my heart, what's wrong with me?).

However, it is the evocation of *l-'arubiya* that becomes central to a sense of self. In the second hemistich of line 7, where Europe is referred as *bləd r-ruman* (lit., country of the Romans), we find an expression that is first and foremost used in the countryside, where it refers to Europe. In fact, while the noun *r-rum* is used to indicate Europeans in rather negative terms, the adjective *rumi* indicates something made in Europe, European, of foreign provenance and, often, something of poor quality. In everyday parlance, in fact, *rumi* is always contrasted with *bəldi*, from *bləd* (country or village), an adjective that indicates anything that is indigenous, local, often rural, and often of better, purer quality.[16]

Another reference that is typically associated with the countryside is found in later verse (line 37), where the mother's emotions are expressed according to an old belief that makes peasant women leery of ingesting food connected, in one way or another, to their children.

> *a l-hut ma nshri / a kal wuldi mən 'əinih*
> Never again I will buy fish / [The fish] ate my son's eyes

As one of my interlocutors commented upon hearing to this verse: "As long as she lived my mother never ate liver, because she believed that since the liver, rather than the heart, is where sentiments reside, she would somehow hurt us." An even more apparent association is in the last line of the song, where the mother asks her son not to wound her liver, referring to it by the diminutive *l-kbida*, rather than *l-kebda*. Because diminutive forms are mostly used by women to express endearment, they inscribe verses with a sort of "feminine speaking" (Kapchan 1996) that further dramatizes the poetic discourse.

L-'arubiya is also reiterated with the extended use of vocative particles such as *wa*, *a*, *ya*, and *yak*, placed at the beginning of each line. These indicate that a person is being spoken to, much as in everyday conversation in the countryside. Furthermore, the continuous elongation of final vowels, as in the emphasis placed at the end of *ghadi-(a)*, mimics ordinary speech and at the same time—as my interlocutors pointed out—the weeping of professional wailers traditionally hired for funerals in the countryside. This connection is reinforced in line 28, in which the migrant asks his grandmother to summon the wailer for his funeral:

wa dada hiya dada / wa jibu shi ʿaddada
Grandmother, grandmother / Bring a wailer

In the narrative, however, there are also a number of terms indexing a different linguistic register referred to as *ṭafṣiḥ d-darija* (the eloquence of the vernacular), which consists in rendering the vernacular closer to the form of standard Arabic that, as noted by Stefania Pandolfo, is increasingly used by a large section of postcolonial Moroccan society (2007, 333). Terms such as *khwan* (brothers) and *uṭən* (nations), in line 6, thus make reference to those of the younger generation, who have formal schooling and whose language and sense of self are also affected by other ways of being. Similarly, the Arabic adaptation of Italian terms such as *lanshia* (from *lancia*), in lines 14 and 27, or *lamərin* (from *la marina*), in line 23[17]—in both their phonological and written forms—is yet another articulation of the postcolonial in this song.

It is also important to notice the deviation from a linear temporality in the narrative, particularly the mixing of tenses that accompanies the different perspectives of the voyage. Lines 1–3, for example, use the future tense to express the decision to burn and the dream of "making it," the change in status which can be displayed through material goods such as a car,[18] here designated by the term *ḥdid* (iron), rather than by *ṭomobil*, which is another everyday expression used in the countryside. Line 6 instead uses the past tense to represent the reality of the voyage, while the physical rendering of approaching death, the claustrophobic sensation of being trapped with death, is recounted using the present tense (lines 14–15). Throughout this first section, the mother's plea, "where are you going?," continues to resonate and to juxtapose itself with the narrative of the son.

The refrain, marked by a change in the poetic and musical structure (lines 23–25), is sung over the same pitch in unison and antiphonal fashion by the ensemble, building up to a crescendo and a tension that is resolved in line 26, as the second section begins. In line 23 a communal voice, appearing for the first time in the song, observes that "all the burners are worried." It addresses first the mother and then the son, interjecting itself into the dialogue between the two, in the first-person speech that both mother and son use to narrate their personal experience. This communal voice reinforces the mother's message in the first half of line 25 that "your country is better than Europe" and her comment in the second half of the same line, that Europe has a "poisonous heart." The vocal quality used in the refrain deserves special attention: aside from indexing the rural speech of the region, the crying quality of the solo voice—signaled by breaks in the voice or crying—sounds a text that my interlocutors understand as reflecting not only a mother's weeping for the death of her son, but also her rage against a country that forced her son to migrate, as is particularly evident in the second section of the song.

Section 1

1. *wa mmwimti basləma rani ghadi*

Farewell, my mother, I am leaving

wa mmwimti wa nar l-ghorba ḥrəqtini

My mother, the fire of the exile burned me

wa fin ghadi wa fin ghadi l-wlid
Where are you going, where are you going, son?

wa fin ghadi wa fin ghadi l-wlid
Where are you going, son?

2. *wa fin ghadi wa mmwimti ghadi nḥarrəg*
Where are you going? My mother, I am going to burn[19]

wa fin ghadi

Where are you going?

ya u ndir bḥal nas
I am going to do like other people

wa fin ghadi
Where are you going?

3. *wa njib ḥatta ana ḥdid*
I, too, am going to bring back a car

wa fin ghadi
Where are you going?

nkharrəj yiddi mən l-jaj u nzid
For my hand to hang out the window, and drive

wa fin ghadi
Where are you going?

4. *ya wəsh 'ajbek l-ḥal darwish*
Would you like the condition of a poor man?

wa fin ghadi
Where are you going?

ma bqit laqi bəsh n'ayəsh
I can't find a way to make a living

wa fin ghadi
Where are you going?

5. *wa bghit milliun u l-flus*
I want a million and more[20]

wa fin ghadi
Where are you going?

ya galluli ndwzək mən l-qadus *wa fin ghadi*
They told me they will smuggle Where are you going?
me through the tunnel

6. *a uṣəlna s-sebta ya l-khwan* *wa fin ghadi*
We arrived at Ceuta,²¹ brothers Where are you going?

ya lqina n-nəṣṣ mən kull l-uṭən *wa fin ghadi*
There were people from all nations Where are you going?

7. *ya shi mṣəbbaṭ u shi ḥəfyan* *wa fin ghadi*
Some with shoes and others Where are you going?
barefoot

ʿəinihum fi bləd r-ruman *wa fin ghadi*
With their eyes turned toward Where are you going?
Europe

8. *ya basləma ya l-mmwima* *wa fin ghadi*
Farewell, my dear mother Where are you going?

ya basləma rani ghadi *wa fin ghadi*
Farewell, I am leaving Where are you going?

9. *ila mat ghir mmwimti ṣəbri* *wa fin ghadi*
If I die just be patient, my mother Where are you going?

wa ila ʿayesht daba nwulli *wa fin ghadi*
If I survive, I will be back Where are you going?

10. *wa yak l-frəq l-yum ṣʿib* *wa fin ghadi*
Today the separation is hard Where are you going?

ya balghi slami kull l-hbəb *wa fin ghadi*
Say hello to all the loved ones Where are you going?

11. *məlli ṭəllit ʿla l-bhar* *wa fin ghadi*
When I looked toward the sea Where are you going?

wa yak l-mwaj kəthdar *wa fin ghadi*
The waves are speaking Where are you going?

12. *wa fin kənna u fin walina*   *wa fin ghadi*
Where we were and where we   Where are you going?
are now

rah rabbi li hadina   *wa fin ghadi*
God is watching over us   Where are you going?

13. *wa yak ṣ-ṣak 'la ẓahri*   *wa fin ghadi*
The backpack on my shoulders   Where are you going?

wa yək l-mwaj ktəjri   *wa fin ghadi*
The waves come faster   Where are you going?

14. *zadt l-lanshia ya khut*   *wa fin ghadi*
The boat left, brothers   Where are you going?

wa rah l-ḥəbs ḥda l-mut   *wa fin ghadi*
Next to the prison there is death   Where are you going?

15. *ya kulha ishiyar b-idih*   *wa fin ghadi*
Everyone waves to be rescued   Where are you going?

wa yak l-mwaj l-ḥbib   *wa fin ghadi*
Only the waves, my dear   Where are you going?

16. *fin kənna u fin walina*   *wa fin ghadi*
Where we were and where we   Where are you going?
are now

wa yak l-'ali hadina   *wa fin ghadi*
God is watching over us   Where are you going?

17. *ya basləma ya l-mmwima*   *wa fin ghadi*
Farewell, my dear mother   Where are you going?

a basləma rani ghadi   *wa fin ghadi*
Farewell, I am leaving   Where are you going?

18. *ila mat ghir mmwimti ṣəbri*   *wa fin ghadi*
If I die, just be patient, my mother   Where are you going?

wa ila ʿayesht daba nwulli
If I survive, I will be back

wa fin ghadi
Where are you going?

19. *wa yak l-yum l-frəq ṣʿib*
Today the separation is hard

wa fin ghadi
Where are you going?

ya balghi slami kull l-hbəb
Say hello to all the loved ones

wa fin ghadi
Where are you going?

20. *məlli ṭəllit ʿla l-bhar*
When I looked toward the sea

wa fin ghadi
Where are you going?

wa yak l-mwaj kəthdar
The waves are speaking

wa fin ghadi
Where are you going?

21. *basləma ya l-mmwima*
Farewell, my dear mother

wa fin ghadi
Where are you going?

basləma ya l-hnina
Farewell, my sweet one

wa fin ghadi
Where are you going?

22. *həzzit ṣ-suaq ʿla ẓahri*
I carried the backpack on my shoulders

wa fin ghadi
Where are you going?

Refrain I

23. *a l-ḥərraga a lalla kulshi məshṭun*
All the burners, lady, are worried

a lamərin tqəlləb wa kulshi məkhzun
The Italian navy is searching, everyone is hiding

24. *wa kilo ḥəmməṣ mmwimti huma bash nkun*
A kilo of chickpeas, my mother, in order to survive

a mən ḥərr l-khəlʿa a lalla fi qobbi məkhzun
Because of burning fear, everything is hidden in my hood[22]

25. *wa rjəʿ l-bladək a wulidi wa qil bləd r-rum*
Come back to your country, my son, leave Europe alone

a bləd r-rum a lalla ra qəlbu məsmum
Europe has a poisonous heart

Section 2

26. *wa gulu lya wa gulu lya l-bənat*   *wa gulu lya*
Tell me, tell me, my daughters   Tell me!

a wash bṣəḥḥ wuldi mat   *wa gulu lya*
Is it true that my son is dead?   Tell me!

27. *tqəlləbt l-lanshia ya khut*   *wa gulu lya*
The boat turned over, brothers   Tell me!

ya mən sebta təsmʿa l-ghwat   *wa gulu lya*
From Ceuta you can hear the   Tell me!
screams

28. *wa dada wa hiya dada*   *wa gulu lya*
Grandmother, grandmother   Tell me!

wa jibu shi ʿaddada   *wa gulu lya*
Bring a wailer   Tell me!

29. *ʿla wuldi mat bla shahada*   *wa gulu lya*
For my son who died without   Tell me!
prayer[23]

ʿla wuldi mədfun bla l-ʿada   *wa gulu lya*
My son buried without tradition   Tell me!

30. *ya l-mmwimma diri n-naʿy*   *wa gulu lya*
Dear mother, prepare the funeral   Tell me!

wa wuldek mḥal iji   *wa gulu lya*
Your son may not come back   Tell me!

31. *ya kun tshufi ya l-mra*   *wa gulu lya*
If you saw, woman   Tell me!

a l-ʿisha f-wust l-ma   *wa gulu lya*
What life is like in the middle of   Tell me!
the sea

32. *wa shabab rahum day'in*   *wa gulu lya*
The young people are lost   Tell me!

wa fi flaik rahum hargine   *wa gulu lya*
They are migrating in small   Tell me!
boats

33. *ya bqau zərda sardines*   *wa gulu lya*
They have become food for the   Tell me!
sardines

ahya l-ghorba ya bti   *wa gulu lya*
The exile, my daughter   Tell me!

34. *wa kya sa'ad lli ma dərti*   *wa gulu lya*
The fortune you did not make   Tell me!

wa 'la shaban lli day'ati   *wa gulu lya*
To the children you lost   Tell me!

35. *'la ṣabyan lli qədmti*   *wa gulu lya*
To the children you offered   Tell me!

a l-hut ma nshri   *wa gulu lya*
never again I will buy fish²⁴   Tell me!

36. *a kal wuldi mən 'əinih*   *wa gulu lya*
[The fish] ate my son's eyes   Tell me!

wa 'la shaban lli day'ati   *wa gulu lya*
To the children you lost   Tell me!

37. *a 'la ṣabyan lli qədmti*   *wa gulu lya*
To the children you offered   Tell me!

a l-hut ma nshri   *wa gulu lya*
Never again will I buy fish   Tell me!

38. *ya kal wuldi mən 'əinih*   *wa gulu lya*
[The fish] ate my son's eyes   Tell me!

ya l-mmwimma diri n-naʿy
Dear mother, prepare the funeral

wa gulu lya
Tell me!

Refrain 2

39. *wa rjaʿ a wulidi la tkhəllinish wahida*
Come back, my son, don't leave me alone

klam n-nas ra shəlla wa bhər mwaju madida
People's gossip is too much, and the waves of the sea are long

40. *ʿaishək rjaʿ ya wulidi la tkhəlli jərhka fi l-kbida*
Please come back, my son, don't leave your wound in the liver

The feminization of mourning elicits a collective emotional response to pain, suffering, and loss that is central to the poetic and sonic representations of crossing and death, in which the role of the mother is crucial. This compositional device is not unique to "L-ḥərraga," as a song by the *ʿabidat r-rma* troupe of the Ouled Brahim shows (video ex. 2.2).[25] Commenting on a shipwreck in which an undisclosed number of Moroccan youths were lost to the sea—only twelve bodies of young men were found—the song presents the point of view of the mother expressing grief, pleading with the sea, denouncing the infidel (*l-kafər*) for taking her sons away,[26] killing them on their way to Europe. Accompanied by circular frame drums and goblet-shaped hand drums, the absence of an instrument playing the melody allows the verses to be performed according to the traditional intertwining of speech, cries, and singing, accentuating the somber character of the song.

mgabəl l-bhər u tbki
wa ya l-bhər luh li wuldi
miyyət ula hay

I face the sea and cry
Sea, throw my son back to me
Dead or alive

ra ddahum dhak l-kəfr
qtəlhum fi bərra
rani ndəḥḥi u nkabər
fi qəlbi jəmrə

That infidel took them away
He killed them abroad
I make so many sacrifices and try to endure
But in my heart are live coals

mgabəl l-bḥər u tbki
wa ya l-bḥər luḥ li wuldi
miyyət ula ḥəy

I face the sea and cry
Sea, throw my son back to me
Dead or alive

ra mshau a ulad b-thlatha
ghərqu a f-znata
wuldəthum waḥəd
wa saru a fi dəqqa

My three sons left
They drowned in Zenata[27]
I gave birth to them one by one
And they left at once

mgabəl l-bḥər u tbki
wa ya l-bḥər luḥ li wuldi
miyyət ula ḥəy

I face the sea and cry
Sea, throw my son back to me
Dead or alive

muja tbəʿ muja
u bqa nətrəjj
wa ya l-bḥar luḥ li wuldi
baqi ma ja

Wave after wave
I still hope
Sea, throw my son back to me
He has not returned yet

mgabəl l-bḥər u tbki
wa ya l-bḥər luḥ li wuldi
miyyət ula ḥəy

I face the sea and cry
Sea, throw my son back to me
dead or alive

VOICING THE MEDITERRANEAN

The high level of anxiety about the growing presence of Muslims in Europe has focused debates on what Europe owes to Islamic civilization and, in turn, on a particular construction of the past that continues to affect the present. Building on influential scholarship from both sides of the Mediterranean, academics have directly or indirectly explored ways to promote a configuration of the Mediterranean that is based on historical connections to Islamic civilization and culture through Andalusian music, the cultivated urban musical tradition traceable to medieval Muslim Iberia or al-Andalus (Davila 2015; Shannon 2015; Glasser 2016; Reynolds 2020). Despite their undeniable significance, the sonic construction of the Mediterranean advanced by these and other works focusing on a musical tradition associated with the elites, the urban bourgeoisie, and the Andalusian heritage has centered on flows, mobility, and exchanges.

Mobility and exchanges have also informed, albeit from a different perspective, writings on the emergence of hybrid, syncretic, or "contaminated" music, in a Mediterranean understood as a locus of communications that allows different musical experiences to coexist and interact (Chambers 2008; Plastino 2013). Tullia Magrini recognizes the possibility that the Mediterranean can be a barrier (2003, 20); other scholars often downplay this reality of the contemporary Mediterranean, inevitably dismissing the omission of this sea from Abdelilah's map or minimizing the migrants' traumatic memory of the terrifying waves. As we examine the ways in which the Mediterranean is evoked in the songs analyzed in this chapter, we recall that "the Mediterranean is the site of a number of powerful fantasies about migrants and migrant culture, in which music—which indexes migrant bodies, but can at the same time so easily be separated from them—has played a particular important role" (Stokes 2011, 29–30).

Nabil Matar has challenged the perspective of the Mediterranean Sea as a unifying force for the people and civilizations around it, effectively demonstrating how the Arabs have held entirely different views regarding both its name and its significance. The European construction of the Mediterranean connectivity was made possible by the European colonial conceptualization of the Mediterranean, which ignored Arabic writings and Arab voices that, as early as the Middle Ages, viewed the sea as a barrier (*ḥājiz*), a space separating, rather than connecting, two adversarial shores, using the term *Baḥr al-Rūm* to indicate the adversarial other. The nomenclature *Baḥr al-Mutawassiṭ* (In-Between Sea)—of Roman Latin derivation—was in fact rarely used until the nineteenth century, when we begin to see a significant change in the Arabic term for the sea (2019, 18–28).

Nowadays, the Mediterranean is central to the understanding of the global process of mobility, transformation, and social change (Vacchiano 2013, 337). The rebordering of the Mediterranean, which also entails the reconfiguration of tactics and techniques of border policy and immigration enforcement (De Genova 2017), not only influences the control of the so-called migration crisis or emergency, but is also a way of wielding sovereignty, perceiving membership, and producing citizenship in Europe and beyond (Suárez-Navaz 2004).

Naor Ben-Yehoyada posits the possibility that the Mediterranean may provide a fruitful way to challenge a view of Europe that has served Europeans in staging the "distinction between the West and the 'rest'" and argues that new transnational constellations may emerge in the Mediterranean of modern times (2017, 23). If, as Ben-Yehoyada proposes, the Mediterranean can provide a counterexample to a Eurocentric modern view of the world and in the process be attentive to the historical marginalization of Arab voices in its formation, "L-ḥərraga" should be thought of as sounding an alternative experience of the sea, and as giving voice to a counterexample emerging *in* the sea. All there is left to do is listen.

INSCRIBING THE CROSSING

In her work among Moroccan youth, Stefania Pandolfo traces the debates related to the experience, but also the imagination, of undocumented migration to Europe, focusing on the way Islam provides a framework within which despair, and the existential stakes of life and death, are understood and creatively reconfigured (2007 and 2018). In what follows I attempt to connect Pandolfo's attention to ways in which the Moroccan youths she writes about understand and describe their predicaments in two particular lines of "L-ḥərraga," a song about the hazardous crossing of the Mediterranean suffused with despair and death, in an attempt to present this song as a sonorous travelogue that engages with a moral dimension of departing.

ya wəsh ʿajbek l-ḥal darwish / ma bqit laqi bəsh nʿayəsh
Would you like the condition of a poor man? / I can't find a way to make a living

and

məlli ṭəllit ʿla l-bhar / ya l-mwaj kəthdar
When I looked toward the sea / The waves are speaking.

The first line unequivocally expresses the despair, alienation, closure, depression, loss of hope, and sense of stillness experienced by the migrant, which address and reflect on the reality and experience of youth in Morocco, themes that are also debated in academic writings about migration in and from Morocco (Pandolfo 2007 and 2018; Alaoui 2009; Badimon and Bogaert 2014; Bianco 2015; Menin 2016), and in Moroccan literature (Binebine [1999] 2012; Elalamy 2000; Fāḍil 2000; Lalami 2005; Ben Jelloun 2006), popular song, and popular culture (Sabry 2005).

My focus, however, is on how the second line presents the crossing, and in particular on how it captures the state of mind of the young migrant, his vision of the Mediterranean as a horizon, a frontier that as a horizon extends the "insistent reality of the here and now into that optative space or time—the space-time—of the imaginary" (Crapanzano 2004, 14). As the geographer Claudio Minca reminds us: "[A] horizon that paradoxically provides us with the sense of boundary and also the possibility of crossing over, it reminds us that it is the difference and the thrill toward the elsewhere that articulate who we are and, most of all, who we would like to be" (2004, 1).[28]

The horizon of the Mediterranean, however, is inevitably shaped by the shore from which one departs, and on the voyage one chooses or is forced to undertake. In this context *Baḥr r-Rum* (lit., Sea of the Romans), as the Mediterranean is commonly referred to in Morocco, is also a barrier whose waves are indelible in the memory of the burners, a frontier: "Every time I listen to that song it sends chills down my spine. I came to Europe from Khouribga in 1999 as an *ḥərraga*. We left Tangier at night and arrived at Almeria in four hours. What do I remember of that night? All I remember were the waves, those terrifying waves. There were so high and I was so scared. But I made it" (Abdelilah Ta., personal communication, 28 December 2017, San Giustino). In this context, victory in the noble and heroic death of trespassing becomes a symbolic recognition that is intimately connected to a theological and moral dimension of departing, as articulated by Redouane during a discussion about the song: "The aim, the horizon of migration [*l-wijha dyal l-hijra*] in our region is Italy, everyone dreams about Italy. There is nothing here for the young people; we needed to send a message" (Redouane El Aibed, personal communication, 13 August 2015, Khouribga). By comparing the perilous journey of young Moroccan migrants to that of the Prophet Muhammad and his followers from Mecca to Medina (622 CE), Redouane adapts the doctrine of *l-hijra* to a rather different interpretation from what is commonly used to describe the flight from a country governed by unbelievers in order to join the Muslim community.[29]

Muhammad Khalid Masud has shown how the doctrine of *l-hijra* has been quite adaptable to varying political contexts as in the case of Ibn al-Arabi—the great Muslim mystic and philosopher of the eleventh and twelfth centuries—who had already permitted *hijra* from a land of disease and financial insecurity to a better place (1990, 42). According to him, a new dimension of *hijra* has emerged in contemporary times as Muslims have traveled to and even settled in non-Muslim lands for reasons of education, training, and employment. Indeed, a number of distinguished scholars of Islamic law in the Middle East have argued both the necessity and the lawfulness of this type of *hijra* (42). In this context, it is possible to see how undocumented migration—often viewed as the only alternative to what is compared to a slow death (Pandolfo 2007, 350)—may take on a rather different dimension. As Eickelman and Piscatory remind us, "pilgrimage and migration in Muslim societies are forms of political and social action" (1990, 3).

> That song tells the truth, it talks about what really happens. There was nothing for me in the village where I was born, nearby Khouribga. One must make sacrifices in order to leave, in order to ameliorate one's life . . . and death, at times, is necessary . . . it is part of the sacrifice. (Hassan Ja., personal communication, 5 November 2018, Umbertide)

The trope of migration as a risky adventure is also central to male narratives in Morocco, where "facing the risk of clandestine migration with courage, and risking one's life for the sake of one's family and one's future, becomes a masculine performance" (Menin 2016, 29), a "masculine ritual" allowing the passage from *shabb* (young man) to *rajəl* (Juntunen 2015, 2). Undocumented migration, in fact, is experienced as a real undertaking, a test of courage and virility, whereby it is possible to become a man, to obtain one own's independence and demonstrate one's worth (Antonelli 2010, 90).

These responses, however, also need to be understood in local social, economic, and political contexts as well—that is to say, in reference to the historical denigration of the population of the Moroccan Atlantic plains and plateaus. The notion of *l-ʿarubiya*, which the voice of "L-ḥərraga" articulates, has historically been associated with negative values and linked to the uneven development of rural areas. The heroic act of crossing, framed in a theological and moral dimension of departing, effectively refutes such denigration at home and, as we shall see in the following chapter, in Italy.

In this context, migration becomes an adventure, a necessary risk to take if one is to cross over to the other side of the Mediterranean with all that such a journey entails: anticipation, fear, skills, but also excitement (Pandolfo 2018, 194). By narrating this perilous undertaking, the text of "L-ḥərraga" conjures the concept of *riḥla*, a term that can be translated as "journey" but that also defines a whole genre of travel accounts. *Riḥla* was particularly linked with the pilgrimage to Mecca and Medina, a long and risky voyage necessitating a written record that in turn served as a useful guide for future pilgrims (El Moudden 1990, 69). Al-Samaany writes about such descriptions in seventeenth- and eighteenth-century Moroccan *riḥlāt*.

> Al-Murābiṭ compiled his *Riḥla* in poetic form, including invaluable advice from an expert guide, to make pilgrims aware of the most significant points to be taken into consideration while passing in or through these stages. Each stage is followed by a particular [piece of] advice. For instance, when pilgrims arrive at Wādī Khālid, they should supply themselves with water and after visiting the Prophet Khālid's grave to entreat his aid against aggressive Bedouin attacks, every precaution should be taken to fight them. In addition, pilgrims should avoid passing through al-Zāb, where vile Bedouins [might] attack them. When they arrive at Biskra, they must obtain supplies to meet their needs until the next stage, then they should visit 'Uqba b. Nāfi''s grave in Twazar to entreat him. (2000, 115)

From the sixteenth century onward, *riḥla* literature flourished in North Africa and especially Morocco. As argued by the Moroccan historian Abderrahmane El Moudden, because travelers were not detached but often involved in the situation described (1990, 74), by presenting their accounts as eyewitness a *riḥla* is best understood as an autobiographical travelogue.

As the anticipation and the excitement recounted in the first person in lines 2, 3, and 5 give way to a more detached depiction of the arrival in lines 6–7 and the fear along with the display of skills in line 24, it is possible to conceive of "L-ḥərraga" as a *riḥla* whose mass-mediated circulation reminds future travelers—but also the loved ones who are left behind—about the risky voyage.[30]

> The song speaks about a voyage just as a *riḥla* does. It is about someone who decides to travel to change his life, the useless life he has in Morocco,

and in order to do so he must make this dangerous journey by sea. It is an imaginary voyage, but it is also a voyage that is well-known to all Moroccans. For us Muslims, the *hijra* is omnipresent; this is why there is always a sacred dimension to a voyage . . . the *hijra* is a model for us. We salute anyone who departs by saying that he is in the hands of God [*f-idd Allah*]. (Hassan Na., personal communication, 28 October 2018, Rome)

The sound of the *tburiḍa* (from *baruḍ*, gunpowder; to fire muskets) closes the song. This is an equestrian display—also known as *fantasia* in Morocco and abroad—in which a troupe (*sərba*) of six or more riders dressed in traditional attire (the colors, style, and decoration of which vary depending on the region) and armed with muskets charge their horses for two hundred to three hundred meters (650–1000 feet) before abruptly stopping as they simultaneously fire their guns into the air. The *tburiḍa*, which evolved from cavalry charges, is nowadays a celebratory display at local saints' festivals (*moussems* or *mwasim*),[31] tourist events, competitions, and wedding celebrations in the countryside. As a ceremonial practice, but also a military maneuver intended as a demonstration to the sultan of the warriors' prowess, the *tburiḍa* is intrinsically connected to *furusiya*, a concept that describes Arab horsemanship, chivalry, knighthood, heroism, and valor. Ideals of manhood are therefore critical to this all-male environment.[32]

Canova discusses how the strong relationship between Arabs and horses was particularly evident in the critical role that horses and horsemen played in early Arab poetry, which often focused on the spirit of the warrior and on Bedouin pride (2010–11, 238–39). This trope of men and steeds is not mentioned in the poetic text of "L-ḥərraga," but it is sounded out clearly at the end of the performance in the *tburiḍa*. The rhythmic crescendo, the change to loud dynamics, the use of vocal cries imitating those used to incite the horses to gallop or charge (*a, ha, hay*), and the fast antiphonal singing all link the song to Bedouin values, the beauty, honor, strength, and vigor of the horses and the noble horsemen in their battles.

"If we lose *'abidat r-rma* and the horses, we lose everything . . . our pride, our blood, our origins!" This is what a young man in his twenties, originally from the Casablanca-Settat region, told me as I conducted interviews among Moroccan youth in a correctional facility near Rome. The thirty-something Hassan Ha., a welder residing in Umbertide, described with great pride how his father, the leader (*muqaddem*) of a troupe of the region of Sidi Hajjaj, taught him horsemanship: "He taught me how to ride at a young age, and now I go back every year to be part of the *moussem* of our region and ride with the troupe." Despite generational changes, migrant Moroccan men from the Atlantic plains and plateaus remain intimately connected to *l-'arubiya* and, in turn, to specific ideas about manhood embedded in this and other songs. The gendered voice of "L-ḥərraga" challenges, at least symbolically, the humiliating conditions these men experience in their daily lives, restoring dignity to their crossing, reinforcing values questioned in the context of migration, and reminding them what it means to be a "real man" (*rajəl*).

"L-ḥərraga," I posit, becomes a sonorous "site of memory," a sonorous travelogue that offers the possibility to listen to how migrant Moroccan men experience and narrate the Mediterranean Sea, endowing them with dignity and personhood even under circumstances in which they are usually portrayed as utterly undignified and desperate, investing these men with agency as they challenge the view from the shore. In penetrating the Mediterranean, the song questions and upholds its very foundations, acting as a counterpoint to the mass-mediated images of silent bodies at sea, tracing the voice of those who travel in search of different possibilities of life, making them audible, turning into a testimony of their crossing, allowing migrants to generate and share knowledge about their crossing, calling to mind the journey and the feeling of it all.

20 November 2019, Umbertide

"I arrived in Italy on 14 July 1992. I remember that day and the crossing as if it were yesterday," Mustapha Da. says, staring at me with an unsettling intensity. He is eager to tell me his story, and today we met just for that. At nineteen he was already a good welder, and even though he was making a decent living in Morocco, all he wanted to do was come to Italy to realize his vision. "We left Beni Mellal early in the morning by bus and arrived in Tangier the next day. We stayed at a hotel in Tangier for sixteen days, waiting for the voyage to be organized. At the time it was only us, Moroccans, who were doing the crossing, not like now. We waited until nightfall, and at about 10:30 we started the crossing. We were twenty-seven men and one woman, packed together in a wooden boat that began to take on water halfway across." "Were you afraid?" I ask him. "No, no . . . I was prepared." "But can you swim?" "No, not really . . . it was a risk," Mustapha says stoically. And yet, I know how traumatic his crossing was and of the tears he shed in private. "I was not wearing shoes," Mustapha continues; "they were in my backpack together with a pair of pants, a jacket, audiocassettes of music from l-ʿarubiya, *and roasted chickpeas to sustain me." I remind him a line from "L-ḥərraga": wa kilo ḥəmməṣ mmwimti huma bash nkun (a kilo of chickpeas, my mother, in order to survive).*

It took us four hours; we arrived in the middle of the night in Spain.
"Tarifa?" *someone asks.* "I do not know, I can't recall . . . I had never
left Morocco before." "It must have been Tarifa, that is where everyone
leaving Tangier landed at the time." *Tarifa, a municipality located at
the southernmost end of Spain and right across the Strait of Gibraltar, is
known as a surfer's paradise and for its spectacular views of North Africa
from "just across the sea." One cannot help wonder how different the perspective must be when looking out from across the other side of that same
sea, the different experience of a shared space.*

"We arrived on a beach with tents. You know, those where people
stay." "It must have been a tourist campground," *someone else says.* "We
quietly crossed the beach heading to the forest [Mustapha is referring
to the national park in Tarifa], and we walked all night through to the
morning. When we finally got to rest in the woods, my feet were all swol-
len and bruised. I did not have time to put my shoes on; we had to move
fast, and I was afraid of being left all alone behind! We only moved at
night, and so the next night we started walking again. However, in the
middle of the next few nights, a van picked us up and drove us to France.
It was a commercial van, with no windows and little air to breathe. We
were there for a long time until we got to the customs [dogana]." "How?"
I ask. "You were undocumented." "We got off, and as the van continued through customs, we went around, went up into the woods, and
crossed by foot there." "Yes, I see them doing that whenever I go through
Ventimiglia [the frontier between France and Italy]; it is enough to look
up at the surrounding hills and woods to see them," *someone else comments.* "In the evening we got back in the van and went on to Ventimiglia,
got out and in again, and finally arrived in Genoa; in the 1990s that's
where everyone ended up, because it was the preferred route for those
traveling without documents—the invisibles."

For Moroccan men from the Atlantic plains and plateaus engaged in
the practice and in the imagination of migration, men whose rural sense
of self has historically been excluded from other sonorous formations of
the Mediterranean, "L-ḥǝrraga" allows them to counter such exclusion by
experiencing the rural at both a local and a transnational level, introducing
a different network of sites linked by people, history, narrative, genealogy,
movement, and affect (cf. Glasser 2016, 31) and providing a basis for reflecting on the complex and asymmetrical connection between regions, broader
modalities of power, and a critical undercurrent transforming the contemporary Mediterranean.[33]

CHAPTER 3

Spectral Guests,
Marocchini, and "Real Men"

r-rajəl huwa l-kəlma
The real man is he who keeps his word

r-rajəl huwa l-maʿqul
The real man is he who is serious

r-rajəl huwa lli imut ʿla bladu wa wladu
The real man is he who dies for his country and his family

A small town with a population of about 11,230 in the Alta Valle del Tevere, San Giustino has little to offer to tourists with the exception of the fifteenth-century Bufalini Castle and the Historic-Scientific Museum of Tobacco housed in the former Tobacco Farmer Consortium, a warehouse built at the end of the nineteenth century that remained active until 1992, when tobacco processing was transferred into the nearby industrial zone (Saccia 2012).[1]

Created in one of the areas where the cultivation of tobacco is most consistent, the uncritical narrative of the museum aims to reassess the damaging effects of tobacco; among them the high incidence, by Italian and international standards, of stomach cancer in the Alta Valle del Tevere. Lorenzo Alunni refers to what has been analyzed as an incidental connection between the phytosanitary products used for the tobacco plants and stomach cancer as a *sotto-storia* (underground history), a *rumore di fondo* (background noise) with which the residents of the area are forced to coexist (2017, 155–56), a coexistence that inevitably affects migrants working in the tobacco fields.

9 August 2017, San Giustino-Capanne

Yassine has just gotten back from work; he is exhausted, and the visible redness in his eyes is characteristic of an infection. He welcomes us with a smile into the modest apartment he shares with Ali, his father, Mina, his wife, and their two small children; except for his father, everyone else is back in Morocco for the summer. The apartment is located on the second floor of a desolate farmhouse in San Giustino-Capanne. The unkempt courtyard, where in the past peasants would lay out wheat and barley to dry, is used as a space for parking, for drying laundry, for airing blankets, and, weather permitting, for socializing. Moroccan mint, cucumbers, tomatoes, and peppers are grown in the small vegetable gardens tended by some of the migrants.

The farmhouse is isolated, located right underneath a state highway and surrounded by a large field of weeds. It is owned by the local diocese, which rents the apartment for 250 euros a month—a nominal fee, an example of so-called buonismo *(do-goodism)[2]—but the farmhouse is condemned, no longer fit to be occupied. Of the fifteen to twenty residents—virtually all men, documented and undocumented migrants working in the nearby tobacco fields—there are only two women who rejoined their spouses. With the exception of a Tunisian couple, everyone else is from the Atlantic plains and plateaus; they are all from* l-'arubiya *here. The solidarity among those coming from the same territory, families, and even tribes—a solidarity that played a critical role in the internal rural-to-urban migration discussed in chapter 1—continues to be paramount in migratory paths to Italy, where nowadays the majority of Moroccan migrants are able to enter legally through family affiliations.*

Yassine's Italian is quite good; he speaks as someone who arrived in Italy at a young age, while few of the older generations do. It was his father, Ali, who brought him along to work in the tobacco fields; at the time Yassine was in his teens, a minor. This was the classic migratory model for most Moroccans in Italy, as well as in the rest of Europe. The male head of the household would migrate alone and rejoin his family in Morocco whenever he could—although it was impossible for many of the migrants to see their families for years as they waited to obtain their legal documents. As the situation in Italy became more stable, the migrant would come back to Italy with one of his sons and, once he had fully regularized his status, with a contract and a suitable home, he would ask for his wife and the rest of his family to be allowed to join him via the family reunification law. Many of the men, however, chose to leave their families in Morocco, sending money home with the intention of moving back once they retired.[3] Yassine, now in his late thirties, is thankful for the opportunity his father gave him; he is aware of the high level of unemployment plaguing the male population of his region in Morocco.

It was a particularly difficult day; aside from having to work in the unbearable heat, Yassine had to endure the toxicity of la medicina *(the medicine); this is how tobacco laborers refer to the chemical products used to treat tobacco plants. By law workers are supposed to go back to the fields twenty-four to forty-eight hours after the treatment, but Yassine and the others were sent back to work immediately. Yassine is angry. "One of us, a Nigerian woman,[4] fainted . . . she couldn't take it. I had a terrible headache and felt nauseated all day . . . others vomited . . . but we couldn't stop working."*

Ali enters the room and quietly joins us; he is a poised, white-haired man with gentle eyes. I wonder how his thin-framed body could endure working in the tobacco fields for more than two decades; he does not look like the others in the room. Originally from Bradia, Ali hails from a rural commune where 86 percent of the migrants chose Italy as their destination after the agricultural crisis hit the region hard (Harrami and Mahdi 2006, 38); they were among the first to arrive after losing their lands, years of drought, and chronic unemployment.

Yassine shows reverence and affection to his father. He stands up to make a place for Ali to sit down among us, offering him something to eat and to drink, but his father gently declines, placing the palm of his right hand onto his stomach. The room turns quiet and everyone looks down. "My father was ill, he had to have surgery, and now he goes to a local hospital for treatment." "I am better now, thank God!" Ali announces as he interrupts his son. He does not wish to make a fuss about his health; he is a modest and honorable man, a former imam in Morocco, whom everyone respects. The men respond with traditional formulas of good wishes: " 'la slamtək, 'la slamtək, bi shifa inshallah" (greetings, greetings, may you be healed, God willing)."There was something in his stomach," Yassine continues; "they had to get it out . . . thank God he has the red passport[5] and could get treated here for free . . . he would have died in Morocco, they do not care about us!" I realize that the "something" Yassine refers to is stomach cancer, the rumore di fondo *of the Alta Valle del Tevere.*

In order to reassess the effects of tobacco, the museum has emphasized the socioeconomic role that the cultivation of tobacco has had in the area, claiming that tobacco "has always signified welfare, economic development, employment, social emancipation, and tradition" for the population. The principal goal of the museum is in fact "to preserve the cultural, social, and economic legacy deriving from the cultivation and the manufacturing of this product [. . .] the intent is instead to restore dignity and to reevaluate the labor of *all of those* [emphasis mine] who have worked and work

Figure 7. l-Kbir, Ahmed, and Ali

Photo by the author

in this important sector" (https://www.museotabacco.org).[6] And yet, in room after room, image after image, and caption after caption, one cannot help noticing their absence, the silence surrounding their presence, as if languishing in the "waiting room" (Chakrabarty 2000, 7) of the history of a multimillion-euro industry in which Italy excels as the top producer in Europe, with Umbria supplying about 30 percent of a national product that couldn't be manufactured without the work of migrants filling jobs abandoned by, rather than stolen from, Italians (Cruzzolin 1997; Duca 1997; Sereni 2010; Muzi and Tondo 2019). I am reminded of the sign that Abdelilah Am. keeps on the bare walls of one of his offices at the CISL/ANOLF;[7] it is there that I was first introduced to many of my interlocutors.

Make me understand the concept according to which an immigrant in Italy "steals jobs" while an Italian abroad "fights for his own future."[8]

With the exception of Abdelilah Am., none of my interlocutors has ever visited the museum, even if Moroccan men were among the first migrants to replace the now celebrated *tabacchine*—female tobacco workers who, from the 1930s to the early 1980s, made up 85–90 percent of the manual laborers in the tobacco industry of the Alta Valle del Tevere (Saccia 2012, 65). The lives, memories, struggles, and victories of these women, who worked long hours for low wages and under challenging conditions, have become part of the local and national history (Capitani, Piras, and Scarpelli 1983; Del Prete 2012).[9] But as the museum proudly displays the *tabacchine* in exhibitions that place them in the history of tobacco cultivation, the invisibility of these men—who nowadays constitute about 70 percent of migrant laborers in the tobacco industry in Umbria[10]—is even more striking. Being invisible, however, is not limited to their treatment by the museum but is part of their everyday life.

For Fiorella Giacalone, the overall invisibility of Moroccan migrants in Umbria is the result of their distribution across the region.

Part of the reason is that they are scattered in many centers: many are in Perugia; another important community is in the Alta Valle del Tevere; and other communities are in Gualdo Tadino, Bastia, in the area of the lake. [. . .] But more than Perugia, they are in the suburbs and in villages. (2003, 14)[11]

For Carlo Capello, who conducted research in Turin, the invisibility of these migrants is caused by an imperceptible barrier erected by the Italians, the "invisible prisons" Moroccan migrants inhabit.

[I]mmigrants are separated from the autochthonous by an invisible barrier of discrimination, prejudices, suspicion. By spending time in working-class neighborhoods and the suburbs of the city, it is easy to recognize the condition of subalternity and exclusion of most migrants. Now rooted in the urban space, Moroccan migrants live in the same neighborhoods, go to the same places, the same bars, and their children spend time in the same schools and the same playgrounds of the working class of Turin. [. . .] And yet, despite exceptions, the social relations with the natives are still limited, marked by prejudice and diffidence. [. . .] Excluded from social and everyday relations, migrants lead a separate social life with respect to the social reality of Turin, mostly relying on intra-community relationships and relations. (2008, 133)[12]

For Valeria Ribeiro Corrosacz, who conducted research among metallurgical workers in Modena, the invisibility of the large percentage of Moroccans working in the industry is apparent from the fact that they are prevented from advancing in their profession, and from their lack of everyday interactions with Italians.

> [F]or example, there are no Moroccan supervisors, and there are many [Moroccans] here since the company is rather big, [. . .] I am talking about the professional level, since I do not socialize with them outside of here. (2008, 58)[13]

Francesco Bachis, whose research focuses on migrant Moroccan men of the Mzab tribe working as itinerant vendors in Sardinia, discusses their mimetic strategies, arguing that, in contrast to Albanian migrants, Moroccan men aim not to pass for Italians but rather to reduce their social visibility (2009, 24).

More compelling, however, is how my interlocutors acknowledge their own invisibility and what is like to be ignored. The description given me by Abdelilah Ta.—a metalworker from Khouribga residing in San Giustino—of the encounters Italians chose to have or, better, chose not to have with him is painful.

> They only see us when they want to see us. For example, my neighbor, who never says hello to me . . . always acting as if I do not exist, recently spoke to me, telling me how from now on it was not going to be easy for me here, now that Salvini and the Lega Party had won the last European elections. She had never addressed me before. (Abdelilah Ta., personal communication, 1 June 2019, San Giustino)

Just as poignantly, the reserved l-Alami—another metalworker originally from Settat—reveals that he no longer extends his hand expecting a handshake from Italians, since they do not usually respond to his gesture. And Yassine, whom we have already met, complains that the school bus does not even stop at the house in San Giustino-Capanne; it is as if his children do not exist. The outspoken Abdelilah Am. complains that "Moroccans do not [seem] to exist except as criminals," dramatically juxtaposing their everyday invisibility with overexposure in the media and a popular imagination that reflects profound anxieties about the ghostly presence of these migrants.

27 July 2017, Assisi

Sara is eager to tell me about a joke that Bouchaib Bo., her husband, apparently did not quite get. Sara heard the joke at a local radio station, but she tells me that she is not sure she can imitate the dialect of Città di Castello, since she was born and raised in Assisi. As in the rest of Italy, in Umbria dialects remain important markers of personhood and belonging.

"Hello, Dad."

"Hello, Marco, how are you?"

"Not so great, Dad . . . I got a 4 in geography"

"Good God! How come? What did they ask you?"

"Well . . . they asked me where Morocco is."

"So? Weren't you able to answer?"

"No, Dad, I don't know where it is."

"Good God! Come on, I'll help you. Get the atlas and we'll look at it together, let's go."

The son takes the atlas down from the bookshelf and brings it to his father, who opens it.

"So, let's see . . . so, here's Castello, here's Citerna, San Sepolcro, Pistrino . . . , my son . . . it should be just around here, because they [Moroccans] ride their bikes to work, and it only takes them around fifteen minutes!"[14]

I laugh politely but am puzzled by the joke. On the one hand, I recognize how the hilarious ignorance of geography on the part of the father—who places Morocco in Italy—reflects Italian anxieties about what they see as a profound transformation of the population and the territory by a spectral presence. On the other hand, one could also interpret the joke as being about relatedness, a metaphor for the everyday relations between Italians and Moroccans, as well as complex ideas about connection and affinity.[15]

Donatella Di Cesare argues that migrants are spectral guests that no law of hospitality can turn into neighbors, someone similar or someone close, and that there is no place in the nation for a phantom who is always a felon and condemned to a life of inexistence (2017, 139).[16] However, because in Italy not all of these spectral guests share the same status,[17] it is necessary to analyze what defines migrant Moroccan men, and what distinguishes them from other migrant men in Italy. As Adelaida Reyes posits, for studies of migration "variables such as culture of origin, circumstances of departure from place of habitual residence, legal status, and attitudes toward migrants within the receiving society must be given due significance if migrant life, musical and more broadly social, is to be understood and accounted for" (forthcoming). In this chapter I introduce a discussion of terms that exemplify the difference I refer to, terms that my interlocutors acknowledge, engage with, and react to either directly or indirectly. From there I trace how a collective trauma caused by an earlier colonial encounter, between the

French Expeditionary Corps and the Italian population at the end of World War II, has profoundly influenced the perception and the image of migrant Moroccan men in Italy. This discussion aims to locate the ways in which the manhood of these migrants has been problematically constructed, fetishized, and criminalized, and, in turn, how these men negotiate with this construction in their everyday lives. The chapter concludes by juxtaposing my interlocutors' construction of manhood with their notion of what it means to be a "real man" (*rajal*), which is inseparable from that of *l-'arubi*. The final discussion centers on an informed analysis of a popular song by one of the most famous interpreters of *sha'bi*, Abdelaziz Stati, admired by migrant Moroccan men in Italy and beyond—a song that is understood as providing a "moral map" for its listeners (Caton 1990) on what it means to be a "real man" and how to enact it.

MAROCCHINO AND *VÙ CUMPRÀ*

Here, dear mother,
we are all more or less the same,
the dirty window washer
the delinquent drug dealer
and the ignorant "vu cumprà"
we are all as one
and we are no one.[18]

(from "Nostalgia" by Aziz Bouzidy)

7 December 2018, Umbertide

"I came to Italy in 1987, and started working as vù cumprà *in streets and markets, and on beaches selling the usual things: carpets, beachwear, cheap custom jewelry, sunglasses, and so on," recalls the sixty-something-year-old Driss, originally from Ben Ahmed and now residing in Umbertide. "It was tiring to work for hours, walking up and down under the sun; but it used to be good money. I would come to Italy to work for the whole summer, and afterward I would go back to Morocco and spend all the money I made. It was only years later, when I settled down, that I started working on a tobacco plantation, like most of us around here."*

A stocky, good-natured man in fragile health, Driss speaks with a candor that has often gotten him into trouble: "You know what they say about

Figure 8. Driss

Photo by the author

mzab . . ." is how Driss has often jokingly explained his temper.[19] We have spent hours discussing life and politics, gossiping about the Moroccan community in Umbertide, and, needless to say, talking about music. Driss is passionate about ʿaiṭa and the *shikhat*, and I suspect that most of the money he worked so hard to earn during those summers was spent in their company. The display of wealth, after all, is part of the selected information, the enchanted memories, the imaginary that migrants bring back when returning home. It is part of what Abdelmalek Sayad refers to as the "collective lie," whereby migration is produced and reproduced because, when the peasant mind and way of life come under attack, migration is imagined as the only possibility left to prove that one can make a man of himself, that one does not have to resign oneself to the humiliation of being a sharecropper or worse, and that it is possible to break the vicious cycle of proletarianization (2000, 161–63). However, in describing his occupation with the phrase *vù cumprà*, Driss allows us to look behind the "lie."

Alessandro Dal Lago argues that, even before being actually discriminated against, migrants are stigmatized by the language that society devises to represent them (1999, 43). The linguistic adaptation of *vuoi comprare* (do you want to buy)—the question itinerant vendors used to ask when approaching potential customers—*vù cumprà* turned into an enduring racist stereotype that mocked migrants' difficulties with Italian pronunciation and verb conjugation, stigmatizing, as well as criminalizing, undocumented migrants believed to be engaged in illegal trade. *Vù cumprà* was particularly problematic for Moroccans who constituted a large segment of these vendors,[20] who were compared to invaders and constructed as a menace for beachgoers.[21] An expression widely used in the 1990s, *vù cumprà* is said to have replaced the earlier stereotype of the *marocchino* (Moroccan man), which referred to a migrant man who came from Africa, the Middle East, or South Asia (Faloppa 2011, 31–41)—that is to say, a non-European, dark-skinned migrant. Miguel Mellino argues that one cannot understand contemporary Italian racism against migrants without considering the cultural, political, and economic construction of its main predecessors, that is, the "historical racism against the southerner and the colonial Other (during the early liberal and Fascist period), the Jew (in the Fascist period), and the southern migrant worker in the second postwar republic" (2012, 87). The term *marocchino* was in fact used in northern Italy to indicate a southern Italian male migrant.[22] Nowadays, *marocchino* continues to be a negative epithet, an insult used to refer to any *extracomunitario* (non-European migrant man) who is considered to be a criminal, or whose mere presence troubles Italians;[23] as my interlocutors remind me, "*Marocchino* is used for all of those who are not good people."

21 November 2019, Umbertide

Oussama, Abdellah, and Zakaria are twenty-three, twenty-seven, and twenty-six years old, respectively. Only Zakaria, who arrived in Umbria at the age of five, could be defined as part of the second generation of Moroccans in Italy. Abdellah and Oussama, on the other hand, arrived a few years ago through the family reunification law and, in the case of Oussama, as an undocumented migrant. He traveled for three months before reaching Italy: he went from Morocco to Libya, crossed the Mediterranean in a small boat, and, after reaching Turkey, walked all the way to Italy through the Balkan route, which, at the time of his arrival in 2015, was one of the main migratory paths into Europe. Oussama had burned his documents, as many ḥərraga do, in an attempt to enter Italy as a Syrian refugee.

They are all from Casablanca, from difficult peripheries such as Sidi Moumen—a neighborhood that became infamous after the 2003 attacks carried out in Casablanca by a group of young suicide bombers from the

Figure 9. Oussama, Abdellah, and Zacharia

Photo by Omino Rosso

neighborhood—and Sbata—a neighborhood within the larger former bidonville of Ben M'sik. Their parents had migrated from the regions of Marrakesh-Safi and Casablanca-Settat during one of the rural exoduses discussed in chapter 1.

They have met here, in Umbertide, where they reside with their immediate families or more distant relatives. They are inseparable, and at first glance one would think they were "integrated." But when our discussion shifts to their hopes and aspirations, they are painfully aware of being marocchini, because "the social audacity of the second-age emigrants predisposes them to a sharper and more frequent experience of racism" (Sayad 2004, 48). Zakaria laments that he is always the one who has to make the move, go toward the others (i.e., Italians), who would otherwise ignore him: "altrimenti . . . è come se non esistessi" (otherwise . . . it is as if I do not exist). The young Moroccans of the second generation, in fact, continue to be perceived as strangers (Orlandi 2010, 226)."Do you know what they call us in Perugia?" Oussama is quick to answer: "'marani' and 'marocchinacci.'" They stare at me in silence, while Abdellah shakes his heads with a halfhearted smile.

While marocchinacci is a pejorative form of marocchini,[24] the contemporary use of an old term such as marano among the youth in Perugia is worth explaining. Derived from the Spanish marrano, it refers to Jews and Muslims who, fearing persecution, converted to Christianity after the

Reconquista. Marked by a strongly negative connotation, the term was first used in Italian chivalric epics to indicate anyone who did not respect or abide by the mores of chivalry and courtesy. To this day *marano* indicates a traitor, someone who cannot be trusted, a vile and dishonest person, someone without honor, as well as someone who is not a Christian.[25]

Sara Ahmed argues that particular modes of proximity—as in the case of those produced by migration—create the figure of the stranger whose difference is impossible to grasp in the present. Ahmed urges us to ask "how contemporary modes of proximity *reopen prior histories of encounter*" and to explore the complex relationship between histories of colonialism and contemporary modes of encounter (2000, 13–14). In what follows I trace how the difference of migrant Moroccan men in Italy was produced by the earlier colonial mode of encounter, and how this encounter—that is, the memory, imagination, and "affective judgments" of such an encounter—has been problematically rearticulated in contemporary Italy.

MAROCCHINATE

Maghrebi migration is deeply rooted in the socioeconomic structures brought about by French colonialism and, in particular, by the types of agricultural and land-dispossession policies analyzed in chapter 1. Even as these practices forced people off their land, the demands of the French empire for cheap labor to work in factories, mines, and the military attracted migrants to the cities of Morocco, then to Algeria, and finally to France.

The Atlantic plains and plateaus, and particularly the Casablanca-Settat region, where almost all the land had been taken over by colonial agriculture, were an important reservoir for the recruitment of soldiers (Baroudi 1989, 74);[26] although it was called "voluntary," recruitment was often forced through violent and brutal methods (Atouf 2014, 41–46). The violence intrinsic to colonial wars and pacification campaigns, once transferred into the so-called civilized wars, legitimized men who came from a country brutalized by Europeans to exercise violence.

> On 21 May they came like devils from the mountains. We were expecting liberators, and, in fact, in Mangiavacca, where we were, people came out with a white flag; we thought that they were the liberators. Instead, as they arrived, they took the women and began to commit crimes. In Lenola there was a real massacre. It was said that these Moroccans had come to break the front line. Germans had a lot of fortresses, and so Moroccans took a risk, not thinking about their lives. [...] [M]oroccans did cross the front line, but it was fire that crossed over. There, no one made it. In Lenola they killed three and even a fifty-year-old woman, they

cut her with scissors. A man killed a Moroccan who had raped all three of his daughters, three beautiful daughters, right in front of him. In short, an entire village was on its knees. Poor little ones, they did to them what they did to Christ's tunic, those girls. (Gribaudi 2005, 529)[27]

This emotionally charged recollection by one of the women of southern Lazio who survived the acts of violence committed by the French Expeditionary Corps during World War II is one of the oral testimonies collected by the historian Gabriella Gribaudi. In her discussion of the mass rapes that took place in central and southern Italy in 1944, Gribaudi weaves the testimonies of the survivors in and out of her text, juxtaposing an academic language with the vernacular of the women she interviews, sounding and amplifying their words so that readers may feel the violence, the suffering, the humiliation, and the injustice these women had to endure even after the rapes.[28]

Marocchinate (Moroccan deeds) is the unfortunate term commonly used for the charges of murder, rape, theft, and other acts of violence committed against Italian civilians by the French Expeditionary Corps, 70 percent of which was composed of colonial solders—commonly referred to as *goumiers*—from North Africa who fought in central and southern Italy toward the end of World War II, and who played a decisive role in winning the famous Battle of Monte Cassino against the Germans in 1944.

Marocchinate—a term that captures a prior encounter between Moroccan men and the Italian population—stems from *marocchinare*, a verb that originally described the tanning of goatskin by means of a technique introduced to medieval Iberia by the Arabs but that also came to mean "to subject to violence, to violate, to rape (in reference to the violence that Moroccan troops carried out in central and southern Italy during the last period of the second World War).—Also: to infect with syphilis"[29] (http://www .gdli.it/JPG/GDLI09/00000834.jpg).[30] Despite the presence of Tunisians, Algerians, Senegalese, and French soldiers in the Expeditionary Corps, the term *marocchinate* unequivocally implies that, in the Italian collective memory, it was only Moroccans who were committing these acts of violence.

A number of scholars (Baris 2003; Gribaudi 2005; Riccio 2008; Atouf 2014; Maghraoui 2014; Gershovich 2016; Maraini 2017) have examined the problematic status of these colonial soldiers in the French army, arguing that it was an important instrument of colonization reflecting the colonial order with troops headed exclusively by French officers, and also arguing for the need to examine the documents and the narrative of the era in a postcolonial framework. In his effort to acknowledge the contribution of soldiers excluded by European historians writing about World War II, Driss

Maghraoui considers the history of these soldiers as an example of "minority history" that has been suppressed and posits how, aside from being deprived of recognition for their contribution to fighting, these troops had to carry the stigma of savagery and dishonor for the crimes of a few. The Moroccan historian also notes that little was ever said about the practice of the *razzia* (pillaging) as "part of the logic of tribal warfare as the Moroccan soldiers perceived it," blaming French officers for having actually encouraged it (2014, 580). While acknowledging the troubled legacy of these soldiers, Maghraoui aims to restore their honor by locating the responsibility for the violence onto France.

Notwithstanding her focus on the victims and survivors, Gribaudi also acknowledges the complexity of a situation where colonized men, coming from countries that had been brutalized, were turned into French soldiers and given license to commit violence by hypermasculine white French officers in charge of the troops (2005, 557–61).[31] For Gribaudi, the reasons for this violence are multiple, but she stresses that it is also a part of conquest, another way to subjugate a population that had been defeated—particularly because, in societies in which women's honor reflects that of men, violating women meant violating the men who were unable to defend them. It is in this context that the Italian historian reflects on how the rapes, which took place in groups, could be read as a sign of virility and solidarity among men, an expression of triumphant masculinity, a way to reciprocate the type of treatment the colonized themselves received from the colonizers, and which included the freedom to have white women (2005, 564), just as the colonizers had access to indigenous women in the Maghreb.

For their part, the French blamed only the troops of "color" for their savage nature, their lack of sexual inhibition, and their primitive, uncontrollable appetites—a representation uncritically adopted by a population that had been exposed to similar racist propaganda of the Fascist era, since sexuality, as Sander Gilman reminds us, is the most significant marker of otherness figuring in any racist ideology (1985).

The nonscholarly, popular treatment of this dramatic and complex scenario unfolding at the end of World War II in Italy has been quite problematic, beginning with the literary representation in *La ciociara*,[32] the celebrated novel by Alberto Moravia (1957) and Vittorio De Sica's even more popular cinematic adaptation (known in English as *Two Women*), starring Sophia Loren (1960). The historian Moshe Gershovich comments on the central rape scene in the film, writing that if the garb leaves very little room for doubt about the identity of the assailing soldiers, the dark face of one of the assailants, twisted into a "hideous grin," and the incomprehensibility of the "noises" uttered by the soldiers turns them into "aliens in uniform"

(2016, 77).[33] However, what the film uncritically captures is not the aliens, but the traumatic memories of the victims, distorted by racist stereotypes—including sonorous ones—which dehumanize the soldiers through a "zoological" language (Fanon 1963) that links them to nonhumans, primitives, and the uncivilized (Baris 2003).

In the last few years, the term *marocchinate* seems to have taken on new meanings and to function as a "usable past" in political discourse. This is painfully apparent in the controversial use and reworking by the neofascist nonparliamentary party Forza Nuova of a 1944 poster that the Fascist regime employed to rally against the Allied troops.[34] In the original poster, the depiction of a lustful black racialized male figure, a savage with distorted facial figures and rapacious animal-like claws, is holding on to his victim, a white woman, as he attempts to rape her. The image is juxtaposed with the urgent message, "Defend her! She could be your mother, your wife, your sister, your daughter."

Forza Nuova's reworking of the poster lies in a small but crucial change in the text rallying against non-European migrants: "Defend her from *the new invaders* [emphasis mine]. She could be your mother, your wife, your sister, your daughter." In communicating the danger of "the new invaders," the poster urges (even commands, through the use of the imperative) the Italian man—that is, the fascist idea of a patriarch whose honor is dependent on that of his female relatives (your mother, your wife, your sister, your daughter)—to act.

My interest in this poster lies in its circulation and particularly in its choice as the cover of a 2018 book on the *marocchinate*,[35] whose narrative borrows from the racist anti-Arab and anti-Muslim propaganda of the Italian Far Right and the writings of one the most controversial authors of the twentieth century, the Italian Curzio Malaparte, characterizing the *goumiers'* hypersexual deviance.

> The goumiers drew a sordid gratification in having sexual relations with white women, considered—according to their tradition, indulged or at least not banned by the French Command—spoils of war, or also a religious revenge against the Christians, remembering what the Knights Templar had done against the Muslims. [. . .] Curzio Malaparte, in his book *The Skin* [. . .] studied them in their glances, full of cupidity and desire for white women. (Ciotti 2018, 2–3)[36]

In the current unstable political climate, in which we are witnessing the radicalization of the Right, an alarming support for fascism, and a resurgence of anti-Semitism—being that fascist ideology has always been on the margins of, and has never disappeared from, Italian politics—the *marocchinate* have become an effective "usable past" through which it is possible to draw a direct link between ghosts of the past (Moroccan soldiers) and ghosts of the present (migrant Moroccan men).

25 November 2019, Umbertide

The International Day for the Elimination of Violence against Women. A crucial day for a country like Italy, which has an alarming number of victims of femicide—with a woman killed every seventy-two hours— and many more subjected to daily violence. Today, a history program on national television focuses on the issue of wartime rapes in the twentieth century. The host of the program, standing behind an iconic image of Sophia Loren in the film La ciociara, *opens up the discussion by citing the sexual violence committed by French Moroccan soldiers.*

"We learned about the marocchinate *in school," Zakaria tells me. "What is that?" Abdellah asks. Oussama begins to explain, but Abdellah is quick to interrupt him: "I do not believe that . . . my grandfather was in that war!" The conversation switches to Arabic, an intimate but also safer language to discuss such a topic in a crowded café where the three young men are the only Moroccans. "Moroccans were recruited because they were fierce fighters. They fought in Monte Cassino; they were the ones who defeated the Germans. You can see them fighting in close combat; you know what I am talking about, right?" Oussama is excited: he can see them in combat, imagine their strength and their valor on the battlefield. There is no room for other scenarios, particularly for the one he had to learn in school. School here refers to the training courses (*corsi di formazione*) that a migrant like Oussama has to undergo in order to facilitate his integration in Italy. "They discussed the* marocchinate *when they taught us Italian history and culture." "And what did you say? How did you feel?" I ask. "Nothing . . . what could I have said?" Zakaria has turned quiet. He sits tall on a stool; he, more than his friends, had to endure the humiliation of the* marocchinate *in school. "All of us have had bad experiences that we could tell you; after all, I am the son of a* vù cumprà!*"

Although unique to Italy, the equation of Moroccan men with rapists cannot be divorced from the highly sexualized and complex figure of the

Arab man in France (Shepard 2017), nor can it be abstracted from the politicization of sexuality taking place in European debates about migration, where the presence of Arabs and Muslims is often portrayed as a sexualized invasion or rape (Mack 2017). Thus, if this discussion of the *marocchinate* has intended to situate the stigmatization of migrant Moroccan men in its specific Italian context, it has also aimed for such stigmatization to be framed in the larger European perspective, historicizing their alterity and tracing the problematic construction of the Moroccan male subject and of his manhood within the context of previous colonial encounters.

Marked by the *marocchinate*, my interlocutors in the Alta Valle del Tevere must, on the one hand, negotiate a manhood that is considered to be an uninhabitable way of being in Italy and, on the other, mobilize a manhood that cannot be separated from their sense of self as *'arubi*. But which ideal of manhood do these men conjure in response to their particular social and historical contexts? Which construction of manhood do these men feel they need to enact in order to remain anchored to tradition? And how is their everyday performance of manhood influenced by specific settings in Italy; that is, how do they negotiate the notion of being a "real man" in their daily lives?

The chapter now turns to examining my interlocutors' conception of manhood and their notion of what it means to be a "real man" (*rajəl*). It is not my intention to discount the concept of "emergent masculinities" (Inhorn and Isidoros 2018), or to overlook the danger of perpetuating a hegemonic discourse about manhood, however, in remaining attentive to my interlocutors' tropes about the importance of being a *rajəl*, I follow Karin van Nieuwkerk's call for the need to examine the "enactments of hegemonic models, not hegemonic masculinities per se" (2019, 27), and to analyze what such enactments mean on the ground.[37] The manhood my interlocutors enact is "primarily a stance or posture" (Nieuwkerk 2019, 86), a response to the situations they face in their everyday life and to local narratives. These migrants perform a manhood that is not innate but rather needs to be acknowledged by others, a manhood that allows one to construct oneself as a worthy individual. Most important, because of the interplay between *rajəl* and *'arubi*, for my interlocutors, to be an *'arubi* entails to be a "real man."

The discussion that follows centers on an informed analysis of a popular song by Abdelaziz Stati, a performer admired by migrant Moroccan men in Italy and beyond. The song is understood as providing a "moral map" (Caton 1990) and is particularly valued because it is directly related to migrants' own preoccupations: displacement, masculinity and morality, that is, what it means to be a "real man" in the face of migration, and how to perform it.

THE "REAL MAN" AND *L-ʿARUBI*

rjal mshat ḥərga
ya ʿamt fi bḥur ghərqa
wa li rajəl ya rəbbi tsəhhəl ʿəlih
ya waḥed ʿəinu zəlga
ya ʿəshqu məskin fi ṭənga
msha rajəl ya wili rjəʿ thaqb udnih

Men left clandestinely
They navigated deep seas
May God help the real man
And cause the eyes of the other to fall out
The poor fellow, his passion is in an earring
He left as a man but unfortunately came back with pierced ears

waḥed ghbər nhar wa raḥ
rjaʿ b-mlayən ṣəḥḥaḥ
qlaʿ l-qəḥra ʿla rasu khutu məʿ waldih
waḥed nəqqəz wa raḥ ṭaḥ
jaib sh-shauha bla rbaḥ
wa ʿəshr snin fi bərra wa mazal mmu katʿaṭih

One disappeared for a day and left
Came back with real millions
Snatched himself, his brothers, and his parents away from misery
One jumped but fell
He brought disgrace and no profit
Ten years abroad and his mother still supports him

waḥed ḥərg məʿ rjal
jərrəb n-nas wa rah jal
ḥram nḥsədu ya rəbbi isəhhəl ʿəlih
l-akhor ʿa l-muḍa rah isal
fi klamu rah bsal
ma ʿla balush l-mustaqbal ma ḥasəb lih

One migrated clandestinely with other men
Experienced people and traveled
It is forbidden to envy him, may God help him
The other follows the fashion[38]

His words are also nonsense
He does not worry about the future, he does not take it into account

ya ṣaḥ smaʿ u rwa
lli kbir mənnak ila dwa
smaʿ klamih inafʿak wa wakha mədirsh bih
fut l-qum l-harda
wa ṣəḥab l-hadra wa blah blah
kif ma walu təlqihum
ki hna kif lhih

Hey, friend, listen and learn
If someone older speaks to you
Listen to his words even if you do not follow his advice.
Even if you are not going to put them to use
Keep away from bad people
From those who gossip and their blah blah
You will find them futile
Here and there

"Rjal mshat ḥərga" (audio ex. 3.1), a *shaʿbi* song expressing the hopes and fears of migrants in Europe, is a warning tale about the potentially negative effects of migration (Capello 2008, 100–101). Of particular interest, however, is how in addressing male migrants the song focuses on the importance of being a "real man" (*rajəl*), or, as Herzfeld proposes in his discussion on the manhood of Glendiots, "in being good at being a man" (1985, 17)—that is, in performing a particular idea of manhood in the face of migration whose danger is recognized in the loss of one's sense of self, in the risk of "becoming Italian" (Persichetti 2003b, 225–28), in the loss of traditions, fundamental mores and values and, consequently, on the moral integrity of character that, as shown by Flagg Miller, is also an important trope in Yemeni poetry (2005). The absence of a female voice emphasizes a masculine discourse that, unlike the endearment and the affection expressed in the use of diminutive forms in the previous songs, amplifies the masculine discourse of a stern older narrator upholding tradition and demanding attention from a younger male audience through the use of the imperative, as the first three lines of the last stanza show: "Hey, friend, listen and learn / if someone older speaks to you / listen to his words even if you do not follow his advice."

Each poetic stanza of "Rjal mshat ḥərga" is divided into two parts: one provides an example of what is good behavior to follow, and the other provides a counterexample of what behavior should not be followed. It is in this sense that the song may be thought of as having a pedagogical function, providing a "moral map" for its listeners, engaging with values and judgments that are central to my interlocutors, for whom being a *rajǝl* is also fundamental in their listening—that is, "when they finally get to exhale."

19 November 2019, Umbertide

Bouazza is a fifty-something-year-old mason from the town of Ben Ahmed who resides in Umbertide with members of his family; he is waiting for his wife to join him in Italy, but today he seems worried because the documents he needs to submit for the request are expensive and not always easy to obtain. Bouazza arrived in Italy in 2004 with a visa for nine months to work in the tobacco fields, but like most of my interlocutors, he ended up staying in Italy as an undocumented migrant until he was able to regularize his status under the 2009 sanatoria.

A pensive, soft-spoken, yet resolute man whose dark eyes avoid meeting mine out of respect, Bouazza sits composedly on the chair of an unadorned office of the CISL in Umbertide; it is there we decided to meet before heading to a nearby café. His graying mustache and beard soften a face whose deep lines are said to mark the face of a real ʿarubi, like the furrows that a manual plow produces when drawn across the soil. The first time I met him he was parsimonious with his words, proud, stoic, and, although polite, cautious. But today he speaks in a seamless flow in which he reiterates words, thoughts, and fragments as if to mark their importance, mixing Moroccan Arabic with an Italian that, although hesitant, is infused with the local dialect.

Stati is one of Bouazza's favorite performers—a rajǝl, *Bouazza is quick to assert as he continues to list the names of male* kamanja *player-singers and leaders of their own troupes. Ould Mbarek, Daoudi, Mustapha Bourgogne, and Abderrahim l-Meskini are some of the names of the* shiukh *who are regularly invited to entertain mostly male audiences—in their twenties and thirties—who frequent nightclubs such as the Manhattan in Lucca, the Triple Five in Padua, and the Mazazik in Perugia; like their audiences, these performers have roots in the countryside of the Atlantic plains and plateaus, and their* shaʿbi *is rooted in* l-ʿarubiya, *since, in the words my interlocutors, "the* shaʿbi *of cities like Fez is cold [*bǝrd*]." The sonorous difference between the country and the city continues to be meaningful even in a genre that has the capacity to absorb a great variety of local music practices. Stati, who built his reputation accompanying some of the best* shiukh *and* shikhat *of ʿaiṭa before*

Figure 10. Bouazza

Photo by the author

leading his own ensemble, is a virtuoso of the kamanja, *able to interpret both the old* qaṣa'id *of* 'aiṭa *and newly composed poems such as "Rjal mshat ḥərga." All of my interlocutors have at least one song by Stati on their cell phones; this is not always the case with other performers, who, by "moving too much on stage," "not having the right voice," "not saying the right words," or "not been dressed as they should," fail to perform a particular ideal not only of manhood, but also of the countryside.*

The absence from Bouazza's list of one particular well-known male performer catches my attention; it is not the first time his name has been omitted by my interlocutors. When I ask Bouazza about the performer he neglected to mention, he chuckles and, nodding his head from one side to the other, comments: "He is not a rajəl. . . . *I do not listen to him." For Bouazza, listening is shaped by the perceived manhood of the performers, which, in turn, he uses to reaffirm his own manliness. "But who is a* rajəl*?" I ask.*

A real man [*rajəl*] is someone who is serious [*məˈqul*], who cares about his family [*ˈaila*], who cares about his wealth [*malu*], who cares about that which is his [*dyalu*], his virility [*rjultu*], his dignity and generosity [*karma dyalu*]. Who is not a man . . . a person who is a liar [*bugiardo*], a person who is a thief [*ladro*], a person who even when he sees something bad lowers his head [*abbassa la testa*] because he does not care [*non gli frega niente*]; this is not a *rajəl*, he is not called *rajəl*. Who is not a *rajəl* is called a *diyyut* [cuckold] someone who sees something bad in his family but does not say anything, does not defend [*midfaˈ*] his family. For him everything is the same. (Bouazza, personal communication, 19 November 2019, Umbertide)

A flashy solo on the *kamanja* built on various melodic riffs opens "Rjal mshat ḥərga." If the riffs and the sound of the viola unequivocally situate the recording in the musical sphere of *ˈaiṭa*, the heavy use of reverb, the unchanging rhythm and melody, and the instruments accompanying the soloist locate the song in the domain of *shaˈbi*, providing a good example of the porosity of a genre able to draw from diverse music traditions while remaining anchored in the popular. In the recording, the sound of the *qanun* (box zither, an instrument commonly used in the art music traditions of the Mashreq but not as common in Morocco, with the exception of *musiqa ˈaṣriya*[39] and, occasionally, *al-ala*); the *nay* (an end-blown flute also found in *al-ala*, the art music and Sufi music traditions of the Mashreq and Turkey); and the bass (a Western instrument whose role in the recording is to double the low sound played on a percussion instrument signaling a accented beat, as well as the first degree of the *maqam* [*mḥaṭṭa*, lit., station, stopping place], emphasized by the *ˈud* [Arab lute]) are all produced by a keyboard synthesizer referred to as *l-org* (from the French *orgue*).

A short unmetered instrumental introduction is followed by the rendering of the first stanza of "Rjal mshat ḥərga," which, later in the song, turns into a refrain sung by backup male vocalists between each stanza. Performed in the style of a *mawwal*—unmetered solo singing—it borrows from the opening of *raï* songs.[40] Stati is known to have mastered different regional interpretations and for his ability to interpret different styles. He is keen to the sound of *raï*, whose *ṭariqa*—manner of performing—he describes as *waˈəra* (wicked). The choice of permeating the song with influences from *raï* is undoubtedly because the genre is very popular with young people. This is a performance aimed at dramatizing the meaning of each verse, and at heightening the emotions associated with poetic lines that bless the "real man" while cursing and vilifying "the other," who was corrupted after he left home—a corruption embodied in the images of the earring and the pierced ear, which, as understood by my interlocutors, can only be displayed by someone who is considered effeminate (*rwijel*), someone who has lost his virility and is no longer a *rajəl*. The Moroccan sociologist Abdessamad Dialmy, in fact, defines *rajəl* as "a hard man" and *rwijel*—a pejorative diminutive—as "a soft man" (2008, 76).

Although a perceived loss of virility is not limited to fashion, appearances are an important means through which male youth can be reprimanded if they are viewed as not adhering to tradition, to specific ideas about Moroccanness (Rachik 2003; Jansen 2016), and as not embodying local ideas of manhood. Shikh Sharqi, a renowned performer of *'abidat r-rma*, distinguishes good troupes from bad troupes of *'abidat r-rma* partly in terms of the clothing they wear, which, in turn, is associated with particular modes of performance.

> Nowadays the young troupes wear ripped pants, comb their hair in a certain way, put on a T-shirt and they walk on stage. Can you imagine a horseman who wears a shirt and a pair of ripped jeans? Impossible! It is shameful to dress like that. . . . They think it is enough to put on the *rəzza* and the *jellaba* and that you are *'abidat r-rma*.[41] And then they put on a belt and dance, but it is still *'abidat r-rma*, and the performers of *'abidat r-rma* do not dance sensuously [*nshwiya*]. [Men] must dance with feet and shoulders. But where did they learn to dance like that? From the *shikhat*! (Shikh Sharqi, personal communication, 7 August 2015, Ben Slimane)

Steve Caton has also described how Yemeni male youth are ridiculed for being vain and effeminate, for imitation of Western fashion, and, inherently, for acting like women, in poems in which the voice of a stern and didactic father concerned about young men's abandonment of tradition, addresses them (1990, 232).

25 July 2017, Ouled Ziane

It is Amezzane who opens the door while carrying a magnificent plate of couscous prepared by a woman I will never get to meet, at least not today. Stati's ground floor is a masculine space par excellence, an intimate space in which men can relax and socialize, an all-male space that is silently but effectively marked as such. In this context, and in similar situations I observed, younger male musicians, apprentices, will often perform what are thought to be "feminine" tasks for the leader of a troupe, for a master musician like Stati, whose manhood is evinced even in small and apparently insignificant gestures.[42]

Stati performs a manhood that needs to be reiterated and acknowledged in front of others and is therefore often paraded in photos available on social media. To my initial question about who is an 'arubi, his answer is quick and resolute, uttered with a proud stance and a strong voice that resounds throughout the large open space; it is a challenge that begins with a negation of what is commonly believed.

"To be an 'arubi is not something pejorative! It describes the behavior of a real man [rajəl]. Someone who wakes up at four o'clock in the morning, leaves his wife, and goes to work. Someone who is generous [krim]. Someone who is attached to the land [mərbut m'a lərd], who has never been insulted or denigrated . . . always respected [dima muḥtərəm]. A real man could die for nature [imut 'la l-ṭbi'a], could die for his family [imut 'la bladu wa wladu]. A real man is he who keeps his word [r-rajəl huwa l-kəlma]."

Hassan Na. smiles as points out the similarity in the discourse of Stati and Shikh Sharqi, for whom the notion of rajəl and of 'arubi are entangled. Unlike Hassan, who is familiar with these tropes because of his origins in the countryside, Mounir—a middle-class university professor from Rabat—is taken aback. Issues of class are intertwined with the notion of manhood. I am reminded of Shikh Sharqi's narrative about his two wives, whom, he proudly asserts, he treats the same, as a fair and honorable man must do. I wonder if Shikh Sharqi is aware of what his older wife, Malika, had once conveyed to me about her condition. In an almost silent and dramatic gesture—lifting the palms of her hands to her face and lightly caressing it while letting her hands and arms fall with no resistance, no life of their own, until abandoned to the side of her frail body—she said, in a hushed voice, "walo," expressing how she had been reduced to nothing.

As the viola lands on seventh note of the *maqam bayati*, marking the end of the *mawwal*,[43] the simplified version of the *ḥəddari* introduced by the *bendir*—a ubiquitous compound duple rhythm in Moroccan *sha'bi* associated with the music of the religious order of the Aissawa (Nabti 2010)—signals a distinct shift in the mood of the song. The new melodic line, based on the same *bayati* and rhythmic pattern, will remain unchanged throughout the performance. Rather than obscuring or lessening the pedagogical and moral function of the song, the festive atmosphere seems to allow listeners to embody the text through *nashaṭ* (pleasure, enjoyment, enthusiasm; from the verb *nshəṭ*, to rejoice, to have fun, to be happy)—a specific emotional state of celebration conjured, among other things, by fast-paced rhythm, music, loudness, and movement (Kapchan 2003). Stati's performances evoke such strong emotions and excitement among his mostly male audiences that they can be dangerous to attend—people are often injured and even killed in stampedes.

The inability to care for one's family, and the inherent shame in a son's having his mother support him, is the subject of the second stanza. Like the first, this stanza provides an example of good behavior and a counterexample of what behavior that should be avoided: a migrant who is economically successful and generous, and who saves his family from misery, is praised, while the other, whose failure has brought disgrace to his family, cannot be considered a *rajəl*.

To be able to rely on oneself rather than depending on one's family or, for that matter, on anyone is a critical quality of manhood, as a well-known proverb in the countryside emphasizes: *ju'i f-kərshi, u 'naiti f-rasi* (my hunger is in my stomach, but my dignity is in my head).

Failing to obtain such independence may prevent a man from getting married and starting his own family and it may cause his dignity ('*naya*) to suffer. In chapter 2 we saw how the choice to migrate, to take the risk, to be courageous (*shji'*) and decide to cross was described as a way to recover dignity and to perform manhood when everything else is thought to be lost; in that context too, economic success remained fundamental.

Also present in this stanza is the idea that in order not to lose himself, a "real man" must not forget his family and his origins and must never turn away from his relatives.

> In general, the families that remain in Morocco distinguish two categories of emigrants: men of honor who come back *salim wa ghanim* (safe and sound after having made a fortune) to do good for their loved ones, and those who instead "become Italians," that is, those who forget their relatives and rarely come back to their country of origin; for this reason they are called *wuld al-haram* (bastard, son of the sin). [. . .] The expression "to become Italian" does not only mean specifically to back out of obligations to one's relatives, but in general to lose one's whole system of moral values. (Persichetti 2003b, 232)[44]

The idea of not losing oneself, that is, losing "one's whole system of moral values," is also entrenched in the way in which my interlocutors define an '*arubi*, as they maintain—though somewhat humorously—that an urban man is not a "real man." For them, only men from *l-'arubiya* are *rjal*, real men, because they still live according to the values of their parents and their ancestors (*'əhd dyal walidin u jdudhum*), and as such they maintain their morals (*l-khlaq dyalhum*), their heritage (*t-turath dyalhum*), and their traditions (*t-təqalid dyalhum*).

> *wahed hərg mə' rjal*
> *jərrəb n-nas wa rah jal*
> *hram nhsədu ya rəbbi isəhhəl 'əlih*
> *l-akhor 'a l-muda rah isal*
> *fi klamu rah bsal*
> *ma 'əla balush l-mustaqbal ma hasəb lih*

> One migrated clandestinely with other men
> Experienced people and traveled
> It is forbidden to envy him, may God help him
> The other follows fashion
> His words are also nonsense
> He does not worry about the future, he does not take it into account

The third stanza begins by praising the man who travels, a common trope for a number of Moroccan proverbs that unequivocally gender the experience of traveling, as shown in the proverb "There is no good in a woman who roams about and no good in a man who does not" (Rosen 1984, 24). Traveling, in this context, is seen as a way to acquire knowledge, information a man may use for his network, since the knowledge of others, the experience of other people's ways and connections, can be vital for predicting how they may act and what situations may be most advantageous for a man with such knowledge (Rosen 1984, 25; Alzetta 2004, 255).

The second half of the same stanza juxtaposes this positive image with that of a man who, once again, is scolded for following fashion, accused of his words being nonsense, and blamed for not worrying about the future and thus for failing to perform an important task of manhood: that of being a provider. One may remember how a man's word—that is, the word of someone who does not lie and who does what he says—is one of the essential features of Bouazza's definition of a *rajəl*, a description that is similar to how Stati himself describes an *'arubi*.

Karin van Nieuwkerk discusses the associations that her main interlocutor, Sayyid, draws between *ibn al-balad* (an authentic Egyptian son) and being a man, and how he identifies manhood with the authentic Egyptian son (2019, 24, 87). Like *rajəl*, *'arubi* invokes virtues such as honor or reputation (*'ərd*), toughness (*qasəh*), virility (*fhula*), courage (*shja'a*), generosity (*krama*), self-control (*jmə' rasu*, to have one's head together), and hospitality (*dyafa*), and thus a manhood whose behavioral repertoire must be enacted but also acknowledged by others—a manhood that, rather than innate, requires constant reiteration. It is in this sense that "Rjal mshat hərga" may be understood as a template, a map that helps my interlocutors navigate and negotiate their personhood and their manhood in their every-day life in Italy.

I chose to sing this song to recharge [*kanshhən*] our Moroccan youth with a breath of virility [*nəfs dyal rjula*], so as for them to be men [*rəjjala*] over there . . . here, in this song, I recharge the human being [*kanshhən bən-adam*] . . . I tell him directly how he must behave over there. (Abdelaziz Stati, personal communication, 12 January 2019, Ouled Ziane)

22 February 2019, Ponte San Giovanni

Redouane El Am. works hard; he plans to marry soon and start a fam-ily. A native of the region of Fquih Ben Salah, he arrived in Italy at the age of fifteen, after his father abandoned him. During the day Redouane works as a mechanic, and at night he manages the club Miami Cielo, where I first met him. Located in Ponte San Giovanni, the club is on the ground floor of a two-story building, next to a halal butcher shop. The big parking lot in front of the club is empty at night and, I have been told, not always safe.

Miami Cielo is a relatively small space of about a hundred square meters (about 330 square feet), with a small bar and a dance platform surrounded by booths with low tables where Moroccan men in their twenties, thirties, and forties can sit and relax while smoking a shisha (water pipe), drinking, listening to sha'bi, and watching Arab music videos on the large screen next to the dance platform. The dimmed lights and the blacked-out windows facing the street give customers the privacy they are looking for. The Miami Cielo is a private club, which avoids problems with the authorities and the sale of alcohol; nor can these men be seen consuming alcohol or even smoking cigarettes in front of their family members, out of respect for them. There is no doorman at the Miami Cielo. Redouane explains that the club is open until sunrise and that they prefer to allow customers to sober up on their own rather than kicking them out. When there is live music, the show starts at 11:00 p.m. and goes on until the early hours, just like weddings in Morocco. Some nights there are also belly dancers, a form of entertainment practically unknown in Morocco outside of tourist venues.

Police are known to heavily patrol clubs like the Miami Cielo and to use any excuse to shut them down. The club has just opened up, so they need to be very careful. Police harassment is motivated by the fact that Moroccans in Italy are linked to drug dealing, particularly hashish, but also because, like any place where Muslims gather, the club is surveilled for potential terrorist activity. The club opened up a month ago, and so they need to be careful; they do not want to be closed down.

Redouane has asked his friend Younes to join us that evening. He is the same age and from the same region as Redouane; however, Younes is an Amazigh musician who plays kamanja, lotar, *and* l-org. *Younes makes his living with his own* shaʿbi *group and by accompanying Moroccan musicians who arrive in Italy without their troupes; this is a way for concert organizers to save money. Musicians such as Stati usually receive about 2000 euros per performance,*[45] *but they can also count on* l-ghrama, *the customary tipping of performers.*

Younes—who learned to play by listening to audiocassettes and YouTube—has a rather large repertoire of songs of various genres and styles. He tells me that the young men who frequent this and other clubs love shaʿbi *and* ʿabidat r-rma *but also* raï *and adds, "They listen to* shaʿbi *because they do not really understand the words of the old poems of* ʿaita *anymore, even though they often rediscover the old songs through their new renditions." "And yet," I ask, "no Italian songs or music that does not have its roots in* l-ʿarubiya?" "No, nothing like that." *Redouane is quick to point out that for someone like him, descended from a family of horsemen of the* tburida, *he cannot help but listen to the music and the voice of* l-ʿarubiya, *whether in its traditional or contemporary rendition. He is saving money for his wedding and hopes to hire Stati.*

It is around 11:00 p.m. when our conversation is suddenly halted by the entrance of two carabinieri *(one of the national police forces of Italy) inside the club. They have arrived unannounced and, for that matter, unauthorized. I note their voices, their loud and harsh sound as they half-jokingly say that they will confiscate everything and shut the club down. Arrogant and intimidating, they go around from one booth to another. But the men sit still on the couches, cool and composed. Self-control is an important trait of manhood for these men, similar to that of the tribesman described by Caton: "One is expected to maintain the same self-possession in other equally trying, if less dangerous, circumstances, as in replying to insults or suffering inflammatory accusations. On plenty*

of occasions ill-wishers might like to provoke someone, tweak his pride,
or try his patience, but no matter how maddening these situations might
be, the tribesman ought never to let them get the better of his emotional
equilibrium" (1990, 29–30).

The men inside the club ignore the police officers, nodding to them
silently only when necessary. As the two carabinieri approach our booth,
one of them exclaims, "There is a woman here!" But they are quick to
recognize that I am Italian and, although puzzled, they turn away. My
interlocutors continue to keep their cool, even though there is very little
conversation going on and that the tension is mounting. When they finally leave, Redouane tells me: "They use the excuse that there is a lot of
drug dealing going down to find reasons to shut clubs down, particularly
those of Moroccans; they have closed so many. At least these two were
somewhat friendly." And not long afterward he startles us by affirming,
"I do hope to move back to Morocco. . . . sometime it is just too much to
take in. It is not easy for us here."

CHAPTER 4

Longing (*ḥnin*), Intimacy (*rasi rasək*), and Belonging (*intima*)

Voicing l-'arubiya

zəy bladi ma ittansash
The cry of my country cannot be forgotten

f-l-'arubiya kulshi fiha
There is everything in *l-'arubiya*

huwa klamu 'arubi
The way he talks [i.e., sings] is rural

5 December 2018, San Giustino

"Nowadays we have everything in the countryside; it is better than the city. Now, for example: I have a home in Mohammedia,[1] *but I still go to the countryside. There we still have a big* khəima.[2]*" "You mean a hut* ['əzib]*?" "What hut? What are you saying? It is better than a building or a villa in Casablanca. It is half the size of San Siro.*[3] *Aside from the stables, it has fifteen or sixteen rooms. My father used to have donkeys, cows, and camels!" Abdelilah Ab. responds, visibly annoyed. "As I was telling you," he continues, "you get up in the morning,* mashallah *[God willing], and you go to* l-'arubiya *for some time. The air [*l-juw*] is fantastic. You can sleep at ease, there is no noise, you get up and see the sun . . . and there is absolute silence [*ṣ-ṣəqil*]! Next to us there is a mountain; I always go up there and look at the lights below me at night. You do not hear anything, [only] what is in your head [*kansmə' rasək ash kain fih*]." "The eye rests in the countryside," concurs Abdelilah Ta. "You can look . . . you can listen. It is not like in the city, where you are all closed up, you cannot see, you cannot let your eye wander freely, as we say. Your eye strolls around in* l-'arubiya *[*katsərrəḥ 'ainik fi l-'arubiya*], you hear well [*katsmə' məzyan*], you see well and smell well [*katshuf*]*

məzyan u katshəmm məzyan]. *This is not something you have in the city. You wake up in the morning and smell the animals, you smell the scent of nature [tshəmm riha ṭ-ṭbi'a], the milk goes from the cow directly to your mouth. The countryside is a beautiful place. I was born and raised in Khouribga, I studied there, but I love the countryside; I am an* 'arubi!" "But what about your children?" I ask. "*The children visit their relatives in Morocco, there they have donkeys, horses . . . they go to their grandfather's home and learn how to ride the horse of the* tburiḍa; *that horse is like a human being, you can talk to him like a human being [fhal l-insan kathḍər m'ah]. The children have a horse with whom they can talk.*" "*Yes, I know these horses. A neighbor has one of them. If you tell him* 'come here,' *he comes to you!*" asserts Abdellatif. "*I went to the* moussem *of the Ouled M'hmed and there were different troupes competing,*" Abdelilah Ta. continues. "*There were also those of Ouled Bouria. I am from there[4] . . . it is part of the great Chaouia.[5] There was a troupe [sərba] made up of seventeen horses! All the horsemen are in Italy now.*" "*I know, I know, they are all here,*" the others respond. "*One of them went to his* mqaddəm *[leader of the troupe] and asked him to sell him his horse, but the* mqaddəm *refused and told him that no matter how much they might give him, he would never sell his horse. He told him that the horse is like his son, dearer to him than his son; nobody else can mount him, either. And you have to see what that horse does—he turns his head when he has to lead the troupe . . .* subhanallah *[Glory to be God], it is as if the horse speaks with the other horses. I have never seen anything like that. . . .*" "L-'arubiya," comments Abdellatif, "*is something one has inside.*" "*It means that you have a connection to your grandparents who are* 'arubi *[i'əni jdudək rhəm 'arubi],[6] and when you feel you are an* 'arubi *[u mni nta kathəss annək 'arubi], it is as if you are thinking about your ancestors [i'əni fhal ila katfəkr jduduk],*" says Abdelilah Ta. "*It means belonging [intima], to be attached to tradition [essere attaccato alle tradizioni],*" explains Abdelilah Am., switching between Moroccan Arabic and Italian. "*You always like the place where you are born [l-blaṣa lli zwin fiha dima 'ajbək], even if you live elsewhere.*" "*They call us* 'arubi *in Casablanca . . . but who do you think lives in Casablanca? They are all coming from outside [bərra] the city, from the countryside,*" says Abdellatif.[7] "*Where we come from, people say that the origins of Morocco are* 'arubi *[hna 'lina kaigulu aṣl l-maghreb kull 'arubi]. I have a cousin who asked me once,* "How come someone like you who studied and left for Europe has remained an 'arubi?" *I told her that my origins are* 'arubi, *my grandparents and my parents are* 'arubi!" "*But the son of the city [wuld l-medina], where does he come from? His father is surely*

an 'arubi," says Abdellatif. "Ask them . . . maybe is a Beni Meskini, a
S'aidi, a Mzabi[8] . . . his origins are 'arubi." "The origins of Morocco are
l-'arubiya. What was Morocco before colonization? What was there?
There was only Casablanca!" "Yes, only Casablanca," the others respond; "look at the map, there was only Casablanca." "There was only
one house, white, that is what my father used to say," says Abdelilah Ab.
"There was only one house in Casablanca; they named it Casablanca because there was only one house, a white house. People moved there, and
that is when they called it Casablanca. But there was only one house,
and that is where people would head toward. And look at it now, look
what has become of it. It is a mess; if you go inside you can't come out
of it!" "No matter what people tell you . . . the origins of Morocco are
'arubi, everyone is an 'arubi, they cannot say this is a mdini and this
is an 'arubi. Everyone is an 'arubi," asserts Abdelilah Ta., as the others
nod and agree. "Nowadays they say that central Morocco is 'arubi, from
Kenitra to Marrakesh. All of the people from there are called 'arubi."
"Just like terroni," Abdellatif asserts, keenly aware of the implications
of the term.[9]

The entrance of l-Alami, a young metalworker originally from Settat,
momentarily halts our conversation. He pulls a chair up to our table,
which is in the back of a bar. Nobody seems to pay attention to us, but
the looks of the Italians entering and leaving of the bar speak as loudly as
their silence. Abdelilah Am. reproaches l-Alami for not having said hello
to me, but Abdellatif is quick to excuse l-Alami: "She is Italian and may
not shake his hand, and so, in order not to be embarrassed, he avoids
shaking anyone's hand." It must have been hard for the young l-Alami to
reorient himself, his body and his gestures, in Italy—that is, to reeducate
himself as a migrant.

Now that l-Alami is settled, the conversation resumes. "You must like
the countryside in Umbria," I ask, using the term 'arubiya. I am curious
about their reactions. "Nooooooo, there is no 'arubiya here [makainsh
l-'arubiya hna]!" They explode into contagious laughter. "In Morocco
there are no roads, the car may get stuck somewhere because the road is
rough [ṭ-ṭreq ḥərsha]. Here the countryside has it all: asphalt roads and
everything." "And look, here there are lights, cars, the roads are good,"
another replies. "I work on top of a hill and I see houses with electricity,
with roads, with telephones . . . with everything. The countryside is the
one we have back home, even if now there is electricity in most parts
of Morocco. But in some regions around Beni Mellal, they do not have
lights, there are only vipers [kain ghir l-lfa']!" Everyone starts laughing again. "Here even the animals are clean, nice and educated." The

conversation changes its flow as everyone begin narrating fragments of their life all at once. And as they excitedly recall their stories, their voices begin to overlay into a multivocal rendering of l-'arubiya.

"*In Morocco the animals are bad [*cattivi*], you cannot touch a slougi [North African hound],*[10] *you can touch anything but a slougi. In the countryside, the slougi recognizes only his owner . . . smells the odor [*f-l-'arubiya s-slugi i'rəf ghir maya . . . ishəmm riḥa*]." "You are right! In the countryside you cannot enter a home at night unless the owner comes out and tells the dog to be quiet; otherwise you do not make it home." "The problem is rabies." "No, no," Abdelilah Ta. intervenes, "dogs are vaccinated, but the heat, the sun goes to their heads. Here dogs are cool, in the shade." More laughter follows Abdelilah's statement. "In our region," Abdellatif continues, "humans have rabies! In fact, I do not go to* l-blad *[village] as often. If you argue with a taxi driver, for example, you cannot get out of the taxi. If you try to leave you will find him with a bat [*zərwaṭa*] ready to hit you!" They continue to laugh, acknowledging Abdellatif's comment. "Can you send me those photos?" "Only if you bring me back a donkey," Abdlelilah Am. Responds. "Even four if you like." "How many do you have?" "I had one but he died. My father left the countryside and went to Mohammedia and the donkey was left alone. I told my brother to take him in." "They probably sold him," the others suggest, making fun of Abdelilah Ab. "I think I told you that my father was the only one who could ride that donkey. I could not ride him. But whenever my father wanted to ride him, the donkey would somehow make it easy for my father to mount him. And my father could go anywhere with that donkey. But my father has grown old, and so we left for Mohammedia and that donkey was left behind. Someone from the family would feed the donkey, but I told my brother to take him. And so I asked for someone to go pick the donkey up and take him to my brother. He was there for about a year. They had grass to feed him, and my father would still use him with a cart to carry whatever he needed. But we do not understand what happened, and one morning he was dead. Maybe that one is right, they sold him but did not want to tell me." "Maybe he was disoriented, or maybe they made him work too hard, and he was not used to that." Everyone is laughing hysterically now, but Abdelilah Ab. keeps his composure as he remembers the donkey with affection. The very first time I met him he told me all about that donkey, with the same wonder one finds in myths and legends and epics. His ears were large, he was taller than most, and his bray was powerful; he was nothing like the inadequate little Italian donkeys, he said proudly. "The donkey was used to eating and sleeping, and maybe, once he got to Mohammedia, they exploited him . . . the poor little one [*l-məskin*] was not used to that."*

"You know that many of not only the gestures, but also the sounds, of 'abidat r-rma *mimic animals . . . I used to be a very good dancer and can tell you all about them," says Abdelilah Ta. "Look at how they move their feet. There is that step when everyone in the troupe moves together sideways facing the audience, when they bend and raise one knee and gently put one foot down crossing the other . . . that step is meant to mimic the horse, and especially when the horse moves quietly [*piano, piano*]. Do you know what the significance of that is? You see, during colonialism, they used the performances of* 'abidat r-rma *to send messages and to teach people how to act against the French,*[11] *to move and not to be heard by the French, just like this." Abdelilah Ta. begins to lightly tap the table with the palms of his hands, imitating the quiet pace of the horses. "It is the same thing for the dance with the shoulders [*l-ktaf*]," referring to a rather difficult movement where a dancer, keeping his arms down close to the body, rapidly alternates the slight forward and backward movement of each shoulder, which is accompanied by the rapid alternation of the upward and downward movements of each foot. These fast shoulder movements produce a shimmering of the body, a wavelike motion that is meant to mimic the slithering of a snake. "During the war [*la guerra*] for independence, people needed to hide in the countryside, where there were no buildings or construction. After the harvest the wheat was placed in a pit underneath the hearth, while the hay was kept inside the barns in order to feed the animals. One place where those who fought against the French used to hide was under the haystacks. But in order to slip underneath a stack, they would have to slide like snakes do: that is what the dance represents." "And what about the gestures when you lift your arms in front of you with one wrist sitting on top of the other with the hands moving up and down, as if flapping . . . like the wings of birds do?" I ask Abdelilah Ta. "That is to mimic the pigeons [*l-ḥmam*], the carrier pigeons, the ones that bring messages. There are so many meanings in the gestures of* 'abidat r-rma, *people think that* 'abidat r-rma *is for fun, for dancing, but there is so much in there . . . everything is in there."*

As the past animates performances in the present (Meintjes 2017, 118), the heroic actions associated with these dance movements have the potential to symbolically transform the oppression and the violence (Argenti, quoted in Meintjes 2017, 118–19) of the colonial era, which, with some differences, is still experienced by migrants in the present. Abdelilah Ta. works for a company that builds luxury prefabricated homes, earning 8 euros an hour before taxes. Like the rest of my interlocutors, he struggles to support his family of five. Fearful of being fired, he cannot join a union, so he is unprotected from the demands of an employer to whom he is eager to demonstrate that "we [Moroccans] are not all the

Figure 11. Abdelilah Ta., Abdlelilah Ab., the author, Abdellatif, and l-Alami

Photo by Abdelilah Amahdar

*same!" [*non siamo tutti uguali*]. Abdelilah Ta. feels stuck, unable to move [*immobile*] in Italy. But there is something deeper to his own sense of immobility, another "biographic specificity within a collective history" (Meintjes 2017, 118). His father, a former "French" soldier who was first stationed in Germany and then for years in the former Indochina (the term Abdelilah Ta. uses), came back as a disabled veteran. He died years later of an illness that goes unnamed, only silently acknowledged in Khouribga: cancer. His own sense of immobility and his father's actual inability to move are inevitably entangled in the dances and the heroism he so proudly describes. "Do you still dance, Abdelilah?" I ask him. "No, here I do not have time. I dance a little bit when I go back home . . . at weddings."*

Intensely felt through the senses, *l-'arubiya* is a site of longing (*ḥnin*) and belonging (*intima*), a site of knowledge and experiences that questions and challenges its association with what has been historically linked with backwardness. It is a trope, an experience, a discursive construction as much as a geographical location (Hoffman 2008, 113), a transnational imagination of "home" permeating the everyday lives of these migrants in Italy; it is used to evoke tradition, the way of life of the ancestors, a territory where vision is unhindered and taste is unmediated, where it is possible to smell nature and hear well.[12] L-'arubiya, however, should not be understood as a merely romantic or nostalgic vision of the peasant world or past, since, as discussed in the previous chapters, behind the green and yellow fields of wheat l-'arubiya has historically articulated a geography of disparity, marginality, land dispossession, lack of infrastructure, and a difference that my interlocutors acknowledge and reclaim in their tropes and listening practices, and particularly in what they refer to as ṣawt l-'arubiya and n-nəbra l-'arubiya (the tone or inflection of l-'arubiya).

In the previous chapters I analyzed ṣawt l-'arubiya through songs directly linked to migration; but this is by no means all that my interlocutors listen to. In what follows, I want to push the analysis further and discuss two commercial recordings that exemplify the everyday listening practices of my interlocutors in reference to 'aiṭa and 'abidat rma. I discuss how these mediated performances produce l-'arubiya, allowing migrant Moroccan men—whose origins have not ceased to have value and whose ideas about the countryside do not include that of Umbria—to carry a sense of place along their transnational routes and in their transnational lives, since, although it derives from a specific location, l-'arubiya can travel through people's voices and performances (Chávez 2017, 269). In their everyday lives, for example, Moroccan migrants have reconstructed a sense of place through the Moroccan rendering of the Umbrian territory via linguistic assonances, local similarities, creativity, and imagination. The village of San Secondo becomes Hassan Secondo—in reference to the late king Hassan II; Todi—a town known for its pottery—is renamed Villaggio dyal qəllal (village of pottery); Gualdo Tadino—a town known for its yearly donkey race—is referred to as Villaggio dyal ḥmar (village of the donkey); while Ponte Pattoli—part of the municipality of the town of Perugia—is referred to as kəḥlat l-'yun (black eyes), in reference to the owner of a bar where Moroccans would go to make phone calls in the 1980s and 1990s.

In what follows, I posit that the mediated performances in question can cultivate the rural, to allow a sense of self that has been muted, fetishized, and criminalized to become whole again and enable these migrants to claim place and agency.

26 July 2016, Città di Castello

"In Morocco, they think that we are in paradise, but it is not that way for us here. Their glances [occhiate] are enough! They don't even allow us to slaughter the lamb for the Feast of the Sacrifice. . . . It is only through music that I get to exhale [respirare]." "Any music?" I ask Hassan Be., a

*thirty-five-year-old industrial machine operator originally from Settat.
"I can't really listen to Italian music, the words don't do it for me, it
doesn't put me in the mood. To exhale I need the music of our region,
the music we listen to at weddings back home." "And here?" I ask. "Here
we have clubs, but there's the Internet, television, we have music on our
phones and in the cars."*

Hassan's last statement emphasizes a change in the privileged listening practice of these migrants. Although listening to commercial recordings among friends is not uncommon in Morocco and elsewhere in the
Maghreb (see Schade-Poulsen 1999 for Algeria), in Italy listening has fun-
damentally turned inward and is not unlike what Charles Hirschkind, in his
discussion about the entwinement of sound and subjects that are ignored
within modern spaces, defines as "subterranean" (2006, 21).[13] The recordings I have chosen to analyze are part of this type of subterranean listening
because in Italy, aside from the *sha'bi* performances in clubs, described in
chapter 3, *l-'arubiya* is seldom experienced live unless *'aita* and *'abidat
r-rma* are presented as items of folklore at the relatively few festivals and
events claiming to foster dialogue and exchange among Italy and Morocco.
In those contexts, the genres are presented onstage along with other music
traditions of Morocco—the element of a sonorous collage that is meant to
illustrate, much like a tourist brochure, the country's soundscape—or as
entertainment accompanying the consumption of yet another sensual experience of Morocco: its cuisine. To my knowledge, my interlocutors are not
very keen to attend these types of events. Furthermore, in contrast to the
music and sounds of other migrant communities that have become fixtures
at concerts and festivals (D'Amico 2005; Sabelli 2006), heard in the streets
of Italian cities (Portelli 2014) or at religious functions and liturgical rites
(Facci 2017; Cosentino 2019), and performed by asylum seekers in refugee
centers (Caruso 2019) or by multiethnic groups and orchestras (Dari 2017),
sawt l-'arubiya remains largely inaudible to Italian ears. And yet . . .

27 July 2016, Gubbio

*We meet Simo in the evening in Gubbio. He is closing his shop—a ven-
dor's truck full of leather goods, located at the entrance of the old town.
He greets me with a broad smile, and I immediately take to him. His
cousin, Si Mohammed, is also there; shy, composed, and careful at first,
he is the opposite of Simo. I know their family well in Morocco—or what
is left of it, since, in Gubbio and the surrounding area alone, there are*

more than thirty relatives living there now. This is the type of migratory chain discussed in chapter 3; it all started with Simo's father, who migrated to Italy in the 1990s. I have not visited Gubbio myself for decades now, and apparently nothing has changed except for the prevalence of Moroccan Arabic I hear as we walk to a café nearby.

Simo is taking us to dinner at a place in the nearby countryside, and we all get in his car. He loves ʿaiṭa and the shikhat; his father did too before making the pilgrimage to Mecca, when he stopped listening to music altogether. Every time Simo goes back to Morocco, he hires the best performers for an evening with his male friends. "You should come too next time. We stay up all night, and in the morning I go to the hammam and then home to rest." I thank him for the invitation, but we both know that it would be awkward for a woman to attend these intimate male parties. "And what do you do here?" I ask, eager to know if there is anything happening, "Here I only listen to recordings in my truck, in my car, and when I am out with friends," Simo explains as he begins singing verses from a well-known poem of ʿaiṭa. The others join in, and the voice of l-ʿarubiya fills the interior of the car, spilling out of the open windows into the Umbrian countryside.

As a site where aesthetic behaviors, signifying practices, and performative and speech acts originate (Chávez 2017, 9), as well as a "geographical imagination" (Harvey 1973), I posit that the voice of the rural allows migrant Moroccan men in the Alta Valle del Tevere in Umbria to experience wholeness instead of lack, and to claim agency and reject the exclusion that has been put on them (Chávez 2017, 57).

This chapter focuses on a detailed poetic analysis that examines the role of poetry and vernacular language in the construction and articulation of l-ʿarubiya. It also examines sonic characteristics of the genres in question, particularly those concerning the voice. It investigates how the voice is conceived as a sonic phenomenon in which timbre becomes central because it acoustically embodies nature, the environment, and particular experiences of space, time, memory, intimacy, and male desire. The chapter attempts to convey how migrant Moroccan men draw from sonic practices that index a concatenation of rurality and masculinity, allowing them to reconstruct a sense of the rural and masculine self that has been silenced because of stigmatization, racialization, and the fear of, alienation of, and othering of Moroccan men.

Sound ideologies and ideologies of sound, Alex Chávez reminds us, "are instructive in understanding how migrants live in and hear the world" (2017, 11). It is in this context that I also analyze how migrants adapt images, experiences, and the imaginary of the ʿarubiya in helping them shape a new geography, an alternative sense of place in the Italian present.

The discussion begins with an analysis of "L-ghaba" (The Forest), a song that is critical to the repertoire of ʿabidat r-rma. I analyze this poem to elaborate how a "unique and perceptual environment" (Larkin 2008, 2–3) that is part of l-ʿarubiya is produced and circulated. I aim to inquire into the type of rural epistemology that emerges in a particular performance (Dent 2009, 49), and to capture the essence of what counts as l-ʿarubiya, connecting "L-ghaba" to the tropes of my interlocutors, contextualizing the dialogue with which I opened this chapter with poetry, music, and the voice, for songs and verbal art "are sutured tightly together with everyday talk, too" (Fox 2004, 229). The analysis also focuses on the gendering of l-ʿarubiya, on the importance of the male voice—singing and narrating—connecting it to what it means to be a rajəl.

Any discussion about the gendering of l-ʿarubiya, however, needs to include a discussion about ʿaiṭa and the shikhat. The chapter concludes with an analysis of "Ḥajti fi grini" (I long for my male companion) and a discussion of the role of the female voice and narration in the construction of manhood (rujula and fḥula) at the intersection of history, rurality, and male desire.

"L-GHABA": MUSIC, VOICE, AND THE NATURAL ENVIRONMENT

A celebrated poem in the repertoire of ʿabidat r-rma that continues to be interpreted by different generations of performers steeped in the music and the voice of l-ʿarubiya, "L-ghaba" is known and appreciated by all my interlocutors, who are familiar with renditions said to be inspired by the late Shikh l-Bachir, one of the most renowned interpreters of ʿabidat r-rma (audio ex. 4.1). The choice to analyze one of Shikh l-Bachir's recordings from the 1980s was dictated by the critical role that his performances are known to play in more contemporary interpretations of "L-ghaba" and in the listening practices of my interlocutors,[14] and by my close working relationship with Shikh Sharqi, who, having learned his trade from Shikh l-Bachir, now leads his own troupe.

The circulation and availability of old recordings on today's online platforms have allowed an unparalleled number of performers, performances, recordings, and technologies to coexist and accrete. This copresence has affected listening practices in two substantial ways. It has allowed different renditions of "L-ghaba" to feel the same despite difference, that is, one can listen to and understand each version through its intertextual relationship with other renditions (Ciucci 2012a), and it has allowed older and more traditional artists to be (re)discovered and incorporated in the more diverse listening practices of a younger generation of migrants who are eager not to forget.

ON CRIES

aaaaaaa . . . r-rami
Aaaaaaah . . . the hunter

A cry, a call, a shout. A stretched-out vowel in which speech, cries, and singing are intertwined, their boundaries blurred. The straight, throaty sound of the open "a"—a phoneme that more than any other articulates the materiality of the body singing its language (Olwage 2006, 214). A sound that Arab theorists refer to as *tafaghur* (Al-Kātib 1972, 126) because it is emitted by a wide-open mouth (from the verb *faghara*, to open the mouth wide). An interjection used to gain attention, to alert an audience to listen well; this is what storytellers do when gathering a crowd in a circle (*ḥalqa*) to perform in public squares. The words of Shikh l-Bachir, after all, were known to have meaning, to be more than singing (*klamu mə 'na mash ghunna*).

This is a cry embodying the voice of *l-ʿarubiya*, whose hard (*qaṣəḥ*), high (*tal* or *ʿali*), and hoarse (*bəḥḥ*) qualities are the antithesis of the smooth (*mləs*), light (*khəfif*), sweet (*ḥlu*), and gentle (*ḥnin*) voice emitted by a rounded mouth, a mouth that does not project from the throat as it performs *al-ala*. The distinction is already palpable in this first utterance, loaded with embodied meaning—in the materiality of a voice reinscribing the past into the present. For a voice to be heard, it must, "be materially instantiated" (Meintjes 2017, 13).

Shikh l-Bachir's throat is tight. One hears the physical stress in his voice, imagines his neck protruding and his carotids enlarging as I have seen in other singers, performance after performance. Interpreters of this tradition are always fussy about their throats, constantly touching them, testing them, and coughing in order to clear them. "The voice of the rural must not come from the inside, that voice is bad," Shikh Sharqi explains patiently, pointing to his diaphragm. "The good voice comes from the throat [*ḥəngora*]," he continues, touching his throat with his right hand. He pronounces *ḥənjura* (throat) in accordance with one of the linguistic specificities of the vernacular of *l-ʿarubiya*, often substituting [j] with the rural and ideologically loaded hard [g]. "Singing *l-ʿarubiya* is all in the throat," he tells me, as our conversation switches to his vegetable garden and his love of trees.

The vocal competence of the countryside, the set of qualities governing the aesthetics of a voice able to mobilize, reconstruct, and preserve the ethos of *l-ʿarubiya*, emanates from the throat. For the Zulu, Meintjes writes,

Figure 12. Shikh Sharqi and his troupe

Photo by the author

the throat is where eloquence resides (2017, 65); for my interlocutors, the throat is where the rural resides. The relationship between throat, voice, and the rural is perhaps best reflected in the term ḥəlq, which can be translated as throat, voice, cry, or vocal timbre, or, even more fittingly, in the expression 'əndu l-ḥəlq (he has a beautiful, powerful voice),[15] a compliment given only to a singer whose voice evokes l-'arubiya. Strength and power are important elements of the aesthetics of the voice in this male genre.[16]

"The cry of my country cannot be forgotten!" This is how the fifty-something-year-old Mustapha El Me., a water-well driller originally from Khouribga, had articulated his emotions through sound and, more specifically, through the term zəy—that is, a high-pitched cry associated with such animals as mice, hedgehogs, rabbits, and baby birds. The verb zwa, from which zəy derives, may also mean to play the ghaiṭa, a double-reed aerophone whose sound is generally characterized as high-pitched and loud.

L-'arubiya is pervaded by a range of cries that, in the absence of visual landmarks, are said to aurally demarcate its space. The vocal and emotional qualities of these cries, used in songs as poetic intensifiers, are rendered by a rich lexicon describing the quality of the cry, its function and volume, as in the following examples: ghəuta, a strident cry, a call for help, a scream associated with arguments and disagreements; 'aiṭa, a loud cry, a call, a shout, an invocation, a cry entangled with particular strong emotions and a musicopoetic genre; briḥ, a call, a loud cry, a proclamation made in public spaces such the weekly marketplace; ndih, a loud cry, a voice that stimulates and excites animals; and *hait*, a cry at the top of one's voice used specifically to drive prey toward hunters. Local terminology acknowledges the presence and the meanings of a cry, challenging Orientalist accounts of "exotic cries" cut off from semantics, and reduced to an exclusively corporeal sensation of the European body and ears.

> During the weeks I spent in Morocco I made no attempt to acquire either Arabic or any of the Berber languages. I wanted to lose none of the force of those foreign-sounding cries. I wanted sounds to affect me as much as lay in their power, unmitigated by deficient and artificial knowledge on my part. I had not read a thing about the country. Its customs were [as] unknown to me as its people. (Canetti 1978, 23)

ON ROUGHNESS AND COARSENESS

Amanda Weidman writes that, rather than assume the universal significance of the voice, it is crucial to ask "where and when 'voice' becomes a salient metaphor and what is at stake" (2014, 38). Associated with excess and vulgarity, with that which colonial and, to an extent, Moroccan postcolonial ears continue to perceive as rough, coarse, and unpolished, the voice of *l-'arubiya* has been ignored and denigrated, and its population left as if they had "no tongue" (Najmi 2007, 1:19). I have already described how the concept of *ḥarsh* (rough or coarse) refers to a wide range of phenomena, from speech styles to loudness in one's speech, forcefulness, and aggressiveness. A person, in fact, can be *ḥarsh* in terms of mannerisms and behavior when they lack tact and refinement and thus inherently perceived as lower class, imbued with connotations of illiteracy, poverty, peasantry, and immorality (Hachimi 2012, 330–31, 334).

Roughness or coarseness, however, is not perceived in the same way by those inhabiting—in reality, in their memory, and in their imagination—the rural. If we understand timbre as a perceptual process of relating sounds to their sources (Osborn, discussed in Blake 2019, 144), it is possible to recognize how the connection between the rough or coarse vocal quality, the land, and the way of life of the countryside allow *ḥarsh* to take on a new meaning, to have an emotional affect, and permits particular experiences "to seep into the texture" (Meintjes 2017, 126) of the voice of *l-'arubiya*. It is in this sense that timbre may be conceived as a site "for sonically enacting and negotiating the social politics of identity formation," and, in turn, for challenging "dominant power structures sonically" (Blake 2019, 148).

Ḥarsh is thus reclaimed as central to listening, as well as to a multisensory set of counteraesthetics.

Table 1 The aesthetics of *ḥarsh*

ḥarrəsh	to make something rough or coarse, to irritate, to provoke
ḥarrəsh l-klam	lit., to make someone's words rough, that is, to speak ill of someone
ḥarsh	rough, coarse, rocky, stony, someone who is brusque, tough, as well as full of energy
ḥrəsh	the name of the characteristic pottery of the of the Marrakesh-Asfi region in the Atlantic plains and plateaus, which is considered to be some of the best in Morocco: characterized by its coarse surface, natural earth colors, lack of enamel, and simple, and, to a certain extent, unpolished ornamentation (see Triki, Ouazzani, and Daum 1993), this pottery is contrasted with that of Fez, which is considered more refined because of its urban association and its connection to al-Andalus
ḥrəsh l-ʿyun	rough eyes, meaning beautiful eyes, as in a verse in a poem of *ʿaiṭa*: *sidi ahmed ḥrəsh l'yun* (my lord Ahmed with the beautiful eyes)
ləḥmha ḥrəsh	her rough skin, a sign of beauty for a woman in the countryside
ḥarsha	a metaphor used to describe how a desirable woman's sexual organs should feel
yddih ḥarsha	his rough hand, indicating the hand of a peasant that is not slender or smooth and thus is better suited or more desirable for working the land; the hand of a peasant may be considered almost sacred because of the work it performs
khəshba ḥarsha	a piece of wood on which it is possible to touch its grain and thus feel its soul
ḥarrusha	rocky soil
khobza ḥarsha	high-quality peasant bread with semolina sprinkled on top, also referred to as *məḥrash*
djaja ḥarsha	well-roasted chicken
ḥarsha	pan-fried bread made from a coarse type of semolina
ḥarshisha	long, loose-fitting outer tunic for men made of coarse wool, characteristic of the countryside, with a rough but durable quality
naʿnaʿ ḥrəsh	a variety of mint considered to be the best for making tea

Cornelia Fales posits that "not only does timbre carry the most information about a source and its location, but of all the parameters of music, it
also carries the most information about the environment through which
the sound has traveled" (2002, 57). Thus, if it can be argued that what is
defined as a rough or coarse timbre is found in a number of music genres
throughout the world (Holst-Warhaft 1983; Schuyler 1990–91; Chuse 2003;
Wallach 2008; Willoughby 2012; Dave 2019; Fellezs 2019; Sonevytsky
2019), the roughness or coarseness of *l-ʿarubiya* harks back to the complex
attachments that link my interlocutors to features of a physical world (Basso
1996, 55); it denotes the way in which migrant Moroccan men remember,
perceive, and sense *l-ʿarubiya* through a voice that aurally demarcates a "social and somatic landscape" (Seremetakis 1994, 9), a collective vocal identity that recreates a sensorial and emotional experience of place. In their
"timbre-centered listening" (Levin and Süzükei 2018) soil is central. "There
is the soil [*torba*] in the voice of *l-ʿarubiya*," they explain, referring to a
rocky soil traditionally classified as *ḥarrusha* and thought to be at the origin
of this voice. "It is as if you say that it comes from the soil [*bḥal ila gulti mən
torba*],"[17] musicians explained to me—the same soil seen in the pictures that
migrants carry on their phones, and that they are quick to show when asked
about the landscape of *l-ʿarubiya*.

6 December 2018, Umbertide

*Akrout is originally from Khouribga. Now in his late thirties, he arrived
in Italy with a tourist visa fourteen years ago, and although he has an
Italian passport, he still works on the tobacco plantations. It is the best he
can do for now. He seems eager to talk. We sit down at a table adorned
by a red tablecloth, a reminder that Christmas is near. The café is particularly loud, with a television blasting through thin and unadorned walls
that amplify the screams and laughter of the women behind the counter.
"Stefaniaaaaaaaa," one of them shouts across the bar in a local accent
marked by the Tuscan dialect. Akrout seems unaffected by this cacopho-
nous surrounding; he ignores it, just as the Italian patrons ignore us.*

*"No, no, nothing. I do not listen to that music." Akrout is very clear
about his likes and dislikes when it comes to music. He does not even
care about Malika Ayane, the Italian Moroccan singer who, although
famous, is never mentioned by my interlocutors.*

"I listen to a lot of shaʿbi," *he says, using this term to include* ʿaiṭa
and ʿabidat rma. *"I keep the music on my phone . . . look." The voice of*
l-ʿarubiya *intrudes in the cacophony of the café as Akrout plays a home*

video he took at a wedding in Morocco. Despite the poor quality of the recording and its distorted sound, Akrout does not hesitate to tell me that this is what he likes. "What is it about this voice that you like? Can you tell me?" "Sawt l-ʿarubia," *Akrout begins; "it is the language [é la lingua]. I like this voice, it sings about history [*kayghanni 'la storia*], that which is lived, experienced. It is a voice that makes you think about the past [*l-maḍi], about my childhood . . . about who I am."*

The voice of *l-ʿarubiya* is inevitably linked to the vernacular of the region. It is impossible for my interlocutors to talk about the quality of a voice without considering the quality of the poetic lines. Good singers are evaluated in accordance with how well they know a text and whether the words they sing are beautiful (*klam zwin*)—that is, in accordance with the kinds of emotions they are able to elicit, and whether the words have meaning. Singers who are considered to be only interested in money are said to sing empty words (*klam khawi*). There is a rich and complex relationship between voice and speech, and between a singer and his voice; it is a matter of whether or not the tone of a singer's voice is that of an *ʿarubi*, that is, whether his vernacular also indexes rurality.

Jeffrey Heath writes about how the central type of Moroccan Arabic—indicated by other linguists as *ʿarubi* (Abbassi 1977, 23–24; Boukous 1995, 94; Hachimi 2012, 41)—corresponds to what is commonly referred to as Hilalian dialect, spoken by the descendants of the Beni Hilal Bedouin tribes who settled in the Atlantic plains and plateaus in the eleventh century, a dialect that contrasts with the old urban dialects. The dialect in question is commonly recognized by its robust quality and characterized by some of the following traits.

- The consonant *qaf*, generally pronounced *qa*, becomes *ga*
- The short diphthongs *aw* and *ay* are pronounced *u* and *i*, respectively
- Short vowels usually merge as schwa *ə*
- The extensive use of syncope with clusters of up to three consonants, as in *nktəb*, instead of *nəktəb* (I write)
- The assimilation of *nt* in *tt*, *ft* in *tt*, and *nd* in *dd*
- Consonants at the ends of words are not followed by a vowel; this gives the impression of a rough or brusque ending
- Stress on the penultimate syllable of a word
- Gender merged in the second- and third-person plural
- Feminization of the second-person singular

- Words not being clearly enunciated but rather pronounced indistinctly, with a sort of throaty or guttural enunciation (Heath 2002, 8–10)

ON ANIMAL CRIES

Before turning my attention to the poetic text, I want to delve a bit more into another cry that is critical to "L-ghaba" and, more generally, to ʿabidat r-rma. As servants and performers, the men of these ensembles played a double role: beaters during the day and entertainers at night. Because of this traditional context of performance, the natural environment is said to be present in all songs and narratives, with the forest being one of the major themes of the genre (Amine and Carlson 2012, 36).

Beaters usually move in line as they approach the wild boar and they scream and cry out; they are performing the cry of the dog [hait l-kəlbi] and the cry of the wild boar [hait l-ḥalluf]. They emit cries that imitate the animals as they move toward the prey. (Shikh Sharqi, personal communication, 30 July 2017, Ben Slimane)

Shikh Sharqi refers to these two particular cries as hait, a term indicating a cry that is specifically used to incite the animals and drive the prey toward the hunters. The objective of the hait is to communicate with these animals and, consequently, to mimic their voice. The hait pervades ʿabidat r-rma, and, in the case of "L-ghaba," it is the hait of the slougi.

Characterized by the fast alternation of the aspirated hu and ha, in the hait l-kəlbi the forceful expulsion of air emulates the excitement and the panting of the greyhounds in pursuit of the prey. Except for the leader, the hait is performed by all the members of the ensemble over what is describe as "the dragging rhythm" (l-iqaʿ z-zəḥḥaffi) where dragging describes the gait of someone who has lost or injured their legs.[18] The basic pattern of this 6/8 rhythm is 2 + 1 + 2 + 1, where beats 1, 3, 4, and 6 are accented. This is a rhythm that may also be described as the combination of two distinct units of duration (long–short, long–short), inevitably bringing to mind the aksak or "limping" rhythm (Brăiloiu 1984). Here, however, the rhythm is locally conceived by musicians as consisting of two strokes "inside" (when the instrument is beaten in the center and produces a relatively deep note, in this case beats 1 and 4) and one stroke "outside" (when the instrument is beaten at the edge, producing a higher pitch, in this case beat 3 or 6). The stroke "outside" on beat 6—referred to as "mother" (umm), since it is said to hold everything together—unequivocally comments on the critical role of syncopation in the basic rhythmic pattern.

A fixed and essential component of 'abidat r-rma, in this poem the *hait l-kəlbi* is part of the text; it is the last line of the refrain (*lazima*) that is repeated after each section (*faṣl*), a line resonating longer than any other line in the poem and resounding throughout "L-ghaba."

> *aaaaaaa . . . r-rami*
> Aaaaaaah . . . the hunter

> *wa ana, anana, anana . . .*

> *wurrini waḥshək a l-ghaba*
> Show me your wild animals, forest

> *huha huha, huha . . .*

Ochoa Gautier writes that a number of ethnographies have pointed to the practice of imitating or referring to the sounds of animals as the sonic dimension of the everyday, and that "if . . . incorporating nonhuman entities in sound is not a problem but an objective, then it becomes evident that the human-nonhuman relation . . . present in the voice is not one that debases the person" (2014, 61). Ochoa Gautier's statement is quite pertinent to this discussion, particularly when comparing Shikh Sharqi's objective—to imitate the animals so as to acoustically render the hunting scene in the forest—with a colonial account of a hunting scene, where the sonic utterances of the local population are perceived problematically. In this account, the description of "tremendous noise," "strange cries," animal vocalizations, and human and nonhuman communication unequivocally debases the voice of the population.

> The beaters made tremendous noise, filling the air with strange cries as they commenced the drive towards us. It was amusing to listen to them. A Moor always talks to an animal as he would to a human being. He firmly believes that they all speak "Moorish." So I was not surprised to hear Salem shouting with his huge, resounding voice, "Now come out and show yourself, great Abou Snau (father of tusks)." (Bonsal 1893, 268)

The ability of 'abidat r-rma to "move between the world of the human and the nonhuman by envoicing animal sounds" (Ochoa Gautier 2014, 63) could be partly explained by the fact that unlike in the city, where the general term *ṣiḥ* (bellow, shout) is employed, in the countryside animal vocalizations and onomatopoeic words for animal utterances have made it possible for the animal lexicon to invade the vernacular (see also Heath 2002, 67–70). But there are two more points worth making when discussing the voicing of animal sounds. The first is that humans' and animals' shared capacity to have a voice is embedded in the notion of *ṣawt*, which, in medieval Arab treatises, indicated the communicative medium in the lives of both (Shehadi 1995; Sawa 2019).[19] The second is that although animals figure significantly in Islamic thought and culture, zoology—understood in the narrower and contemporary sense of the word—was not as developed because animals were always regarded in relation to humankind (Eisenstein 2014; Miller 2017, particularly in reference to *Kitab al-Ḥayawan*).[20] In this sense, *'abidat r-rma* requires "a vocalization that is conceived as a multiplicity rather than embodying a sound that represents an entity" (Ochoa Gautier 2014, 64)—a vocal competence that allows one to reconstitute the type of human and nonhuman relations my interlocutors described at the opening of this chapter, and that they recognize as being entangled in their experience of *l-'arubiya*.

"L-GHABA" AND THE MEANING
OF THE MASCULINE VOICE

Section 1

a wa ila katti nəḍḍam[21]	*a wa ila katti nəḍḍam*
If you were a bard	If you were a bard
jib 'la l-ghaba	*wa 'la l-ghaba*
Sing about the forest	About the forest
a l-ghaba nəbbah	*bu'mira hwa sh-shəṭṭah*
Pay attention to the forest	The kestrel, he is the dancer
wa gulu l-ghaba	
Tell the forest	
ila rbəhti rəbbi səmmah	
If you win my God is magnanimous	

Sung at full volume with a quasi-spoken articulation and a straight tone, the syllabic articulation of the poetic lines emphasizes a binary rhythmic flow that, set against the ternary feel of the "dragging rhythm," gives the first stanza a rich polyrhythmic texture and an intense drive. As the fast call-and-response gives way to the continuous performance of the verses, the enjambment between the final two lines amplifies the chase, the excitement and the pace of hunting.

20 November 2019, Umbertide

Abdelilah Ry. loves the countryside, and he is passionate about hunting. He arrived with a tourist visa in Umbria in 1985, before the Schengen regime was put in place, traveling by car from Ben Ahmed to Città di Castello. He sells intimate apparel with his wife, Khadija, in weekly markets throughout the region. Today he is in Umbertide.

Like other hunters, Abdelilah Ry. loves the fresh air, the interaction with nature, the waiting, and the excitement of the actual hunt. "It is difficult to explain," he tells me, but that is what he likes to do when he goes back home. "There's no time for hunting in Italy: family, work, and you know the rest," he acknowledges. His daughter, born and raised in Città di Castello, recently got married in Berrechid,[22] Khadija's hometown. "We had ʿabidat r-rma at my daughter's wedding; I don't listen to anything else. I grew up with that music and am naturally drawn to ʿabidat r-rma. . . . When you listen to their songs it is as if you are right there . . . hunting with them."

Singing, as already discussed, is accompanied by an array of percussion instruments. Among these instruments, made of local materials and animal skins (Amine and Carlson 2012, 36)—the head of the *bendir* (large frame drum) is made of goatskin and the frame of wood, while the *taʾrija* (goblet-shaped hand drum) is made of glazed ceramic and its head also of goatskin—the role of the *məqqəṣ* (sawed-off pair of large scissors) is paramount. Traditionally used while shearing, its unchanging rhythmic pattern provides the time referent for the alignment of all the other percussion elements, while its metallic sound is said to be reminiscent of the hammering of a blacksmith (*ḥəddad*), considered the symbolic leader of ʿabidat r-rma.[23]

Asked to sing about the forest, to bring attention to a natural environment that is very meaningful to the countryside and its population, the poet-as-hunter (Stetkevych 2016) observes and narrates a space that on the one hand is traditionally considered as a public good used for pasturage, land clearing, and the various uses of wood (Ankouz and El Aïchouni 1999, 33), and on the other is a space that legends and tales have associated with frightening characters, the supernatural, and wild animals, as the line from the refrain *wurrini wahshak a l-ghaba* (show me your wild animals, forest) reminds us. As in legends and tales, the role of the poet-as-hunter is to turn the uninhabited space of the forest into an inhabited space for humans, here expressed through the range of emotions and sentiments taking place in this ecological space and, at another level, in the feminization of the forest.

This transformation begins with the introduction into the forest of the kestrel whose epithet, *bu'amira* (the one with the small ornamentations), refers to the small black dots on the bird's rust-red plumage. Kestrels are known to hover by facing the wind and using their tail to help keep them aloft, almost motionless, with an occasional quivering of the wings or gliding that is said to resemble dancing. The portrayal of the kestrel as the dancer draws from these movements and sets him apart from the other wild animals in the forest.

Just as important, the kestrel is associated with falconry and with the Bedouin tribes of the Atlantic plains and plateaus, who have historically engaged in it (Colin 1999, 47).

Section 2

mal l-ghaba mqələqa Why is the forest troubled?	*mal l-ghaba mqələqa* Why is the forest troubled?
mal l-ghaba mqələqa Why is the forest troubled?	*mal l-ghaba mqələqa* Why is the forest troubled?

mən harr l-mənshar khaifa
She is afraid of the heat of the saw

wa t'əyyət a hiya a syadi
She cries, my masters

səkhəitu biya
You abandoned me

In contrast to the previous images, in section 2 the forest is described as troubled, frightened by the "heat of the saw"; as she cries to her masters, "you have abandoned me." The use of reported speech allows different voices to become audible and permits the forest's plea to be amplified; it also signals the feminization of the forest. In this section, fear and crying acknowledge events of the past, turning history into an effective emotional narrative (Dent 2009, 50).

In chapter 1 I discussed how the French colonial image of the Atlantic plains and plateaus as the "granary of Rome" played a pivotal role in environmental and land policy in Morocco; forests were also fundamental to this colonial narrative. As deforestation and desertification—assumed to have been wrought by the Maghreb's large pastoral population—turned into an account used as an excuse to appropriate land, a particular colonial environmental narrative that placed overgrazing at the center of the forest question in Morocco allowed the French to pass new laws and policies that curtailed and criminalized many of the traditional uses of forests, including the centuries-old practice of transhumance. Furthermore, not only did the occupying army burn and cut down trees in an effort to control the resisting population, but the harvesting of cork, timber, and other forest products for export also took their toll (Davis 2007, 157–69). Morocco, which had the highest percentage of forested areas in the Maghreb, is considered to have been the most severely deforested during the Protectorate.

Lacking the polyrhythmic drive of the first section, the singing here follows the triple feel of the compound duple meter, with the exception of the final enjambment and the return to the binary rhythmic articulation in the final lines. The *hait l-kəlbi* saturates "L-ghaba" once again.

Although no longer indicated in the text below, the performance structure of these first two sections is repeated throughout the poem.

Section 3

wa ila katti nəḍḍam
If you were a bard

a smaʿ shi khu ash gal
Listen to what a brother has said

ʿəl l-barud ʿəyyan
About the weak gunpowder

gal lihum mana shi ʿəyyan
He told them, I am not weak

a sh-shikh lli dəkkni
[It is the fault of] the *shikh* who pressed me down [in the musket]

mən ḥərr l-mizan
The burning [is because of] the quantity

It is the gunpowder that speaks in the third section, giving voice to that which is inanimate. It complains about the *shikh* who loaded the musket using the wrong quantity, causing the firing to be weak, tired (*'ayyan*). Connecting hunting with the *tburiḍa*—the equestrian display that evolved from cavalry charges and that culminates in the simultaneous firing of muskets into the air—the verses criticize the hunter or horseman who is unable to load his musket and fire with the expected vigor. Indirectly, the gunpowder's complaint critiques the manhood of the hunter or horseman.

Refrain

aaaaaaa . . . r-rami
Aaaaaaah . . . the hunter

wa ana, anana, anana . . .

wuṟrini wəḥshək a l-ghaba
Show me your wild animals, forest

huha huha, huha . . .

Section 4

a mulay idriss l-ḥbib
Mulay Idriss, the beloved

a lli zark maikhib
Whoever visits you will not be disappointed

wa lli ḥəkk 'lik
Whoever wants to pick a quarrel with you

madar mziya
He did not do anything

'afah khuya 'afah
Please, my brother, please

Mulay Idriss al-Akbar (778–921 CE) was the founder of the first Moroccan dynasty, known as Idrisis. He is buried in Jbal Zerhun, and his remains are preserved in a shrine that gives the town its aura of holiness, particularly because he was a descendant of the Prophet. The naming of saints or holy men and the description of their shrines is a common poetic device in *'abidat r-rma* and, as we shall see, in *'aiṭa*. More telling, however, is how this first verse connects to the following one, which describes a visit (*zyara*) to this holy site. Saints and holy men play a critical role in Morocco, and their tombs are traditionally visited, as they are believed to communicate *baraka* (blessing) to their visitors. The verb *zar* (to visit) here may also refer to visiting a lover, and thus in this case the saint may also function as a metaphor for the lover (see Ciucci 2017). Mulay Idriss is in fact addressed as the loved one (*l-ḥbib*) in the opening verse.

Refrain

aaaaaaa . . . r-rami
Aaaaaaah . . . the hunter

wa ana, anana, anana . . .

wurrini wəḥshək a l-ghaba
Show me your wild animals, forest

huha huha, huha . . .

Section 5

wa ila katti nəḍḍam
If you were a bard

a jib 'la l-ghaba
Sing about the forest

mal l-ghaba mqələqa
Why is the forest troubled?

mən ḥərr l-mənshar khaifa
She is afraid of the heat of the saw

wa t'əyyəṭ a hiya a syadi
She cries, o my masters

səkhəitu biya
You abandoned me

Refrain

aaaaaaa . . . r-rami
Aaaaaaah . . . the hunter

wa ana, anana, anana . . .

wurrini waḥshak a l-ghaba
Show me your wild animals, forest

huha huha, huha . . .

Section 6

shuf l-ḥaif wa l-malḥfa
Look at the haif and the melhaf

wa shaddu ʿa bin la-ktaf
Fasten it only between the shoulders

wa ila zgalti
If you miss [the prey]

tʿaṭi n-nṣaf
You pay the penalty

wa sir a ghdar ṣaḥbu
Go, you who betrayed his friends

madar mziya
He did not do the right thing

allah ikhli khaimtu
May God ruin his tent

ma khla s-suq f-l-ʿashiya
Like the *suq* in the evening

Traditional images of *l-ʿarubiya* are present in this section. We find the *ḥaif* and the *malḥfa*, which refer respectively to a woolen cloak wore by men and to an ample single piece of lightweight fabric that is wrapped around the body, shoulders, and head by the women; the references are to the *suq* and the *khəima* (the traditional black Bedouin tent, but also the household). Of particular interest are the final two verses: *allah ikhli khəimtu / ma khla s-suq f-l-'əshiya* (God empty his tent / like the *suq* in the evening). In her discussion on the *da'wa* (pl. *da'wat*) as curse and blessing, Deborah Kapchan describes it as a local genre of formal speech frequently used in the market-place consisting of a predicate sentence, beginning with the word "God," and says that it is formulaic; in fact, although a *da'wa* can be improvised on the spot, there are stock phrases for *da'wat* (1996, 81–83). Kapchan cites a *da'wa—allah y-khli 'ash-ha kama khla s-suq f-l-'ashiya* (God leave her nest like the *suq* in the afternoon) (1996, 287)—which is almost identical to the final verses of section 6. In the *da'wa* cited by Kapchan and the final verses in this section, the image of the *suq* in the afternoon or evening is one of desolation: empty and littered with trash and flies.

Refrain

aaaaaaa . . . r-rami
Aaaaaaah . . . the hunter

wa ana, anana, anana . . .

wurrini wəhshək a l-ghaba
Show me your wild animals, forest

huha huha, huha . . .

Section 7

a wa ila katti nəddam
If you were a bard

jib 'la l-ghaba
Sing about the forest

a l-ghaba nəbbah
Pay attention to the forest

bu'mira hwa sh-shəttah
The kestrel, he is the dancer

wa gulu l-ghaba
Tell the forest

ila rbəhti rabbi səmmaḥ
If you win our God is magnanimous

Refrain

aaaaaaa . . . r-rami
Aaaaaaah . . . the hunter

wa ana, anana, anana . . .

wurrini waḥshək a l-ghaba
Show me your wild animals, forest

huha huha, huha . . .

Section 8

ḥubbək a ya ʻaisha
Your love Aisha

təjini mʻərsha
Come to me adorned [with flowers]

kif s-sulṭan tabʻu l-basha
Like the sultan followed the pasha

wa khailu msənnəh
His horses are well armed

History and the erotic characterize the final verse of "L-ghaba," a theme that will be explored in greater detail in the discussion to come.

Refrain

aaaaaaa . . . r-rami
Aaaaaaah . . . the hunter

wa ana, anana, anana . . .

wurrini waḥshək a l-ghaba
Show me your wild animals, forest

huha huha, huha . . .

Verse after verse, section after section, "L-ghaba" takes the listener on a journey into the forest, turning the uninhabited into the inhabited, the unknown into the intimate as it draws on that which is familiar. Through the use of terse language and fragmentary syntax saturated with the everyday language of the countryside, Shikh l-Bachir sings of scenes that overwhelm the senses of the listeners, builds images in which they recognize themselves, and evokes that which is already known—customs and traditions—allowing listeners to reconnect in a place (Italy) where "there is no ʿarubiya." The evocative power of "L-ghaba" depends on the extent to which it maps "a place narrative that emotionally resonates with personal, biographical, and historical self-consciousness" (Feld 1996, 125) for my interlocutors. The words of Shikh l-Bachir acquire meaning precisely because he is able to express the community in accordance with an oral tradition in which a poet expresses himself "through expressing the group" (Adonis 1990, 14), and because he is able to "intensify or foreground the aesthetics of communication in the production of verse" (Caton 1990, 50). Silence often follows these moments of sonorous and poetic abstraction from the everyday life of these migrants in Italy.

The verses, which differ in their degree of transparency, are particularly meaningful for those who have been immersed in the music, poetry, and voice of l-ʿarubiya; the invocation of verses in everyday speech demonstrates a history of engagement with the genre, as well as the ubiquity of poetry in everyday conversations.

14 December 2019, Rome

The sidewalks of Via del Corso are crowded. It is a warm winter day in Rome, one of those clear days in which it is possible to take in the city's beauty. We are walking toward Piazza Venezia. Sana is talking to Hassan Na., who is a few steps ahead of us, when she receives a text message from her father, who grew up with Hassan in Ben Ahmed. Sana smiles and hands Hassan her phone, saying, "Ahmed sent you this!" He is quick to smile. "Ah, this is a good one. It is one of Fatna," he says, recognizing the verse and the singer who forged it; "mzinha ʿawma fik a ruma [how beautiful it is to swim in you, Rome]," he recites to the rest of us. This is how Ahmed, in Morocco, chose to salute his friend, now in Rome.

Verses, referred to as ḥabbat (sing. ḥabba, grain), are independent poetic units that constitute the critical elements in the repertory of performers.

The *ḥǝbbat* can be sung independently one after the other or with a vocal or instrumental refrain that connects them. As part of either long or short poems, the *ḥǝbbat* are considered the basic poetic unit. Most *ḥǝbbat* consist of two short lines that are sung in what can be referred to as a call-and-response fashion. Performers themselves describe this practice by referring to the singer as the *bumǝqlaʿ* (the one with the sling), which implies that singers throw the *ḥǝbbat* back and forth as they respond to the first line with a second. Although the *ḥǝbbat* generally have an internal rhyme, this is not a prerequisite, since rhyming is secondary to meaning and should be understood more in terms of similarity of sound rather than as following set rules. Most important, the essence of a *ḥǝbba* resides in its meaning, in the image it is able to depict, in its double entendre, the feelings it conveys, and the history behind it.

8 October 2002, Rabat

"I am going to tell you the story behind this ḥǝbba," *a noted performer once told me, "*khǝllini sakǝt ḥǝtta yduz sǝbt *[Let me be silent until after Saturday]. Once a group of people asked some musicians to entertain them for an evening in their home. For one reason or another, the musicians never showed up. So these people went around and asked an old* shikh *of the region, who was now retired, to perform for them. They were so insistent that the* shikh *accepted and went out looking for some of his old colleagues to join him. When the evening finally started, the problem that immediately arose was that the public was composed of young people who wanted to hear new songs, while the poor* shikh *could only interpret old ones. In order to save the situation, the* shikh *whistled to the young audience to catch their attention and indirectly sang: '"Let me be silent until after Saturday.'"*

GENDERING THE FOREST

> dir lil ya sidna fi jǝbha l-khlila ghaba
> Tattoo, our lord, a forest on the forehead of the beloved

"L-ghaba" should be also analyzed as a gendered constitution of place, a narrative arising from a male perspective, a masculine experience of the forest engulfing the listeners in the sound of a genre that is, first and foremost, understood to be masculine. This articulation takes place in three different registers. At a poetic level we observe an increasing feminization of the forest, either in the description of the forest as a woman or in the presence of women as lovers or as objects of desire. Here it is important to remember that, aside from being an ecological space that is crucial to *l-ʻarubiya*, the forest also represents a space in which it is possible to engage in intimate acts away from public scrutiny.[24]

While the feminization of the forest is most evident in the final section, crucial insights can also be gained from conversations surrounding the poetry of "L-ghaba." Discussions about verses can be quite instructive for understanding the aesthetics of the poetry of *l-ʻarubiya*, what are considered to be the right and the wrong images of a woman, the ways to represent her, and in turn how the sense of masculinity discussed in the previous chapters is cultivated through these images and representations.

7 August 2015, Ben Slimane

Shikh Sharqi insists that the following verses be added to the text even though Shikh l-Bachir does not sing them in the recording. "It is part of the poem," he asserts unequivocally.

> *wa ila katti nəḍḍam*
> If you were a bard

> *jib ʻla l-ghaba*
> Sing to the forest

> *l-ghaba fiha l-ḥdiya*
> In the forest there is a kite

> *labəs wa ndiya*
> Dressed and wet with morning dew

> *siftha ʻəbdiya*
> She looks like a woman from ʻAbda[25]

"See, old songs used to describe the beauty of the woman; ʻabidat r-rma *would sing every part of the body of a woman, the eyes, the ears, the neck . . . everything.*"

> *tta gul a khuya gul*[26]
> Do tell my brother, tell

tta gul 'la 'əiniha
Do tell about her eyes

'əiniha kəhlət tuta b-l-khula
Her eyes are darkened [with kohl], the blackness of the blackberry

ya shuf kətəḥyi l-mut
Look how she revives the dead

tta gul 'la udniha
Do tell about her ears

udniha b-l-mqyas fi l-mfatən huma u l-khraṣ
Her ears are of a perfect size in their beauty, they and the earrings

tәlqau huma l-kas
They met with the glass

zu'u fas m'ə məknas
Swaying[27] between Fez and Meknes

"But nowadays, young groups insult the woman from l-'arubiya, they belittle her," remarks Azzedine, a violist who performs sha'bi on cruise ships. "That is right, they sing verses like these," Shikh Sharqi continues, reciting the verses of "I want to fill the house" [bghәit n'әmmәr d-dar],[28] a popular song interpreted by young troupes of 'abidat r-rma.

jabt liha l-banan dartu lil qoḍban
I gave her bananas and she made them into skewers

jabt liha s-sfәnj dartu dbalәj
I gave her doughnuts and she used them as bracelets

jabt liha l-barabul təṣḥəbu qəṣriya
I gave her a satellite dish and she mistook it for a couscous platter

"This is nonsense! It is humiliating! They do that to make the urban-ites laugh," Hassan Na. is quick to reply. "Remember when we used to have the traditional hand mill [rḥa] at home?" Shikh Sharqi asks the men around the table. "Nobody used to get sick then! Women would grind wheat, henna. . . ." "Argan and almonds," the others respond. "And we *were strong!" Shikh Sharqi asserts proudly. "Listen to this." After clearing his throat, he begins to mimic the circular movements of the hand mill by sliding the bottom of his tea glass on top of the table—mimicking a woman's labor—and quietly intoning a melancholic melody with a voice whose hoarseness adds impact to the verses.*

> *a nana wa nana nana . . .*
> *u ra baita ntsənna ka'ma jiti a khəyy*
> I spent the night waiting . . . you never came, my dear brother

"Allah, Allah!" the others exclaim, unable to contain their appreciation for the verse. Shikh Sharqi hesitates. He is a great performer, and even at this café and in this setting, he wants to keep his audience on edge. He readjusts his upper body into the chair, bends his torso slightly forward onto the table, and, leaning close into his male listeners, he sings:

> *wa t'əqqəl 'la sh-shtiya*
> Remember the little rain

He suddenly stops on shtiya, the diminutive of shta (rain), raising his left hand to indicate the small size of the raindrops with his thumb and index finger. "Shtiya," the others repeat. The use of diminutive forms, characteristic of women's talk, dramatizes the verse further.

> *u klabək nbəhu 'liya*
> Your dogs barked at me

> *ma gəlti tshəbshi 'liya l-khurba z-zəllala*
> You did not greet me nicely, the cruel seductress

"There you go! This is singing about the countryside, about the woman from the countryside. This is how we praise a woman. Shikh l-Bachir sang these verses about her."

> *wuld 'əmmi u khali*
> My paternal and maternal cousin

> *ja lil u ddani*
> Night came and he took me

> *u b-yddu ḥəll ḥzami*
> With his hands he opened my belt

u 'ṭani kəmsha flus
Gave me a fistful of money

bash nəḥdər 'əiniya
To lower my eyes

"Everybody sings this. Stati has sung this as well, it is all part of
'L-ghaba,' and it goes like this."

bərd'uni u səgiu 'li
Saddled me and used me to get water[29]

kandir ila duzuk 'liya
What can I do if you pass by me?

nmut ḥdid u ma nəbqa ḥya
I'd rather die by iron than be alive [30]

diru qəbri fi ṭ-ṭrəq
Put my tomb on the path

diru sh-shahəd ṣ-ṣabra
Set the cactus as the witness

tkun sh-shəba ḥəḍra u l-məqqaṣa kamlin
While the blond one is present, and the ones who play the scissors [i.e.,
'abidat r-rma] are there

"I love the final verses; I sing them all the time when I am with my
[male] friends," Hassan acknowledges.

Masculinity is also constructed in the exclusion and, to a certain extent,
the silencing of a voice that is first and foremost associated with women.
The *zgharət*, the high-pitched ululations that are the domain of women in
Morocco and elsewhere (Kuipers 1999; Jacobs 2007; Meintjes 2017), satu-
rate the refrain. When I inquired about *zgharət*, my interlocutors explained
that it must have been a live recording and that women were in attendance,
although they also confirmed that the *zgharət* are commonly included in
studio recordings to create a festive mood similar to that at weddings. The
indifference shown in their responses, however, signaled to what extent the
zgharət are in fact marginal to *'abidat r-rma* and to its masculine sound.

Finally, a word about the figure of the *rami*. Although translated as "hunter," the term refers more precisely to a skilled shooter, a courageous and religious man, someone of high status who is respected, who is in charge of the safety of his community, a person with *baraka*, a person of authority, and someone whom people seek out when they need to resolve a dispute. In the countryside, people—mostly men—will ask advice from a *rami* before consulting a judge or anyone from the *makhzan* (central government). In this sense, the *rami* is a sacred and honorable figure with symbolic power. As the *shikh* of a well-regarded troupe of *'abidat r-rma*, Sharqi's status is that of a *rami*, a trustworthy, respectable, and just man.[31] When people go to him, he listens patiently and offers a solution to their problems. Before his visitors leave, Shikh Sharqi lays his frame drum on the floor and asks them to seal their oath by jumping across it.

In traditional contexts such as weddings, *shyukh* like Sharqi continue to uphold the role of a *rami*. At all-male gatherings, Shikh Sharqi begins with the recitation of the opening Sura of the Qur'an (Fatiha) for the groom and his family before the actual singing and dancing begin; in between songs, he and his troupe move from one group of guests to the next performing auspicious invocations (*da'wat*) for tips (*l-ghrama*).

> *allah ifərḥna bih*
> May God make us rejoice for him

> *u allah ishafih amin*
> May God cure him, amen

> *u allah idawih amin*
> May God heal him, amen

> *allah ifərḥkum byh amin*
> May God make you rejoice for him, amen

> *allah ifərḥna bih amin*
> May God make us rejoice for him, amen

> *u l-kmal 'li allah u r-rahma u l-ḥməd allah*
> None is perfect but God, and mercy and praise God

Weaving together the fragments of a sense of place, the natural world, history, beauty, and desire, "L-ghaba" has the capacity to connect an "emotional topography" (Dent 2009, 32) to multiple registers of masculinity, and for the voice and the words of Shikh l-Bachir to touch—materially and emotively—those who are listening.

The rural and the masculine, however, are also evoked by the female voice and its cry. In this final section I explore the role of *ʿaiṭa* through an informed analysis of "Ḥajti fi grini" (I long for my male companion). It is in this context that I examine the role of the female voice and narration in constructing manhood and desire.

3 March 2019, San Giustino-Capanne

"Mina is making tea," Yassine announces as he welcomes us inside the apartment. He has invited me to stop by the house after work. He knows I am back in Umbria, and he has promised to make mint tea, the Moroccan kind they grow in their vegetable garden in San Giustino-Capanne. The television is on, and a popular children's cartoon is playing. "The children were watching it," Yassine explains. "They are in the back now. Let me call them. Soufiane, Khadija, come say hello to your auntie!" I hear the footsteps of the little ones running to their father.

It is a sunny but chilly spring day and, with no heating inside the apartment, we keep our jackets on. Some of the men are already there, seated on the couch. A few of them I already know, but it is the first time I have met Mohammed; the only one wearing a beard. In Morocco men like Mohammed are referred to as les barbus *(the bearded ones), a pejorative used to indicate Islamists.*

In the past couple of years there has been increasing tension in the community around the construction of a mosque in Umbertide, which has recently been halted for a number of administrative reasons. Internal tension, however, has also resulted from a division among migrants who are perceived as Islamists and those for whom a mosque—or an Islamic Center, as they are often referred to in Italy—is not as important as other structures that would benefit the community. Old tribal, regional, and familial conflicts also play a role: rather than attenuating, they seem to become exacerbated abroad, feeding off stressful conditions. We are nearing Ramadan, and tension has been rising as every town and province in Umbria is bound to make individual decisions; in Assisi, Bouchaib Bo. was able to secure the sports center for the evening prayers and the breaking of the fast, while in Umbertide the situation remains hopeless; the Muslim community will once again have to rent a space in a building just outside the town.

I look at Mohammed's hands, the rough hands that characterize people working the land. I reflect on these hands as I write this passage during the COVID-19 pandemic. Despite a surge in Italians requesting work as agricultural laborers, Confagricoltura has organized flights carrying hundreds of Moroccan workers to arrive in Italy as part of the so-called Green Corridors; an initiative that is designated to ease the arrival of non-EU seasonal agricultural workers. Italians have forgotten how to work the land, the heads of the agricultural group in question explain, while Moroccans "already know the work" (Brera 2020). While this move could be seen as a recognition of the role and the place of migrants in Italy, an occasion to rethink the way the country works, in actuality it reinforces the view of these migrants as mere commodities. This view is aggravated by the fact that during the pandemic, Muslim bodies, as in the case of Moroccans but also of a large percentage of migrant laborers, have gotten sick and died and are still left unburied in morgues: they cannot be repatriated, nor can they buried in Italy owing to a lack of space (Moual 2020). In a recent strike of agricultural laborers—the so-called strike of the invisibles—migrants have argued that the proposed temporary amnesty for and regularization of hundreds of thousands of undocumented workers, together with the temporary changes of employment permits, places market interests before their rights and their lives. Let's remember that the term used for these laborers, braccianti *(deriving from* braccia, arms*)—a problematic category of workers that Gramsci discussed in his prison writings—indicates those who work with the strength of their arms, inevitably reducing these workers and these migrants to body parts. In contemporary Italy, Mohammed's life is currently valued only for his arms and his hands.*

It takes time for our conversation to begin. The men are worried about the new migration laws, and especially about the new rules regarding their chance to obtain Italian citizenship. They must pass a written exam in Italian, as they need a certificate that attests to their linguistic competence. But most of them halted their formal education at the elementary level; their knowledge of Italian is usually just enough to get by. Their language skills point to a dramatic lack of interaction with Italians, an isolation that inevitably affects their children. "We are together all the time," they explain as they sit close to one another; "we work together and we go home together."

*While some of the men reside in Italy throughout the year, others are seasonal workers who come and go. They begin working in the tobacco fields in January or February and go back to Morocco in October once work dries up. They must miss home when they are here, I say. "Not really," they are quick to answer. Men like these hold on to their pride; it is not easy for them to acknowledge their conditions to others; it is part of the "collective lie" discussed in the previous chapter. "That is," Ali explains, "we are not nostalgic because of the force of circumstances [*non abbiamo nostalgia per forza di cose*]." The others nod, acknowledging a difficult reality: not allowing oneself to feel. It is the same condition that another migrant had described in equally compelling terms: "my head is full" [r-rasi ʿamər*]*," he told me as he explained why he did not have time to listen to music in Italy.*

And yet, it is not long before l-ʿarubiya *begins to emerge through the detailed description of a particular breed of sheep (ṣərdi), beautiful horses, tall mint plants, and vast fields of wheat; as well as through the difficult conditions that forced them to leave. "We are from* l-ʿarubiya *even if we no longer reside there; there is nothing for us in cities and nothing for us here," comments l-Kbir, a former tailor from Khouribga who has been working in the tobacco fields since the late 1990s. "Everything is there [i.e.,* l-ʿarubiya*]," Ahmed is quick to add. L-Kbir, whose large, jovial face is marked by bushy eyebrows, continues, "What do I miss? I miss hearing the cry of the rooster early in the morning, the voices of women and children taking the sheep to the pastures: sh, sh, hya," imitating the sounds made by women and children. "I love cows too," little Soufiane says, trying to get my attention by lightly tapping my arms. "Ash, ash," Ali gently tells his grandson. "They are beautiful," Soufiane timidly continues.*

They seem ready to talk about music now; it always takes a while before they open up. "We like the lotar *and those who sing accompanied by it. With the* lotar *you can only sing poetry. You can sing about the forest, the snow, the countryside, and the peasant [*l-fəllaḥ*]." Although the* lotar *accompanies performances of* shikhat, *it remains an instrument that is played first and foremost by men and is associated with solo male performances. The late Mohamed Rouicha—for the music of the Amazigh— and Ould Kaddour—for ʿaiṭa—are the musicians who are most often invoked when my interlocutors discuss the* lotar. *"But in our region," l-Kbir continues, "we have ʿaiṭa, which is sung with the* kamanja, *and that is beautiful. From time to time we listen to that here . . . there's Fatna Bent l-Houcine and the Ouled Ben Aguida, Ouled Bouazzaoui . . ."*

Ahmed discreetly pulls his phone out of his pocket and begins playing a song interpreted by shikhat. *Originally from El Borouj, Ahmed migrated first to France and then to Italy in the 1970s. Like many others, he started as an itinerant vendor before coming to the Alta Valle del Tevere to work in the tobacco fields. He is now retired, but continues with his back-and-forth, taking advantage of the Italian health-care system. He is serious, reticent, and not much inclined to laughter; it took him a while to speak to me. And yet, as the voices of the* shikhat *filter through the room, he smiles and hands me the phone to look at the video. But l-Kbir is not happy about the choice of the recording. "There are better ones than that," he tells Ahmed.*

I turn to Mohammed; I am curious about the music he listens to. "Before I used to listen. . . ." I notice a certain reticence in his answer. "If you want the truth. . . ." "Come on, tell her what you used to listen to before, even if you are on another path now," the others encourage him. "I have matured now, I have grown, there is only the prayer for me." "But before?" I insist, as the others continue to press him. "Before, yes, I used to listen when I was younger . . . when I was eighteen, nineteen, twenty-five years old I used to listen to everything [kulshi], everything [tutto], . . ." he says, using first Arabic and then Italian. "I used to listen to shikhat and their cassettes and dance to that." The other men are quietly laughing; Mohammed has a volatile temper, and they do not wish to cross him. "But now I have stopped," he repeats as he looks up and points his index finger toward the ceiling, exclaiming, "Allah! I left everything, I listen only to the Qur'an, there is nothing else for me."

It is Yassine's turns now; he begins playing a nashid—a religious chant—on his phone. As the other men enter into a lively debate about the provenance of the chant and to which Sufi order it belongs, Mohammed turns to me. He lowers his voice and begins to explain. "See, in Morocco I had a grocery store, and I used to listen to music, particularly the cassettes of the shikhat, I used to listen to them in the store and even when I was in the car. I used to listen to them all the time." Suddenly he halts and, in a changed tone of voice, says, "but now I have left everything." I wonder about Mohammed's remarks, about whether it is true that as they grow older these men will distance themselves from listening to music and from certain listening practices. Mohammed's assertion reminds me of the wiry and astute Aziz. I had met him with his cousin Abderrahim—a talented butcher who grew up in Gubbio and who describes himself as an 'arubi gubbino. The first time I met them, they had quarreled the whole time about the good and the bad traits of the 'arubi. I had laughed heartily with them while listening to their back-and-forth, which reminded me of the comic sketches of Qachbal and Zaroual, comedians who started performing in the ḥalqa and rose to fame in the 1970s thanks to their rural humor and, in particular, the way they made fun of the differences between the city dwellers and l-'arubi. Unlike Abderrahim, Aziz had adamantly sworn that he had stopped listening to music (i.e., shikhat) and had devoted himself exclusively to the Qur'an. But I knew this to be untrue; members of his own family had told me otherwise.

Mohammed is quiet again. I turn to the others, curious to know how they select the performers they like. "Everything is on the Internet

Figure 13. Yassine and Mohammed
Photo by the author

*nowadays." I press them a bit harder; I am interested in the voice
(ṣ-ṣawt) they prefer. "It must have an* 'arubi *tone. We, for example, say*
nta *[you]," responds l-Kbir, stressing the [t] sound rather than [nt];
"elsewhere, in the north for example, they say* ntina." *There is a huge difference, the others say. "For example," says Ahmed, "we do not use the
[q], we say [g], those of Fes use [q]." "Or take Rabat," l-Kbir continues.
"They say* khay *[my brother],* nta ghadi a khay *[when are you going,
my brother], we do not do this, we say* nta ghadi a khuy." *He accents
the ending of the word rather than the beginning to illustrate the difference in the pronunciation. They laugh about the way in which words are
pronounced in Fes and Rabat, two imperial cities, agreeing with l-Kbir's
knowledge and explanation.*

*It is getting late, and it is time to leave. I promise to return to visit them
for Ramadan. "Inshallah, we have* harira *[soup],* lben *[buttermilk], and
sweets from Morocco for the breaking of the fast," Mohammed reassures
me. "If the family is here it is all right," he adds, "but if there is no family
for Ramadan, then it is really difficult . . . we can only go to the mosque."
As we get back in the car, Abdelilah's comment strikes me. "From the*
shikhat *to the Qur'an . . . and I bet he could recite more verses from* 'aiṭa
than from the Qur'an; the cry [here referring to the musicopoetic genre
'aiṭa, *which, as we saw, literally means cry] never leaves them."*

Much has been written about the *shikhat* in colonial accounts and postcolonial analyses, about their music, poetry, and dance, and about their complex role inside and outside of performance (Chottin 1931, 1939; Schuyler 1979; Abdeljamil 1993; Buhmid 1995; Kapchan 1996; Rakuk 2000a, 2000b, 2001, 2008; Bahrawi 2002; Najmi 2007; Soum-Pouyalet 2007; Ciucci 2010, 2012a, 2012b, and 2017), but not as much on the relationship between *'aita* (the musicopoetic genre they interpret), *shikhat*, and *l-'arubiya*. In what follows I will expand on some of these earlier writings as I focus on a commercial recording of one of the most famous *qaṣa'id* of *'aita* originally recorded as a video (VHS) in 1991 in Casablanca and currently available on YouTube (video exx. 4.1 and 4.2). Here too the choice was guided by the recommendations made by musicians and by my interlocutors in Italy and Morocco. Their recommendations were based on the fact that the late Fatna bent l-Houcine is considered to be the last great *shikha* and voice from *l-'arubiya*, and on the presence of four *shikhat* accompanying her, something that has become less common owing to the increasing male presence in the *'aita* and especially to the changes it has undergone once it entered the realm of *sha'bi*, as discussed in chapter 3. Of particular interest is also the fact that, among the several videos associated with the same recording and available on the Internet,[32] the one my interlocutors suggested was the only one in which the text of the poem is embedded. If this is an increasing practice in contemporary videos in the Arab world, it is a rather recent development for what concerns videos of *ṣawt l-'arubiya*.

The close poetic analysis of the text follows the text transcribed in the video, with some changes suggested by my interlocutors and some made in relation to a written version of the text that the musicians themselves provided to me. I do not regard any version as original or definite; on the contrary, my interest lies in the relationships between different texts and/or performances of the same poem in relation to its durability and, in turn, on the perception of different renditions of a text as being the same—despite differences—for listeners and performers (Ciucci 2012a).

"ḤAJTI FI GRINI" AND THE MEANING OF THE VOICE OF THE *SHIKHAT*

Faṣl I

Each line is sung over a twenty-five-beat cycle, as shown below, with 1 signaling the strong beats:

1 2 1 2 3 1 2 3 1 2 1 2 1 2 3 1 2 3 1 2 1 2 1 2 3

1. *wa ḥajti f-grini wa qaidi wa haduk l-khəyl ya sidi*
   I need my male companion, my caid, and those [are the] horses,
   my lord

2. *wa r-rəkba ya tʿəjjəbni wa nta ghadi a haduk l-khəyl kwitini*
   I admire the cavalcade, you are leaving, those [are the] horses, you
   burned me

3. *u ila a hməzt a ndrəku wa ba a ya ba maikun bas ya sidi*
   If I spur [the horse] I will catch up, father, everything is all right, my lord

4. *u ila mshit nwulli wa ba a ya ba wa maikun bas ya sidi*
   If I am gone, I will come back, father, everything is all right, my lord

5. *wa r-rəkba tʿəjjəbni u labas u labas kassi frid ya sidi*
   I admire the cavalcade, it is all right, it is all right, my glass is lonely,
   my lord

6. *a mmwimti ṣbərni u qaidi [maidum] ḥal ya sidi*
   My dear mother, my patience, my caid, nothing lasts forever, my lord

7. *wa l-ḥajbat iṭəllu u nta ghadi wa haduk l-khəyl kwitini*
   The secluded women look through the window, you are leaving, those
   [are the] horses, you burned me

8. *wa r-rəkba tʿəjjəbni jabuk u jabuni maikun bas ya sidi*
   I admire the cavalcade, they brought you and they brought me, everything is all right, my lord

9. *u sruthum a ṣulu a ba ya ba wa maikun bas ya sidi*
   Their beautiful horses charging, father, everything is all right, my lord

10. *wa l-ḥajbat iṭəllu u labas u labas kassi frid ya sidi*
    The secluded women look through the window, it is all right, it is all
    right, my glass is lonely, my lord

Fatna, Hafida, Souad, Khadija, and Mina follow one another, interpreting each line if they were a single voice. Everyone can recognize the voice
of Fatna—the older, the leader of the troupe, the "diva"—but what about
the others? I name them because they often go unnamed and their labor

unrecognized, particularly when listening rather than watching or experiencing them live; they are absent from record covers, unannounced in old recordings, and, at least in the past, rarely pictured.[33] They are simply known as *shikhat*, women with a complex history in Morocco because they perform at all-male gatherings, always straddling the line between that which is reputable and that which is disreputable, central to celebrations and marginalized in everyday life (Kapchan 1996). Even after a number of Moroccan male intellectuals argued for their revalorization in a not unproblematic, although necessary, postcolonial stance (Najmi 2007) and documentaries celebrated some of the most famous among them (Genini 1987; Essafi 2006) or they appeared on television, in festivals and so forth, they continue to remain *shikhat*. The young Abdellah in Umbertide had told me how he loved *shikhat*, that he listened to them all the time; but when I asked him whose voice he preferred, he was puzzled and answered: "I do not know their names." He is not alone.

If one can always recognize the voice of a *shikha*, it is not the same when it comes to distinguishing one voice from another. The training of a *shikha*, after all, focuses on her ability to express the group through a voice that, just as is the case with *'abidat r-rma*, must embody *l-'arubiya*, express "pain, joy, and that which is already in our blood"; in other words, they must embody a voice functioning as a culturally created symbol that, as such, follows some of the same vocal parameters I have already described, particularly in, but not limited to, its relation to a rough or coarse timbre. But there is something more to this female voice.

If in the past *shikhat* would join a troupe as dancers and begin learning the words and the trade within the troupe, in past decades younger *shikhat* started by memorizing commercial recordings, imitating the voice (*qəlləd ṣ-ṣawt*) and the versification of the most successful *shikhat* before being incorporated into a troupe. Rather than being known for the uniqueness of each individual *shikha*'s voice, these *shikhat* seem to have learned how to embody and to express a particular voice, as some of their oral histories attest.

> With Dabaji I learned in a different way: he used to beat me. One day he hit me with an instrument. When someone asked why he hit me, I told them that Dabaji had hit me for my own good, for the good of *'aiṭa*, so that it would be interpreted well, and so that I would be more careful in the future. (Khadija Margoum, personal communication, 5 July 2002, Safi)

This subordination is entangled with the role of *shikhat* in performance, and with value judgments expressed in the difference between *shikhat* and *shwikhat*. The latter is a diminutive form that negatively marks those *shikhat* who are considered to be poor interpreters, lacking poetic sophistication, who exaggerate the bodily dimensions in performance and thus are quick to be equated with prostitutes and dismissed even by other *shikhat.*

I was always told that a *shikha* distinguishes herself through a number of qualities. She must always be ready; her clothes must be clean and well ironed, since her *shikh* can knock on her door at any time to tell her to be ready for a performance; she must be responsible about her work; she must not waste her time or go visit another *shikha* just to chitchat. A *shikha* must not wear too much makeup—a little bit will suffice—since people do not care about the makeup, they are there to listen to how she sings, how she performs, if she is respectable, well-mannered, with her hair in place . . . a *shikha* should think of herself as a soldier, ready to do her work well, happy, and delighted to do it. (Aicha Nouni, personal communication, 7 March 2004, Safi)

Like other *qasa'id* of *'aita,* "Hajti fi grini" is valued because it is embedded in the precolonial and colonial past of the Arab tribes of the Atlantic plains and plateaus. This history is reenacted and experienced with each performance, creating an imaginary that sweeps their own unheroic present.

In this context, listening together becomes a communal and a gendered practice. It is an intimate mode of listening that allows my interlocutors to "exhale," to let go of themselves, and that allows intimacy with the others. As music becomes something "like a medicine" (*bhal shi dwa*), the ability of the *shikhat* resides in reconstructing and transmitting the past meaningfully, entangling history with the erotic, the heroic with virility, allowing imagination to enter into these men's lives through a female voice constructing intimacy (*rasi rasak*) through *sawt l-'arubiya.*[34]

The eroticization of history saturates the first section, where images of heroic horsemen, beautiful horses, and a lonely glass express a woman's desire through a male's perspective; that is, a female desire constructed in accordance to the male's desire we saw taking shape in conversation with Shikh Sharqi. This is not to say that the *shikhat* do not have agency and a voice; rather, it is to say that it is important to examine the erotic as intrinsic to the poem, the genre, its aesthetics, and the demands of male audiences.

16 July 2016, Casablanca

"In the region of Marrakesh-Safi," Atir continues, "men are difficult, and so if a group of men hires a troupe of shikhat for an intimate evening

among male friends, and the shikhat *turn out to be not good—that is,*
they do not know what to do—the men will ignore them and avoid to
even directly addressing them. Do you know what they do? They simply
turn around and say: a rəgragi ar l-karṭa" *[ragragui,*[35] *bring the cards]."*
This is a type of silencing indexing shame and with profound implications.

Just as the reference to "my caid," indicating a male lover, connects to
an era in which powerful rural governors ruled the Atlantic plains and plateaus, the horses and the cavalcade hark back to the legendary expeditions
(*ḥarkat,* sing. *ḥarka*) of Sultan Hassan I (1831–94). A military column with
as many as twelve thousand men, this huge procession of soldiers, animals,
court officials, traders, suppliers, wives, and concubines slowly moving
across the landscape made a lasting impression as it traveled throughout
Morocco. Just as important, it also gave the sultan the image of a man, a real
man who, rather than being indoors with women, needed to encounter and
confront other men (Dakhlia 1988, 736–37).

"Ḥajti fi grini" is particularly difficult to sing. As a vernacular *qaṣida,* it
is characterized by a succession of *fuṣul* (sections, sing. *faṣl*) separated by
qoṭban (refrains, sing. *qaṭib*). Each *faṣl* contains an indefinite number of
lines (the first line is referred to as *ḥaṭṭa* and the last as *rfud*) and is sung
to a particular melody and rhythmic cycle. While *shikhat* will either take
turns singing each line of a *faṣl* or a *shikha* will sing the whole *faṣl,* they
sing antiphonally or in unison during the *qoṭban.* It is worth noting that the
term *qaṭib* indicates weaving and thus interlacing threads into a cloth, a
term that aptly describes the vocal texture that the voices of the *shikhat*
create. Syllabic poetic meter and rhyme vary from one section or one line
to the other. The poem is characterized by a collection of lines comprising
semantic or meaning-bearing material (in **bold**), stock formulas (<u>under-
lined</u>), and expressive interjections that can be replaced without affecting
the overall meaning and referred to as *mədd* (extension), as illustrated in
the example below.

*wa **ḥajti f- grini***	*wa <u>qaidi</u>*	*wa <u>haduk l-khayl</u> ya sidi*
I need my male	my caid	and those [are the] horses,
companion		my lord

Singing "Ḥajti fi grini" requires great vocal stamina, since this is a long
(*twila*) and difficult (*ṣ'iba*) *qaṣida*; the lines, sung over long rhythmic cycles,
can be difficult to sustain if the singer is not well trained and may therefore
end up damaging her voice (*tədhi b-ṣawtha*). The power of the voice of the
shikhat—the volume, resonance, and strength—is regarded as the preferred

quality to heighten the emotional impact of the text, to express the hard work of the peasant in the countryside. It is the same for the *kamanja*, the other voice of *'aita*, which must also be produced with vigor. Musicians of *'aita* refer to the instrument as *jarra*, a noun that stems from the verb *jar*, which means to drag, pull, or leave an imprint, thus connecting it to the idea of playing hard or digging into; this is the movement of manual plowing in the countryside, my interlocutors explain.

Qəṭib

Lines 11–13 are sung over 105 beats in various groupings.

11.	*wa huwa wa huwa*	*ahya ahya l-ʿədək l-ʿədək yak a dati ahya*
	Here he is, here he is,	let's go, let's go
12.	*wa huwa wa huwa ya sidi idris*	*wa huwa wa huwa ya dhəb l-kwyyəs*
	Here he is, here he is, my lord Idris,	here he is, here he is, the small golden glass
13.	*wa huwa wa huwa*	*ahya ahya u daba a ḥənn mulana wa ʿada l-khayl ya sidi waily*
	Here he is, here he is,	our master will soon be more loving, the horses have come back, my lord

The *qəṭib* is marked by a different musical flow characterized here by antiphonal singing, a rhythm that is variously grouped and subordinated to the poetic lines, and by a different melody. Semantic meaning is not as important during these refrains, which are meant to separate one section from the next. The fragmentary verses of the *qəṭib* allow the collective voices of the *shikhat* to be even more compelling, particularly as their vocables and their nonsemantic expressivity arouse excitement and affective response in listeners (Jacobs 2007), invading the text.

Faṣl II

Line 14 is sung over a twenty-two-beat cycle: 1 2 1 2 1 2 1 2 1 2 3 1 2 3 1 2 1 2 3 1 2 3

Line 15 is sung over a seventeen-beat cycle: 1 2 1 2 1 2 3 1 2 3 1 2 1 2 1 2 3

Lines 16–23 are sung over the previous twenty-five-beat cycle

14. *a baba l-ʿqil ʿndǝk wa ra l-jnawǝḥ khanuni kulshi b-ḥsabu*
    Father, my poor little reason is with you, the wings have betrayed me,[36] everything has its cost

15. *a jabuk wa jabuni haduk l-khǝyl kwitini*
    They brought you and they brought me, those [are the] horses, you burned me

16. *wa r-rǝkba tʿǝjjǝbni u ḥatta l-khǝyl drǝktni maikun bas ya sidi*
    I admire the cavalcade, the horses caught up with me, everything is all right, my lord

17. *a u ila mshit nwulli a ba ya ba maikun bas ya sidi*
    If I am gone, I will be back, father, everything is all right, my lord

18. *a mwalfa b-nʿasu u labas u labas kassi frid ya sidi*
    I am used to sleeping next to him, it is all right, it is all right, my glass is lonely, my lord

19. *a mmwimti ṣbǝrni u qaidi wa haduk l-khǝyl ya sidi*
    My dear mother, patience, my caid, those [are the] horses, my lord

20. *wa ḥajti f-grini u nta ghadi haduk l-khǝyl kwitini*
    I need my companion, you are leaving, those [are the] horses, you burned me

21. *a l-ḥǝṣba u lafa u a ba ya ba maikun bas ya sidi*
    The *hasba* is familiar,[37] father, everything is all right, my lord

22. *a sh-shǝhbat khwatat w aba ya ba maikun bas ya sidi*
    The blond ones are sisters, father, everything is all right, my lord

23. *a u ila mshit nwulli u labas u labas kassi frid ya sidi*
    If I am gone, I will be back, it is all right, it is all right, my glass is lonely, my lord

Fatna's throat is tight as she sings the first line of a new section over a new melody and rhythmic cycle. She holds the sound in her throat before releasing it. Her voice was known to be best suited for the *bayati*, which is said not to wear down the voice of the *shikhat* as a *hijaz* does. But in *ʿaita*, the *bayati* is also said to be hard unlike anywhere elsewhere (*l-bayati f-l-ʿaita qaṣǝḥ makainsh shi dula*), Bouchaib Benshlih, the viola player, tells me. Hard, in this sense, refers to a tuning that is high so as to suit the voice of the *shikhat* (*l-msawiya dyal sh-shikhawiya ṭalʿa*).

The relationship between the *kamanja* and the voice of the *shikhat* is at the core of *ʿaiṭa*. It is said that without the *kamanja* *ʿaiṭa* never comes out the way it ought to (*maʿamra ṭji hya hadik*), and many of my interlocutors do acknowledge that it is "the sound of the *jarra* that makes me dance." But the *kamanja* must be tuned to the pitch of the *shikhat*, follow the melodic line of each singer, and adjust itself to their voice. It is a relationship inevitably riddled with gender dynamics, since the instrumentalists are men—a relationship that can damage the voice of a *shikha* if the viola player is not professional and does not understand the delicate balance.

> Unfortunately, some *shikhat* we know have retired early from the milieu. The instrumentalist plays his *kamanja* as the *shikha* sings, but when he plays in the upper register, the *shikha* follows the instrument [*tʿallaq mʿa l-ala*] until she chokes [*tjiyyaf*]. If she works in that manner, let's say for a period of four to ten years, she loses her voice [*tadhi b-ṣawtha*]. Often an instrumentalist is only concerned about the sound of his instrument while the *shikha* sings. He doesn't know where the harm [*darar*] lies. He doesn't know the difference between what's bad [*silbi*] and what's good [*ijabi*]. In other words, he uses a bad tuning [*msawiya silbiya*]. (Bouchaib Benshlih, personal communication 18 December 2004, Safi)

The four strings of the *kamanja* were originally made of gut, but nowadays the two lower strings are made of metal, while the thick higher strings are made of gut or, more often, nylon, which is referred to as *bandqi*—that is, coming from Venice, a reference to their high quality. To use all metal strings would cause the essence (*maʿna*) of *ʿaiṭa* to be lost. The *kamanja* is most commonly tuned in fifths (c–g–D–A), but these pitches should be thought of as approximate, since absolute pitch has practically no relevance for these musicians. Musicians describe the tuning of the instrument as higher (*ṭalʿa*), medium (*moyen*), a little lower (*habṭa shwiya*), or a lot lower (*habṭa bezzaf*) in relation to standard tuning. Professionals of *ʿaiṭa*, that is those who are specialists in the repertoire, use a different terminology: *ʿabdellahwi* (standard tuning, a term that appears to have been derived from the name of an old *shikh*, Abdellah, who tuned his *kamanja* this way); *ṭiuḥ* (low, which refers to the action of falling down); *mkhansha* (high, which refers to someone who is tense or whose nose is up in the air); and *madsus* (slightly lower, which refers to something that is hidden or concealed). Fatna used to sing all the time in *madsus*, and musicians would tell her what the farmers used to say: the buried stone breaks the plow (*l-mədsusa kathərras l-məḥrat*). The metaphor was used to comment on the strength, vigor, and potency of the voice of this legendary *shikha*, who was described by my interlocutors as *qwi* (powerful); an adjective that, when applied to a man, a *rajəl*, describes his virility.

Qəṭib

Lines 24–26 are sung antiphonally over 105 beats variously grouped.

24. *wa huwa wa huwa*   *ahya ahya l-ʿədək l-ʿədək yak a dati ahya*
    Here he is, here he is,   let's go, let's go

25. *wa huwa ya sidi idris*   *wa huwa ya dak l-kwyyəs a huwa ahya*
    Here he is, my lord Idris   here he is, that small glass, here he is

26. *a waḥida mshat fəgʿana*   *ʿada l-khayl u a ʿad l-khayl jibuha ahy*
    One left angry   the horses, the horses will bring her back

Fəṣl III

Line 27 is sung over a fifty-four-beat cycle:
1 2 1 2 1 2 1 2 1 2 3 1 2 3 1 2 1 2 1 2 3 1 2 3 1 2 1 2 1 2 3 1 2 3 1 2 1 2 1 2 3 1
2 3 1 2 1 2 1 2 1 2 1 2

Line 28 is sung over a fifty-six-beat cycle:
1 2 1 2 1 2 1 2 1 2 3 1 2 3 1 2 1 2 1 2 3 1 2 3 1 2 1 2 1 2 3 1 2 3 1 2 1 2 1 2 1 2
3 1 2 3 1 2 1 2 1 2 1 2 1 2

Lines 29–32 are sung over a fifty-eight-beat cycle:
1 2 1 2 1 2 1 2 1 2 1 2 3 1 2 3 1 2 1 2 1 2 3 1 2 3 1 2 1 2 1 2 3 1 2 3 1 2 1 2 1 2
1 2 3 1 2 3 1 2 1 2 1 2 1 2 1 2

27. *ila ma jiti u nḥasəbək b-dnubi ya məḥbubi a labas a labas a labas a rak
    tabuha wahy*
    If you do not come, I hold you responsible for my sins, dear one, it is all right, it is all right, it is all right, you are her father

28. *ḥatta mən ʿawdu kidu b-ljamu l-ḥbiba u labas u labas u labas ya rasi frid
    wahy*

He guides his horse with its bridle, dear one, it's all right, it's all right, it's all right, my head is lonely

29. *ila ma jiti u nḥasəbək b-dnubi l-ḥbiba u labas u labas u labas a ya rasi frid wahy*
    If you do not come, I hold you responsible for my sins, dear one, it is all right, it is all right, it is all right, my head is lonely

30. *ḥətta mən ʿawdu mqərsu b-ljamu ash kan sbabi u labas u labas u labas ahya rasi frid wayli*
    He pulls his horse by its bridle, what caused me to be this way? It's all right, it's all right, it's all right, my head is lonely

31. *ila ma jiti u nḥasəbək b-dnubi ash kan sbabi wa labas u labas u labas a ya rasi frid wayli*
    If you do not come, I hold you responsible for my sins, my love, it is all right, it is all right, it is all right, my head is lonely

32. *ʿawdu l-gada mqərsu b-ljamu a l-ḥbiba u labas u labas u labas a ya a rasi ʿawwam wahy*
    He pulls his horse by its bridle, dear one, it's all right, it's all right, it's all right, my head is flooded

Hafida, regarded as Fatna's daughter, never left her side until close to her death in 2005. She joined the troupe at a young age as a dancer before becoming the co-lead vocalist; after Fatna retired, she took on the role of the lead *shikha*. Generous but stern, she is said to have inherited these qualities from her family, who were in charge of the Mulay Abdellah's *moussem*, the annual celebration honoring the birthday of a local saint held at his shrine. It is one of the most famous *moussem* in Morocco, and a space where *ʿaiṭa* is performed inside traditional large tents (*khzain*, sing. *khzana*) that are said to be associated with *shikhat*; "every time you see a tent like this, you know that there are *shikhat* in there."

> *ḥətta mən ʿawdu*
> *wa kidu b-ljamu (a)*
> *wa l-ḥbiba*
> *u labas u labas u labas*
> *a wa wa wa ya rasi frid*
> *wahy…*

Figure 14. Shikha Hafida

Photo by the author

Like the other *shikhat*, Hafida breaks the long line that she sings above (28) into small fragments, marking each fragment with a small pause, with moments of silence full of expectations. She continues to tap lightly on the small *t'arija*, the instrument symbolizing the *shikhat*, the instrument with which they learn how to versify and without which they cannot even recall the verses.

Her voice is full (*'amər*), and unlike Fatna, who held her voice back in her throat, Hafida opens up and resounds vowels and vocables—"a . . . wa . . . ya"—as she gives voice to the image of the horseman on his horse and his female lover waiting for him. Her voice is said to crow (*ṣaqəʿ*), to sound like the cry of the rooster, one of the voices that l-Kbir misses from *l-ʿarubiya*.

Qəṭib

Lines 33–35 are sung antiphonally over a twenty-beat cycle arranged as a regular series of two beats.

33. *wa ḥajni ya ḥəmra l-qdam*
    Come, you with the henna on the foot[38]

    watak allah b-l-usham
    God made you well with the tattoo

34. *wa l-fim a ḥmər b-dwam*
    The small mouth is always red

    had l-wlid ila wlidkum
    this boy, if he is your boy

35. *wa ila makəltish wlidkum*
    If you do not say that he is your son

    a nḏri f-qdamu taiban ushamu
    look at his feet and you will see his tattoo

Faṣl IV

Each line except the first is sung over a ten-beat cycle repeated twice:
‖: 1 2 3 1 2 1 2 1 2 3 :‖

36. *wa l-ḥbiba ʿla mən ʿari*
    Dear one, on whom does my shame fall?

37. *a ya ʿla mən ʿari hada jay ləkhər ghadi*
    On whom does my shame fall? This one is coming, the other is leaving

38. *a ya l-qlib a sidi a l-ʿəwdu li shrit ʿlik nibiʿu*
    Little heart, my lord, I can sell the horse I bought for you

39. *a lalla ash kan sbabi hada jay ləkhər ghadi*
    What caused me to be this way? This one is coming, the other is leaving

40. *a lalla ash kan sbabi ʿla klima[39] a khwit bladi*
    Lady, what caused me to be this way? Because of an insult I left my country

41. *a lalla a l-ʿyun ṣrada a ʿishək lalla l-khdud a urid*
    Lady, the beautiful black eyes, please, lady, and the cheeks like roses

42. *ahya ash kan sbabi ʿla klima a khwit bladi*
    What caused me to be this way? Because of an insult I left my country

43. *a 'bush l-ḥəmqa wəsh l-bka ibərrəd naru*
    'bush, the crazy one, does crying cool his fire?

44. *a lalla l-khlif a sidi wa ra l-'əskər shəggjbala*
    Lady, the deputy my lord, the army crossed Jbala[40]

45. *a fin ma qas l-wə'd i'əddəb*   *a 'la klima a khwit bladi*
    Where the promise strikes it   because of an insult I left my
    makes us suffer   country

46. *a hada jay ləkhər ghadi*   *a lalla 'la mən 'ari*
    This one is coming, the other   on whom does my shame fall?
    one is leaving

47. *a 'la klima a khwit bladi*   *wa tta l-khlif a sidi*
    Because of an insult I left my   and you are the heir, my lord
    country

48. *wa l-'əwdu li shrit 'lik nibi'u*   *a lalla a l-'yun ṣrada*
    I can sell the horse I bought for   lady, the beautiful black eyes, to
    you   please you

49. *a 'ishək a ba l-khdud a urid*   *a lalla ash kan sbabi*
    Please, father, and the cheeks   lady, what caused me to be this
    like roses   way?

The ten-beat rhythmic cycle makes possible shorter verses and allows the voices of the *shikhat* to follow one another in closer succession. As the dialogue between the two lovers begins to unfold in a section where the historical dimension of the poem, with the exception of line 44, is no longer at the center of the narrative, the *shikhat* continue to engender the text in performance. Sensory pleasure, as we learned from the discussion with Shikh Sharqi, is obtained by seizing on the description of the body of the beloved, particularly of the woman, and on other forms of erotic allusions through metaphors or masked descriptions that stimulate the imagination.

As each *shikha* begins trading half verses from line 45 until the end of the section, it is Souad, with her full but, unlike Hafida's, high or piercing voice (*ṣawt rqiq*) who sings a poetic fragment that is particularly telling for my interlocutors: *a lalla l-'yun ṣrada*, lady, the beautiful black eyes. The construction of the blackness of the eyes here deserves a closer analysis. *Ṣrada* (sing. *ṣərda*), in fact, refers to a highly valued breed of sheep in Morocco whose characteristics—high-quality white wool and black markings on the nose, mouth, and eyes—were described in great detail by my interlocutors in San Giustino-Capanne. The beauty of the female lover's eyes here is thus connected to that which is once again valued in *l-'arubiya*.

Qəṭib

Lines 50–58 are sung by everyone over 180 beats in various groupings. The performance comes to a momentary halt at the end of line 58.

50. *a ahya ahya ahya waily*

51. *a kulla wa 'lamu a l-khayl hədak nzulu a*
Everyone has his banner, horses, this is their campsite

52. *a baba ya sidi kan 'əndi*
Father, my lord, I had him

53. *wayli ya wayli sidi ṣaḥəb l-'əudu wayli*
My lord, the companion of his horse

54. *a ntuma l-bnət mulu'at b-ghram hədak nzulu*
You daughters are passionate with love, that is their campsite

55. *a təlqha u bqa a idur u sa'əf f-l-amur wayli*
He repudiated her and she still goes around, be kind in your command

56. *ya u həzzi l-ḥaska aw ṭəl'i ṣ-ṣala ya zərwala*
Lift the oil lamp and come over to the salon, blue-eyed one

57. *ya u labəs u labəs w labəs*
It's all right, it's all right, it's all right

58. *ahya miluda ha a l-khayl jat*
Miluda, the horses have come

Unlike the others, this *qəṭib* presents lines with semantic meaning. Of particular interest is the fact that silence follows the last line of the section, as the musicians and the *shikhat* come to a complete halt. This moment of silence (*ṣəmt*) is highly valued by listeners, who comment on its effect, on the need of a pause from the intensity of the performance as they get ready for a final long section dedicated to dancing. "I love this moment," one of my interlocutors commented; "it always has a strong effect on me. There is something very emotional in that silence."

The verses of this last *qəṭib*, interpreted in unison by all the *shikhat*, paint images of the military expeditions of the sultan, entangled with amorous passion. After a few seconds the next *fəṣl* begins with verses that are now sung over the same melody of the very first section, albeit with shorter lines and a shorter rhythmic cycle.

Fəṣl V

Lines 59–63 are sung over an eighteen-beat cycle: 1 2 1 2 3 1 2 1 2 1 2 3 1 2 3 1 2 3

59. *u mwalfək a qaidi yak a sidi kasi frid*
I am used to you, my caid, my lord, my glass is lonely

60. *wa r-rəkba ya t'əjjəbni sidi a ṣbaḥək khuya a msak*
I admire the cavalcade, my lord, [good] morning, my brother, [good] evening

61. *u ila a hməzt a ndrəku yak sidi kasi frid*
If I spur [the horse] I will catch up, my lord, the glass is lonely

62. *a ila mshit nwulli khuya ṣbahək sidi msak*
If I am gone I will be back, my brother, [good] morning, my lord, [good] evening

63. *ḥajti f-s-safi a ṣaḥəb sidi kubb l-kwis*
I need Safi,[41] friend, my lord, pour the little glass

Qəṭib

Each line is sung over a duple compound rhythm.

64. *wa ntiya 'aisha wa faṭna wa rqia huma b-juj*
You, Aisha, Fatna, and Rqiqa, both of them

65. *yak z-zin a slala yak l-wə'd i'ish*
Beauty is a quality that is inherited, and the promise lets you live

66. *a l-ʿədək l-ʿədək ḥuzha tḥuəzk yak dati wayly*
Let's go, let's go, embrace her so that she can embrace you

Fəṣl VI

67. *a lalla lalla lalla lalla lalla nṣrkum ya ouled sidi*
Lady, may God glorify you, the sons of my lord

68. *ya auddi auddi ʿəlfa məstiya tduz f-d-diya*
The swarm of chosen horsemen pushes through for a bloody bounty

69. *a lalla lalla nṣərkum ya ouled sidi*
Lady, may God glorify you, the sons of my lord

70. *u rəbbi mali bat lwila mada a ifada*
My God, what is wrong with me, he spent a little night, but did not learn anything

71. *ayli ayli ayli mal ḥbibi malu ʿliya*
What's wrong with my beloved?

72. *a ba a ba wa ba mul l-wərdi ḥamed balʿarbi*
Father, the master of the rose color, Ahmed Balʿarbi

73. *wa bti a bti u ra dərji kdami nfaji a hwali*
My daughter, march in front of me, I need to find my good spirit

74. *lalla lalla dar b-rasu gaʿma a ʿərfni*
Lady, he turned his head as if he did not recognize me at all

75. *ana ya na mul ziti ra nta zhiti*
The master of the green olive's color, you had your pleasure

76. *ayli ayli ayli bat lwila u mada a ifada*
He spent a little night, but did not learn anything

The change to a duple compound meter signals the final section of the poem, which is commonly known as *sussa* (dust off) and is dedicated to dancing. The *sussa* can be described as having a puzzle-like structure where subsections, demarcated by pattern variations, melodies, instrumental riffs, and manners of performance, follow one another in a never-ending musical flow held together by the circular singing of the *shikhat*, or passages of solo singing performed by a *shikha*, whose basic structure remains the same throughout. In this particular performance, just as in live performances, the *sussa* can indeed be a lengthy section precisely because it is dedicated to dancing, which, in the recording or video in question, spills over into a second part.

Ana ya na a mul ziti ra nta zhiti, sings Khadija with a clear voice (*ṣawt ṣafi*) but with a somber quality (*f-ʿəmuqiya*) that, more than the other *shikhat*, closely resembles actual crying. Although appreciated, Khadija is faulted for her sometimes unclear enunciation. She could never be the last *shikha*, like Mina, the one to close a *faṣl*. Mina's, unlike Khadija's, is described as a warm voice (*ṣawt dafi*) and with a hoarse (*bəḥḥ*) quality that is highly valued. She is the one who closes this section of the *sussa*, a section in which the female voice, sorrow, and complaint have now taken over the text *ayli ayli ayli bat lwila u mada a ifada* (he spent a little night but did not learn anything).

77. *u win a win bali bya l-khayl l-khayl tʿərgiba sh-shawiya*
    Advance a little, the horses, the offering of the Chaouia

78. *u galikum sidi thazmu a kunu rəjjala*
    My lord told you, prepare yourselves and be real men

79. *l-ḥbiba l-ḥbiba a l-kiya jdida u b-ḍaḍ ṣʿib*
    My love, the burning is new, love is difficult

80. *a z-zin l-ʿdu b-l-ʿdu sʿədat li ʿndu*
    Beauty is the enemy, son of the enemy, happy is the one who has it

81. *yaki u lli ʿndu mʿəddəbu ya ʿabd allah*
    Isn't it so? What had he made him suffer, the servant of God

82. *ʿndi kiyya fi l-jdida u t-ṭreq bʿida*
    I am burned [by love] between El Jadida and the long road[42]

83. *khuya ʿndi kiyya l-qṣiba sh-shmaʿiya*
    My brother, I am burned [by love] between El Ksiba and Chemaia[43]

84. *allah ya siadi wash mən wala a itwala*
    God, my lords, is it important who can rule?

85. *allah a sidi a shrit fərdiya u a ghdr biya*
    God, my lord, I bought my pistol and he betrayed me

86. *ila tti zəllala nuḍi saʿfi l-hwa l-hwa b-l-gaʿida a sidi dawha mali*
    If you were a seductress, adjust yourself with love, love with care, my
    lord, they took her, what can I do?

It is Fatna who interprets alone the following series of verses, after which
each *shikha*, one after the other, will follow her lead. I halt the transcription of the poem here, with the voice and the versification of the legendary
shikha, who, with each verse, will continue to resound a voice known by
many as *ḥanut l-ʿaṭṭar*, an herbalist's shop. In such a voice my interlocutors
can listen, smell, and taste a great gamut of herbs and spices accompanying the historical, but also imaginary, heroic expedition across the Atlantic
plains and plateaus all the way into Italy.

Conclusion

Returns

SCENE 1

Editing of a sequence of different shots, like a video clip.

- Close-up on the ululations of Chaibia.
- Zahra dressed in a light, floral-printed summer dress, wearing sunglasses and holding a folding fan.
- "Speak softly love à la mandoline"[1] [. . .].
- The scenes alternate between the joy of Chaibia in front of the house and the details of Zahra's arrival on Lahbib's cart [. . .].
- Chaibia's enthusiasm as she protects her eyes from the sunlight, so that she can look into the distance, placing her hand on her chest as a sign of great affection and longing. On the other hand, Zahra shows femininity and beauty with her luggage, which contradicts the condition of the cart that traverses the rows of palm trees, beginning at the paved road.
- Suddenly Kabbour appears.
- Chaibia notices him.
- Her happiness turns into shock.
- We see that Kabbour is wearing a jacket torn at the shoulder, a hat with a hole in it, and a pair of mismatched shoes. [. . .]
- Zahra from the top of the cart: "Mamma . . . *a bba!*" (video ex. 5.1).

The opening scene is from the script of one of the episodes of the extremely popular television series *L'Couple*. The series, which consists of three-minute-long comic sketches, was broadcast during prime time in the month of Ramadan in 2013 and 2014 by 2M, the second national television channel in Morocco. It is based on the daily life, and daily squabbles, of a couple living in the countryside where Kabbour, the central character, incarnates *l-'arubi.*

Unlike the portrayals with which this book began, Kabbour is greatly admired by all my interlocutors. His success derives from the ability of the Moroccan comedian Hassan El Fad to interpret an *'arubi* that, if on the one hand is anchored in tradition, on the other is also engaged with a type of know-how, an ability to negotiate with situations and surroundings that my interlocutors refer to as "Moroccan modernity," that is, the modernity of *l-'arubi*. Rather than naive or backward, Kabbour in fact embodies the clever *'arubi* (*l-'arubi sh-shaṭar*) (El Fad 2018, 2), where cleverness is not necessarily understood as a bad trait but rather as being skillful, good at negotiating and mediating.

The episode in question narrates the return of Zahra, the daughter of Kabbour and Chaibia, from Italy, where she has emigrated and married an Italian. The opening scene is set up to contrast "traditional" images and the voice of *l-'arubiya*—the ululation of Chaibia, her clothing, a mule-drawn cart in vast fields of wheat—with those of Italian "modernity"—Zahra's Italian style of dress, the way she embodies Italian standards of beauty and femininity, and her numerous bags, trunks, and suitcases, all signaling the Moroccan popular view of "Italian." The return of Zahra is shot as a fantasy, a fairy tale of bright colors, slow motion, close-ups, long shots of the "Granary of Rome," and expressions and gestures of longing and affection between mother and daughter. The score—the love theme from *The Godfather*—adds a note of absurdity to the sequence, a sonorous layer embodying a Hollywood representation of Italian Americans now juxtaposed with Moroccan ideas about Italy.

The entrance of Kabbour, looking like a pauper, marks a different turn in the idyllic scene and causes uncontrollable laughter among my interlocutors. They know what is coming—what it means to go back home and meet family expectations. Kabbour is a dissonant presence in this dreamlike sequence, one that deconstructs romanticized notions of Italy and Morocco, complicating the migrant's returns. His presence also marks the first time we hear the tone or the inflection (*nəbra*) of *l-'arubiya*; unlike Chaibia, to whom Zahra calls out using the Italian term for mother—*mamma*—Kabbour is addressed as *a bba* (Arabic for father), an utterance indicating a rupture from the dream, immediately followed by the scratch of a phonograph needle sliding across a vinyl disk and brusquely interrupting the music and the dream. We are awake!

A second important scene in the episode plays out in a scene between Kabbour and Chaibia in which he worries about why Zahra has returned. The dialogue is infused with the manner of speaking—most noticeably the terseness of the language and most audibly the pronunciation—and the mannerism of *l-'arubiya*. The dialogue, however, also challenges a distinction between Global North and South in the explicit equation Kabbour draws between Italians and Moroccans, lessening difference, emphasizing a possible relatedness, and reminding us about some of the migrants' tropes on the modernity of *l-'arubiya*, about how things have changed.

The subtle belittling of Zahra's husband, who has no job and is supported by his mother, and whose portrait Kabbour later mistakes for one of his grandson, should not go unnoticed, particularly in reference to the final exchange, where Kabbour reaffirms his manhood to Chaibia.

K: *khdəma?*
She works?

C: *khdəma*
She works.

K: *rajəlha khdəm?*
Her husband works?

C: *gləs*
He is unemployed [lit., he sits].[2]

K: *wa . . . hya təkhdəm 'la rajəlha?*
So . . . she supports her husband?

C: *u tta? khdəm 'lya?*
And you? Do you work for me?

K: *fash khdəma?*
What does she do?

C: *mugabala waḥəd sh-shibanya*
She takes care of an old lady [lit., a woman with white hair].

K: *wa wladha?*
And her children?

C: *mugabalhum rajəlha*
The husband takes care of them.

K: *wa rajəlha?*
And her husband?

C: *mugabalh mu*
The mother takes care of him.

K: *ḥatta ṭ-ṭalyan shi mugabal shi . . .*
Even Italians, everyone is taking care of everyone else . . .
[. . .]

yak shaibia yak . . . gləbti wujhək . . . wulliti tqmə'ini . . . tti mashi rajəl tti . . .
Okay, Chaibia . . . you turned your face the other way . . . you are trying to
tame me . . . but you are not a man . . .

Toward the end of the episode we listen in on a phone call between
Zahra and her husband in Italy, where she converses in an Italian characterized by linguistic errors common among Moroccan migrants: the use of the
infinitive in verbs instead of the imperative (*vedere*), the use of the definite
article *el* instead of *il* (*el bambino* rather than *il bambino*), and the lack of articles before nouns (*cercare soldi* rather than *cercare i soldi*). The cackling of
hens under the intimate conversation marks the soundscape of *l-'arubiya*.[3]

z: *Pronto Luigi, come stai? Bene? . . . Tutto bene. Vedere Luigi, cercare soldi per*
mangiare ragazzi. Vedere Luigi, fai attenzione con nostri ragazzi, soprat-
tutto el bambino Rayane. Buono? Un bacio amore, ti amo tanto, ti amo tanto
amore. Ci vediamo, ci vediamo amore.
Hello, Luigi, how are you? Well? Everything is well. Look, Luigi, look for
money in order to feed the boys. Look, Luigi, take care of our boys, particularly the baby, Rayane. Okay? A kiss, love, I love you, I love you a lot,
I love you a lot, love. We will see each other; we will see each other, love.

Kabbour is going through his daughter's suitcase, taking out packages of
pasta; he is clearly annoyed.

k: *tti had ṭ-ṭalyan fiha 'a l-məqərunya?*
You, there is only macaroni in Italy?

z: *la bba! jəbt lək m'aya grəfaṭa, bil, smaṭi, təqshər, tlata l-grasən, qar'a dyal*
r-riḥa . . . va bene?
No, father! I have brought you a tie, a flashlight, a belt, socks, three pairs
of underwear, and a bottle of cologne . . . okay?

k: *va bene!*
It's fine!

In this short dialogue it is possible to apprehend a rural speech where the
vernacular is peppered by Italian expressions (*va bene*), the Arabic rendering of Italian and French terms (*grəfaṭa, məqərunya*), and other grammati-
cal constructions present in the songs I discuss, such as *tti* rather than *nti* for
the feminine second-person singular.

L-'arubiya incorporates a broad variety of experiences in which the
lives of those who leave and those who stay are inextricably linked with
expressive representations—that is, through music, poetry, the voice, and,

last but not least, the visual. As I have shown in the preceding chapters, *l-'arubiya* lies at the core of the tropes that migrant Moroccan men use with one another. It is a complex notion that continues to be regarded as being at the very basis of their personhood; on the one hand it informs their listening practices, and on the other, it allows them to draw from it. "To listen to the *sha'bi* of Fez," l-Bachir once told me, "you need to be rich. They listen to that music because they are rich. But we, in order to forget, but also remember where we come from and our hardship, we listen to our *sha'bi*, to the *kamanja* [viola] of our region, which is not relaxing like the one of Fez. The *kamanja* of our region brings pleasure [*nashaṭ*]."

The fact that none of my interlocutors listens to Italian music, that they reject music associated with the bourgeoisie and urbanites, and that the younger generation continues engage with *l-'arubiya* but only in the realm of popular music does not turn these migrants from the Atlantic plains and plateaus in the Alta Valle del Tevere into subjects stuck in a romanticized past. Rather, it highlights the social, political, and economic inequities they suffer. That is to say, their past informs their present conditions, and so listening to *ṣawt l-'arubiya* becomes a political act, an act through which it is possible to express concerns and perspectives across history and borders, in order for these men to assert manhood and human dignity against their conditions and positions in Italy.

To focus on the role of a particular notion of the rural also implies asking what its role is in reconfiguring a hegemonic Italian and European identity and an idea of modernity that insists on sharp distinctions between tradition and modernity, rather than on their complex relationships. Modernity has always been associated with a certain place, a synonym for the West or the Global North, and with urban cultures. Modernization, Timothy Mitchell argues, has in fact been commonly understood as a process that began and ended in Europe, whence it has been exported across ever-expanding non-Western regions into those areas whose destiny it has been to mimic the West (2000). Kabbour does not mimic the West; he negotiates with it, and in doing so he inevitably questions and challenges it. He does not offer a folkloric version of *l-'arubi* to the European gaze because, just like *ṣawt l-'arubiya*, his audience is from *l-'arubiya*, which now, however, needs also to be placed in a transnational context. Kabbour's act, therefore, may be understood an act of decolonial refusal.

Throughout the book I have posited that *ṣawt l-'arubiya* sounds the turmoil of late modernity and late capitalism through shadow circuits, through everyday "subterranean" listening practices, media practices, social practices, and digital passages. Shadow circuits work through the connection of distant places across borders; they contribute to reshaping, disrupting, and transforming a seamless narrative, opening up the possibility of aurally remapping Italy and the ways in which migrant Moroccan men choose to inhabit it. From this perspective it is possible to argue that ṣawt l-'arubiya voices the dynamics of contemporary Italy, enabling people who emigrate in search of a better life to be heard. Ṣawt l-'arubiya travels where people travel, but it also travels where people cannot go, allowing its audience to elaborate and share life aspirations and political representations, building new forms of participation at a distance.

In these pages I have attempted to trace and capture both the poetic and the sonorous fragments of the rural as articulated through the songs and poetics of l-'arubiya—fragments tying the past to both the present and the future; fragments connecting that which is meaningful even when the "head is full"; fragments embodying vital musicopoetic traditions that are essential resources to the preservation of a sense of self and the expression of belonging; fragments whose resonance is concerned with a complex geography of space, with the dialectical relationship between the colonial and the postcolonial, tradition and modernity, the Moroccan rural and the Italian present; and in all the ways these dialectics emerge through ṣawt l-'arubiya. Anchored at the intersection of ethnomusicology, history, memory, affect, and poetics, the book has attempted to introduce the voices and perspectives of these migrants in order to examine the complex processes involved in redefining new and conflicting notions of subjectivity and belonging that are washing up on Italy's shores in more ways than one.

31 July 2020, Selci-Lama

"My name is Yassine. I was born in Bradia, a village in the region of Beni Mellal, the thirteenth of November, 1981. I miss it so much! I came to Italy in 1998; I was young. I came to Italy by myself, but my father, Ali, was already here. At the time we lived in Naples. I could not work because I was a minor, and I could not go to school because I was undocumented. My father used to work illegally, so he could not sponsor me. Back in Bradia he used to be an imam: he has the entire Qur'an memorized. No matter what part of the Qur'an I read to my son Soufiane, my father knows it by heart. Since he arrived in Italy in 1992, he has always worked as an agricultural laborer. He plans to retire soon and become an imam in Foligno or Città di Castello. . . . . It was only when we came to Umbria that my father was able to normalize his status and then mine. He started working in the tobacco fields and is still working there. Once in Umbria, I went to a trade school in Perugia and became a carpenter. I worked as

Figure 15. Yassine, Soufiane, Mina, Hnina, and Ali

Photo by Omino Rosso

a carpenter for eight years, but because of downsizing I lost my job, and so I went to work in the tobacco fields. It is hard work. Now I work as a furniture finisher. . . . I had some difficult times. It is not easy for someone who comes here as a minor; you miss so many things. You feel bad, but all you can do is keep it inside. . . . Mina and I married in Morocco; we celebrated our wedding there with the music of the kamanja: 'aiṭa, shaʿbi— *our* shaʿbi. *This music is in the blood [*è nel sangue*]—as soon as you hear it you start dancing all by yourself; it is like having some sort of inner vibrations [*è come se hai delle vibrazioni dentro di te*]. It is a feeling [*sentimento*] that you use to break that . . . absence [*che usi per spezzare quella . . . mancanza*]; I cannot explain it, I cannot talk about it. You feel bad; the absence of your country is inside you. I want to go back because that is where my origins are. Here I feel like a foreigner [*straniero*]; here 'integration' does not exist. People here do not trust you."*

Acknowledgments

I grew up around antique "oriental" rugs piled on top of one another, hung on the walls, or simply lying around on the marble floor of a store in Rome. The store owner, my father, taught me about their sophisticated and intricate weaving—the choice of fiber, the knots, the beauty of natural dyes, and the importance of each thread in the overall design—by looking at the underside of a rug. As he always said, it is from the reverse side of a rug that one can understand its texture, what gives structure to the design we admire in a rug. The texture of this book, like that of a rug, weaves the words, the voice, the sound, the knowledge, and the experience of those who shared their lives. This book belongs to them; without their support and engagement it could have never been written.

Abdelilah Amahdar participated in my work throughout the years, welcomed me in the Moroccan community in Umbria, introduced me to many of those who appear in these pages, sat with me through many conversations in the book, and helped me to understand Moroccan migration in Umbria.

I am grateful to Bouchaib Boussairi for his friendship and for the many hours we spent talking about Italy and Morocco, sitting in his truck or traveling from one market to the next.

I am forever indebted to Abdelilah Ab., Ali Ab., Abdelkhalek Am., Redouane El Am., Hassan Ar., Hassan Be., Akrout Ben D., Driss Be., Abdellatif Da., Mustapha Da., Oussama Fa., El Alami Fa., Mohammed Ga., Hassan Ha., Zakaria He., Hassan Ja., Aziz Kh., Ahmad La., Bouazza Ma., Mustapha Ma., Ali Ma., Yassine Ma., Mustapha El Me., El Kbir Me., Abderrahim Mo., Simo Mo., Abdelilah Ry., El Bachir Sa., Abdelilah Ta., Abdellah Za., Mohammed Zi., and their families.

My ears would have never become attuned to *ṣawt l-ʿarubiyạ* without the patience and instruction of a number of remarkable musicians who generously shared their knowledge, accepting me like a member of their troupes, opening their homes, and caring for me as if I were part of their families. I am especially grateful to the troupe of Ouled Ben Aguida, particularly Bouchaib Benshlih and Hafida Hasnaoui; Shikh Sharqi; the troupe of Abidat Rma Khouribga, particularly Redouane El Aibed; the troupe of Ouled Bouazzaoui, particularly Khalid and Saleh Amras; and Abdelaziz Stati. I am also thankful to two brilliant comedians: Mohamed Atir, who taught me about the scent of *l-'arubiya*, and Hassan El Fad, who generously shared the scripts of his television series *L'Couple*.

This book also took shape in conversations that occurred over a number of years with teachers, colleagues, and friends in the United States, Italy, France, and the Maghreb; I remain deeply indebted to them for making these discussions possible and for helping me to reflect upon and transform my own thinking. I name some of the people who helped me along the way and who have been more immediately engaged with this book, hoping that those whom I do not name here will recognize themselves in the resonance of my thanks.

I have been fortunate to have had exceptional teachers who nurtured me as a scholar and kept me grounded during critical moments in my life. Decades ago, through a serious of fortunate circumstances, I entered the office of Adelaida Reyes and began talking about ethnomusicology. Although the site of our conversations has changed throughout the years, she has remained a constant source of inspiration. Her pioneering work on music and migration has shaped much of my own thinking about the study of migration as an ethnomusicological concern, and on what it means to construct a sound argument. Her encouragement and her "gut" are what led me here today. Many of the ideas I developed during the years of my doctoral study under the guidance of an extraordinary and generous listener, with a profound knowledge and passion for the music and the poetry of the Middle East and central Asia, have come together in this book. I thank Stephen Blum for pointing out lines of inquiry that remain central to my work, for continuing to challenge me, for teaching me the beauty and the effectiveness of clear prose, and for his undying support. Thanks are also due to Vincent Crapanzano, a generous and attentive reader who inspired me to think outside the box. My interest in the music of Morocco developed during a graduate seminar I took with Philip Schuyler; I am indebted to him for sparking my interest, for his encouragement throughout all these years, and for sharing his profound knowledge and love for Morocco.

I benefited immensely from the generous support of my colleagues from the Department of Music at Columbia University. I especially want to thank Ana María Ochoa Gautier for her mentorship and for being present in the development of this book from its inception; her influence on my thinking can be seen and felt throughout these pages. I am also indebted to her as the former chair of the Department of Music, for making my research, writing, and teaching life easier. I send my heartfelt thanks to my fellow ethnomusicologists Aaron Fox, Kevin Fellezs, and Chris Washburne; I am grateful for their generosity, their support and for providing me with an intellectual environment that has allowed me to thrive. I am also grateful to Susan Boynton for being so attentive to me and my work, and for her support as the former chair of the Department of Music. Thanks are also due to Ellie Hisama, Benjamin Steege, Mariusz Kozak, Julia Doe, and Zosha Di Castri.

Some of the ideas of the book came together while I was teaching undergraduate and graduate students at Northeastern University and Columbia University. I hope those students have learned as much from me as I learned by working with them. There are too many to name, so I must thank them collectively.

My colleagues in Italy, Nicola Scaldaferri, Francesca Cassio, Giovanni Giuriati, Serena Facci, Grazia Portoghesi Tuzi, Gabriella Santini, Ignazio Macchiarella, Francesco Giannattasio, Gigi Garofalo, Mauro Geraci, Fulvia Caruso, and Giuseppina Colicci, provided me with an invaluable perspective.

In France, I thank Miriam Rovsing Olsen and Scheherazade Hassan for their encouragement and for sharing their knowledge with me. Thanks are also owed to Denis Laborde.

The research and writing of this book was made possible by the generous support I received from the Rome Prize—providing me with invaluable writing time—and by the support of Columbia University. I wish to express my appreciation to the Center of Ethnomusicology and the Schoff Fund at the University Seminars at Columbia University for their help in publication.

Some of the ideas in this book were discussed in presentations at several conferences. I benefited from discussions at the Symposium on Musical Traditions in North Africa at Sidi Bou Said, Tunisia (2014); the Sixth Annual Symposium of Anthropology and Music in Constantine, Algeria (2015); the conference on Musical Displacement, Economic Dispossession and Climate Change in Bayonne, France (2019); at several meetings of the Society for Ethnomusicology and the International Council for Traditional Music; and at conferences at Columbia University. I also benefited from discussions at invited talks at the Fondazione Cini in Venice (2017), Sapienza Università di Roma (2018), Università degli Studi di Milano (2019), and L'École des Hautes Études en Sciences Sociales (2019).

Eric Bianchi, Stephen Blum, Susan Boynton, Serena Facci, Kevin Fellezs, Aaron Fox, Ana María Ochoa Gautier, Evan Rapport, Nicola Scaldaferri, Philip Schuyler, Berna Turam, and Grazia Portoghesi Tuzi read excerpts or the entire manuscript at different stages and offered insightful critiques.

Nick Patterson has been an invaluable editor throughout the working and reworking of the manuscript submitted to the press. Sana Darghmouni's help in translating and transcribing the lyrics and many of the conversations that appear in this book was also vital.

Thank you to friends and colleagues who have been important interlocutors at different times in my life, including Hisham Aidi, Roberto Alzetta, Susan Asai, Elena Avellino, Amilcar Barreto, Zakia Bekkas, Carmen Belmonte, Taoufik Ben Amor, Naor Ben-Yehoyada, Timmy Boyle, Virginia Danielson, Anthony De Ritis, Laurie Fellezs, the Gaines family, Anas Ghrab, Jonathan Glasser, Eben Graves, Rana Hamadeh, Hubert Ho, Invernomuto (Simone Bertuzzi and Simone Trabucchi), Richard Jankowski, Mohamed Reda Karam, Brahim Kerkour, Seth Kimmel, Toni Maraini, Mujah Maraini-Melehi, Hafida Mesdouri, Maria Concetta Miniaci, Alessandro Molinari, Gianni and Carla Nardi, Deborah Nemko and Lira Nikolovska, Hassan Rachik, Abdellah Redouane, Brian Robinson, Francesco Rossi and Candida Giordano, Leandro Pisano, Hilary Poriss, Maya Saidani, Mounir Serhani, Ron Smith, Mbarek Sryfi, Jane Sugarman, Pier Mattia Tommasino, Jadranka Važanová, Carmela Vircillo-Franklin, Ameneh Youssefzadeh, Claudio Zambianchi, and Enrico Zambianchi and Isa d'Alessandro.

At the University of Chicago Press, I wish to acknowledge the incredible support of Elizabeth Branch Dyson, Philip Bohlman, and Timothy Rommen. I also thank Mollie McFee for her careful editorial assistance and Barbara Norton for her painstaking copy editing. I am grateful for the insightful reports by the two the anonymous reviewers whose suggestions strengthened the book's argument.

Chapter 2 is derived in part from an article published in the *Journal of North African Studies* (2020) ©Taylor & Francis, available online at https://www.tandfonline.com/doi/full/10.1080/13629387.2019.1639152.

To the memory of my father, Francesco Ciucci; to my mother, Rosa Peruzzi, for her strength and her devotion; to my brother, Andrea Ciucci, for his presence; to Lorenzo, Martino, Doralice, and Luca Ciucci; and to the one who, despite his unwavering support, prefers to remain unnamed.

Notes

1. Although the term *'arubiya* may also indicate a female Bedouin or a rural woman, throughout these pages the term will be used only to indicate a specific notion of rural and the countryside, as well as the territory of the Moroccan Atlantic plains and plateaus.

2. The Alta Valle del Tevere is in the northern part of Umbria and includes eight municipalities: Citerna, Città di Castello, Lisciano Niccone, Monte Santa Maria Tiberina, Montone, Pietralunga, San Giustino, and Umbertide.

3. In 2014 a number of migrant Moroccan men held in a reception center in Rome sewed their mouths shut in protest for the lengthy detention. It was not the first time that the act of sewing their mouths shut—and consequently their silence—was used as a desperate measure to force the authorities to take notice of their situation.

4. Sidi Said Mashi is a saint whose shrine is in the region of Settat.

5. Olive trees are considered to be holy and will therefore often mark the tomb of a saint.

6. Hussein Rathnani is a saint whose shrine is in Essaouira.

7. A tribe with saintly lineage in the Chiadma region.

8. Ahmed Ghlimi is a saint whose shrine is in Settat.

9. Mulay Abdellah Ben Hussein is a saint whose shrine is in Tamesloth (Marrakesh).

10. Omar Qadmiri is a saint whose shrine is in Berrechid.

11. The term *kamanja* may refer to the violin or the viola, but in the case of *'aiṭa* it always refers to the viola, which is otherwise indicated as *kaman* or *kamanja kbira*.

12. More precisely, the term *rma* refers to those who shoot with shotguns or with bows and arrows, while *ṣayyada* refers to hunters.

13. While Mouline Othmani and Nassim Haddad are contemporary examples of the embodiment of the feminine in male vocality, the theatrical troupe Kabareh Cheikhats—made up entirely of men—embody the feminine in their appearances as they perform dressed as *shikhat*.

14. See https://www.tuttitalia.it/umbria/72-umbertide/statistiche/cittadini -stranieri-2020/.

15. "'Cuore verde d'Italia,' viene scelto come sintetico autoritratto, dove 'cuore' allude al centro geografico del paese, ma vuole riferirsi anche al possesso dei caratteri nazionali tradizionali più autentici, almeno per tutta la fascia dell'Italia centrale che, con Roma e Firenze, costituisce comunque l'area più rappresentativa del paese; 'verde' evoca l'ambiente naturale quale componente dominante del paesaggio . . .

sostanzialmente preservato da una aggressiva urbanizzazione e, pertanto, da intendersi ancora 'intatto.'"

16. The theme of the 2018 edition of the festival is rather telling: "Barbari: La scoperta degli altri" (Barbarians: the discovery of the others).

17. As of 1 January 2020, Italy has 5,039,637 migrants, constituting 8.4 percent of the overall population; Romanians (1,145,718), Albanians (421,591), and Moroccans (414,249) are the three most important communities. Moroccans make up 8.22 percent of the migrant population; see https://www.tuttitalia.it/statistiche/cittadini-stranieri-2020/. These numbers do not include undocumented migrants, whose presence in Italy is difficult to estimate. In 2020, however, it was estimated that there were 517,000 undocumented immigrants in Italy. See https://www.ismu.org/xxvi-rapporto-ismu-sulle-migrazioni-2020-comunicato-stampa-23-2-2021/.

18. "I Marocchini sono venuti qui in un primo tempo per i lavori stagionali, come la raccolta del tabacco, o per l'edilizia; questo tipo di immigrazione è iniziata con gli anni Ottanta, ed era soprattutto 'agnatica,' cioè basata su gruppi di fratelli o cugini, comunque maschile, e non su famiglie: quando hanno trovato un lavoro stabile hanno cominciato a far venire le mogli e i figli."

19. Over the second half of the twentieth century, Morocco has become an important country of emigration, first to France and Belgium, the Netherlands, and Germany, and only later to Italy and Spain (Berriane, de Haas, and Nattar 2015, 503).

20. These *sanatorie*, often associated with a new migration law or decree, followed the Foschi law of 1986; 1990 with the Martelli law; 1995 with the Dini decree; 1998 with the Turco-Napolitano law; 2002 with the Bossi-Fini law; 2009 with the Security decree; and the 2012 law 92 of 28 June.

21. It was surpassed by the Albanians in 2002 and by the Romanians in 2008.

22. Despite the increasing rooting of migrants in the Italian territory, the dynamics and policies of exclusion and discrimination are considered to be a source of disaffection and to form the basis of migrants' desire to abandon Italy, particularly among the youth and the more qualified (IDOS 2019, 10–11).

23. See https://www.tuttitalia.it/umbria/statistiche/cittadini-stranieri-2020/. This percentage does not include undocumented immigrants.

24. For more examples on popular discourse on the character of *l-'arubi* and migration in popular culture, see Sabry 2005.

25. Many of the processes and phenomena described in this book have their counterparts in Algeria (MacMaster 2020) and Tunisia (Valensi 1985; Anderson 1986).

26. "Un bédouin qui quitte les steppes continue à partager avec ses confrères les anciennes valeurs, les anciennes perceptions des relations sociales et de l'espace, le savoir lié au cheptel, aux plantes."

CHAPTER ONE

1. In her study on Moroccan migrants from the town of Ben Ahmed to the Alta Valle del Tevere in Umbria, Giacalone acknowledges the category of the *'arubi*, describing how they are considered as having conserved the customs, clothing, linguistic expressions, and Bedouin values more than anyone else in Morocco (2003, 3, 82). Roberto Alzetta, in his study on the Beni Meskine migrants in Genoa, writes that *l-'arubi* is described as a person who, because he lives in the countryside and works exclusively in the field of agriculture, is seen as someone who leads a simple life in

economic and cultural terms. Alzetta adds that an 'arubi is often described as someone who is naive and thus characterized as being unsophisticated in thinking and manners, and whose condition results from living in a situation of social immobility, stagnation, and primitiveness (primitività) (2004, 240–41).

2. For discussions about the division between rural and urban before colonialism in Morocco, see Le Chatelier 1902; Mission Scientifique du Maroc 1915; Mazzīn 1986 and 1992; Bū Salām 1991.

3. In one study, Alessandra Persichetti compares the changes in the kinship and social structure of a group of families of the Mzab tribe from the town of Ben Ahmed—in the Atlantic plains and plateaus—that emigrated to Umbria. Persichetti notes that the majority of her interlocutors proudly define themselves as Arabs; furthermore, even though some have a Berber parent, they define themselves as children of Berbers but of Arab descent (2003a, 63 and 87).

4. "ɛṛəb / ɛṛāb 1. lă-ɛṛəb / lə-ɛṛāb les bédouins—f lă-ɛṛəb: chez les bédouins, à la campagne [. . .] pl. péj. ɛṛəbbān: bédouins grossiers [. . .].—2. lă-ɛṛəb les gens de race / de langue arabe, les Arabes; les arabophones."

5. "āɛṛāb / ɛṛāb 1. l-āɛṛāb les Arabes bédouins [. . .]."

6. "ɛăṛbi 1. arabe [. . .].—2. de type arabe [. . .].—3. bédouin; campagnard, paysan; péj. rustre, croquant, frustre (comme un bédouin)."

7. "ɛṛōbi 1. [. . .] bédouin; campagnard, paysan [cont. mdīni]; particulier aux bédouins—[. . .]—ɛṛōbiya femme bédouine. 2. lă-ɛṛōbīya: les bédouins (considérés dans leur ensemble); le milieu bédouin, la population bédouine.—3. ext. les campagnards."

8. Kosansky writes how this system of transcription, which was more accessible to French administrators, officers, and colonials who required basic skills of communications with the natives, marked French presence and French domination (2016, 16).

9. The literature on Ibn Khaldun is vast; however, for a discussion of the ways in which Moroccan scholars have engaged with the writings of Ibn Khaldun since the 1960s, see Mansouri 2014.

10. The title of sharifian, given to the descendants of the Prophet Mohammed through his daughter Fatima, the wife of his cousin Ali Ibn Abi Talib, is very prestigious in Morocco because the Saadian and Alawi dynasties are both of sharifian descent. Sharifian families are also well represented in the Moroccan merchant aristocracy and religious leadership. Murabiṭun are Muslim saints or venerated holy persons recognized as having been blessed (baraka). Murabiṭun were ascetic, saintly men and women who withdrew from worldly life and gathered a circle of disciples who spread their beliefs. Nearly every town and city in Morocco has its patron murabiṭ whose tomb is regularly visited by the faithful. Aside from spreading Islam, murabiṭun also served to reinforce tribal organization and beliefs.

11. Abdallah Baroudi argues that, although absentee, the bourgeois of rural origin working in the administration were able to recuperate a part of their patrimony from small, impoverished landowners, and that the 1971 Moroccanization Project turned into a new "feudal land tenure," where the "new colons"—powerful urbanites in the high administration—possessed the best part of the rural patrimony in Morocco (1989, 91 n. 109, 92).

12. Susan Ossman remarks on the fact that the "contrast of Fasi ways to peasant ('rubi) manners is a constant theme in Casablanca conversations" (1994, 23).

13. In his article on the term *chleuh* Rachid Agrour writes about how French colonials and urbanites classified the *'arubi* and the *chleuh* in rather similar terms—albeit always distinguishing between Arab Bedouins and Berbers—expressing disdain with regard to the person from the countryside (2012, 788–91).

14. "[L']exploration scientifique a précédé de loin la colonisation directe. [. . .] Mais ce n'est qu'après l'établissement du Protectorat qu'une idéologie colonial sur le plan socio-culturel, en fonction des 'réalités indigènes' va se structurer et devenir un des piliers de la colonisation. Et ce sera surtout dans le cadre de l'Institut des Hautes Etudes [*sic*] Marocaines, fondé en 1920, et dans sa publication Hespéris, qui va se déployer une frénésie de la recherche et une spéléologie culturelle des plus spectaculaires. L'I.H.E.M., patronné par Lyautey, le théoricien suprême du Protectorat marocain, va se donner pour tâche immédiate 'l'exploration scientifique du Maroc.' [. . .] Des vocations se développèrent au sein de cet organisme et des théoriciens s'affirmèrent : littérature (Basset, Laoust, Justinard), géographie (Célérier, P. de Cénival, Raynal), histoire (Michaux-Bellaire, de Castries, Laoust), musique (Chottin), linguistique (Biarnay, Lévi-Provençal, Laoust), arts (P. Richard, Herber, Marçais, Terrasse)."

15. "On discerne, en effet, dans les formes musicales de ce pays, une double influence, celle de deux genres de vie qui se juxtaposent, le nomadisme et le sédentarisme; de deux civilisations, rurale et citadine;

> 1° *La phase rythmique*, qui assujettit le primitif, l'être inculte, toujours aux prises avec la nature, à ses nécessités périodiques, à ses alternances de toutes sortes, des jours et des nuits, des saisons, des travaux, des migrations;
> 2° *La phase mélodique*, qui est l'apanage du civilisé, du raffiné, de l'homme accroupi au milieu des coussins, bercé au murmure indistinct de l'eau s'écoulant dans les vasques, insensiblement comme s'écoule pour lui le temps, aux instants fondus dans la pénombre et la tiédeur toujours égale des patios."

16. "Chez les Aroubi [*sic*], Mi Lalla récupère la Taârija au fond de son placard et place au bœuf chaâbi : véritable jam session de aïta, qu'elle soit haouzia, jeblia, gharbaouia, marsaoui ou encore mellalia." Refers to the different styles of *'aiṭa*, each associated with a different region in which it is performed.

17. Throughout his writing Chottin rarely engages with Moroccan musicians. This particular form of Eurocentrism effectively relegates local musicians and their knowledge to providing only the raw material for Europeans to observe and systematize, a practice that, as argued by Scheherazade Qassim Hassan, was also evident in the 1932 Cairo Congress of Arab Music (1992).

18. "Tel est l'état de conservation de la musique venue de l'Espagne, représentative d'une culture raffinée par laquelle s'est développée la civilisation des villes dites *hadariya*, c'est-à-dire de formation urbaine, par opposition aux agglomérations de nature rurale. Ces dernières représentent donc mieux, à certains égards, l'élément nationale du pays, celui qui s'exprime dans ce parler bédouinisant que l'on pourrait appeler le dialecte marocaine moyen."

19. "1° *La Musique classique*, d'origine andalouse, art de cour et art bourgeois, complexe, savant et raffiné; 2° *La Musique populaire*, généralement imprégnée de chant andalou, parfois aussi influencée par le chant Berbère, parfois encore d'origine étrangère: turque dans la musique de cortège, nègre dans certaines confréries."

20. According to Shannon, *muqa'qa'* continues to be considered a less desirable vocal quality in contemporary Aleppo (2006, 152).

21. "La *'aïta* [...] est, à l'origine, un cri lancé à travers la campagne pour faire savoir à tous une nouvelle importante. De là ces longues vocalises, sur une note élevée dont les légères ondulations sont comme les signes subtils d'un langage secret. La *'aïta* [...] est surtout cultivée par les femmes, les chanteuses chikhât, qui l'associent à leurs danses. [...] Lorsque le chante est terminé, l'air est repris par le violon ur un mouvement rapide à 6/8 et la danse du ventre commence, hiératique et froidement suggestive."

22. Abdelkebir Khatibi discusses a similar juxtaposition in the paintings of Delacroix (2019, 148).

23. "[N]ous allons connaître le Maroc libertin et jouisseur. Ce 'visage' est agréable à regarder, mai que de fard sur les joues, que de khol sous les yeux, que de bijoux vrais ou faux scintillant autour de lui ; quelle profusion de couleurs vives et quelle surcharge d'ornements parmi les parfums anesthésiants qui s'en dégagent! Et j'ai bien peur, hélas! que là-dessous, il n'y ait qu'une pauvre et menue figure, pâlotte et fripée de viveur, qui se consume à poursuivre un bonheur sensuel impossible. [...] Voilà donc cette musique si attirant et si décevant à la fois; sur une ligne mélodique qui pourrait être charmante, elle plaque le fard des 'grupetti,' la verroterie des 'vibrati,' elle s'enveloppe d'une expression soupirante trop souvent affectée. [...] Ce rire et cette joie fusent et éclatent dans le rythme, rythme étourdissant, rythme enchanteur qui endort les soucis et les peines; rythme-vampire dont les ailes s'agitent pour anesthésier la douleur causée par sa morsure fatale. Ainsi le *tar*, semble-t-il vous mordre sourdement l'âme, à chaque battement que voile le frétillement doucereux de ses cymbalettes. Un orchestre de Chiakh et de Chikhat comprend essentiellement des chanteurs et chanteuses munis de leur *tar* ou tambour de basque. Un seul violon accompagne et soutien leur chant. Les élèves chanteuses qui ne connaissent pas le maniement du tar se contentent de marquer les temps forts du rythme en battent des mains."

24. "[L]a position du Maroc à la croisée des chemins, à la pointe ouest du *monde ancien*, le prédisposait à avoir, 'greffé' sur le substrat berbère, un cumul d'apports: le rythme africain saharien et subsaharien, les survivances rituelles gréco-romaines, phéniciennes et africaines, le modalisme arabe et le raffinement andalou."

25. "Les plus jeunes parmi les *chikhât* exécutent devant le public des danses sensuelles (jeu de ventre et des hanches, ondulations et frémissement du corps, balancement de la chevelure ...). [...] Aujourd'hui, ce côté divertissant et parfois érotique prend le dessus sur le vrai sens de la 'aïta."

26. "Le violon de Bouch'aïb lance un son râpeux, suintant de mélancolie. [...] Fatna d'abord, entonne ce cri plein de souffrance, *'houahhaaaa...,'* cri rauque, à la limite du sanglot. [...] C'est un grand moment de la *'ayta*. Cette version de *Kharboucha* est gorgée d'émotion rurale à l'état brut."

27. "Les voix plus gutturales de Safi sont à la recherche d'un tragique et d'une tension, qui ont été transformés dans la version de Casablanca: cette version plus plaintive, voire sentimentale (sinon 'glamour'), concrétise musicalement les effets sociaux de la migration des populations de la campagne vers la ville: moins de rudesse, plus de sentimentalité."

28. " لأن 'كورونا' هي تجل من التجليات لهذه التغييرات التي تقع في العام لأن. والشخصية المغربية ان تُبنى حول الثقة في الإمكانيات الذاتية أولا، والثقة في القدرات المحلية، و التي تتجلى في ندرة، وفي خصائص البداوة، كما يقول ابن خلدون، و ليس بفهوم 'العروبية'. البداوة بمعنى التعامل مع شظف العيش ومع الندرة و مع الصعوبات اليومية و هذه هي نقط القوة للمجتمع و هذه هي نقط القوة التي يجب أن تستثمر في بناء مغر جديد."

CHAPTER TWO

1. "Considerare il migrante dalla riva [. . .] equivale a rinsaldare la barriera tra 'noi' e 'loro,' il confine tra residenti e stranieri. Soprattutto vuol dire non mettersi dalla parte del migrante, non vestirne i panni, non assumerne il punto di vista." My thanks to Franco Baldasso for introducing me to the work of Di Cesare,

2. The distance between El Borouj and Casablanca is about 150 km (93 miles), and thus, as others have remarked, it is not likely that Abdelilah covered such a distance with a cart pulled by horses or donkeys. Abdelilah's statement is best understood as an example of a narrative in which the boundary between reality and imagination is blurred.

3. Although colonial ethnography tends to focus on "local differences rather than human similarities" (Rachik 2020, 50–51), Brunot (1920) provides interesting documentation of the area's complex relationship with the sea.

4. In 2018 the unemployment rate in Khouribga was 12.4 percent, against the national average of 10.2 percent. In 2020 the national unemployment rate jumped to about 12 percent, but no data are available for Khouribga.

5. Similar pressure, although from different sources, led to migration from the High Atlas and the Rif. Thank you to Philip Schuyler for pointing this out to me.

6. "Comme des armées des jeunes gens attendaient longtemps que l'OCP les tire des griffes de la misère noire, ils se sont jetés à corps perdus dans les pateras de la mort. Certaines ont eu de la chance et ont réussi à atteindre l'autre rive. Par contre, d'autre malheureux ont perdu leur vie, noyés dans la mer. À titre d'exemple, les jeunes du quartier 'Labrique' et ceux du village rural 'Foqra' qui ont connu une mort collective au large à cause de l'immigration clandestine vers l'Eldorado italien. L'Italie, le pays de prédilection des jeunes chômeurs khouribguis."

7. *L-ḥarg*, the burning, refers to clandestine migration, and *l-ḥarraga* to the burners.

8. The members of the group Abidat Rma Khouribga are Redouane El Aibed, Rachid and Tarik El Asli, Mohammed Hachimi, Icham Msid, Salah Boufed, and Icham Jabeur.

9. The so-called triangle of death is an area delimited by Khouribga, Beni Mellal, and El Kelaa des Sraghna.

10. The song, which appears in a full-length film titled *Latiqa fi 'atiqa*, was produced by the same group of *'abidat r-rma* and is available on YouTube; see https://www.you tube.com/watch?v=JKy7rlBQ3Xw.

11. Khouribga is the site of a yearly festival dedicated to *'abidat r-rma* sponsored by King Mohammed VI, the Ministry of Culture, the province of Khouribga, the OCP, and the communal councils of Khouribga, Oued Zem, and Boujad.

12. An episode of the television program *Suna' al-furja* was dedicated to *'abidat r-rma*; see https://www.youtube.com/watch?v=ZvPCCszrLQs.

13. The logo of the OCP appears on all the jackets of their CDs. As the official sponsor of the group, the OCP supports their studio recordings, videos, and public performances in Morocco and, to a certain extent, abroad. The sponsorship of the OCP, however, must be contextualized in the personal history of the group. The fathers of all the members of the troupe used to work for the company, and all but one have died of cancer. Their widows receive a meager pension from OCP of MAD 500–3000 per month (US$55–330).

14. Ubiquitously used in Morocco, the most common first degrees of the *bayati maqam* are D (D–E-half-flat–F–G–A–B-flat–C–D) and A (A–B-half-flat–C–D–E–F–G–A).

15. McMurray cites an earlier song about migration by Walid Mimoun, a singer from Nador in the Rif region, also structured as a dialogue between a mother and the son from whom she has been separated (2001, 104–5).

16. For the *rumi/bəldi* dichotomy in Morocco, see Rachik 2016b.

17. While it is true that the term *lamarin* has been used to refer to the French navy, in this song *lamarin* refers to the Italian navy.

18. Menin also writes that "cars embody a powerful token of mobility and success in contexts where the donkey was the usual means of transport" (2016, 26).

19. Referring to the illegal crossing.

20. A man's ability to make money (*flus*) and thus to take care of his family through migration is indeed associated with being a "real man" (see also Menin 2016, 32).

21. Ceuta is a Spanish enclave in Morocco about fourteen kilometers (eight and a half miles) from Spain. Aside from its proximity to Europe, Ceuta is one of only two places (the other being Melilla) from which Africans can reach European soil without risking their lives in the Mediterranean Sea. Both enclaves have become significant for migration flows. Furthermore, the fact that Ceuta and Melilla were fenced off by the Spanish government has given special significance to these territories, turning them into paradigmatic examples of EU migration policies and of metaphors for Fortress Europe. In this context, the second half of line 6 may be considered as reflecting this new experience of migration for Moroccans.

22. Here it refers to the hood of a *jellaba*. In the countryside the hood is often used as a pocket.

23. The Islamic profession of faith, the act of declaring, "There is no God but God, and Muhammad is the Messenger of God." It is also recited in the moments before death.

24. The danger of being eaten by fish is a common theme, one that is also found in Tunisian songs about the *ḥarraga* (Salzbrunn, Souiah, and Mastrangelo 2015, 45). Recently, another trope about the same dangerous fate for undocumented migrants who attempt to cross the Mediterranean has begun to emerge in Morocco on social media. An image of the display of fish in a market is juxtaposed with that of an overcrowded boat in the Mediterranean with the following comment: "Moroccans do not eat fish because it is too expensive, but the fish eat Moroccans since they are cheap" (*l-mgharba mayakulush l-hut ḥit ghali wa l-hut yakul l-mgharbḥit rkhaṣ*).

25. The troupe is from Dar Ouled Zidouh, in the region of Beni Mellal.

26. The figure of the infidel (*l-kafər*) is commonly used to indicate a lover who has wronged the beloved and thus as someone who is ungrateful, as one verse shows: *l-kafər iḥsan 'awnak a rwisi* (The ungrateful! God have mercy on me). In the context of this song, however, *l-kafər* refers to the sea.

27. This refers to the Zenata beach, near Casablanca, where the bodies of some of the young men lost in the shipwreck were found.

28. "[U]n orizzonte che paradossalmente ci fornisce il senso del limite e anche la possibilità del suo superamento, ci ricorda che sono la differenza e il brivido dell'altrove a dire chi siamo, e soprattutto chi vorremmo essere."

29. Clifford Geertz writes about a similar usage of the notion of *hijra* in relation to Sefrou. In the 1970s and '80s, a large rural migration to Sefrou created tension between Real and Outsider Sefrouis. The Outsider Sefrouis felt that they were being treated like barbarian intruders, and that they were unwelcome and their material needs neglected. Geertz writes that they responded by reframing their identity: "The term they usually used to indicate their move from the country to the city is not the Real Sefrouis' rural exodus, which makes them sound like tattered refugees, but *hijra*, the Arabic at once

for emigration and immigration, and, of course, for the Prophet's move from Mecca to Medina that inaugurated the Muslim Era" (1987, 299).

30. In the last few years, a different generation of potential Moroccan migrants—younger and university educated—have turned to vlogs, which supply useful information such as the best place to cross a border, the amount of money needed to pay bribes, the names of lawyers helping migrants with paperwork, or the charities that provide shelter. The tremendous pull of these vlogs is said to attract a growing number of the educated and employed making the crossing legally. As one of the vloggers stated in a recent interview: "I help North Africans break the fear barrier and fulfil their dreams of reaching the West." See https://www.economist.com/middle-east-and-africa/2020/07/23/vloggers-show-how-to-migrate-illegally-on-a-jet-ski.

31. An annual celebration honoring the birthday of a saint and held at his shrine, it is also an event at which recreation and entertainment are central. The *tburida* is part of the ludic aspect of a *moussem*, and it always attracts a large crowd of spectators, who watch the equestrian display and comment on the performance of the troupes of competing horsemen (see Berriane 1989).

32. In recent years I have witnessed the emergence of a number of troupes of all-female riders. Nonetheless, the *tburida* continues to be associated first and foremost with manhood, as also discussed by Talley (2020). For more on the relation between *tburida*, manhood, and virility, see Combs-Schilling (1989).

33. Stephen Blum warns that the term "influence" is "an appropriate choice when scholars would rather not specify how they are thinking about one or another process of exchange among individuals or groups," suggesting that music scholars memorize the list of forty-six verbs proposed by the art historian Michael Baxandall (see Blum 2015, 205). "Transform" is one of these forty-six.

CHAPTER THREE

1. Thanks to Daniele Bistoni, who kindly accompanied me to visit the museum and explained its history.

2. Peculiar to Italy is the widespread presence of religious associations caring for migrants that, in one way or another, have filled the gap left by the absence of government and its institutions.

3. For an ethnographic inquiry into the women left behind, see Sadiqi and Ennaji 2004; Elliot 2016 and 2021.

4. Nigerians are the only women working in the tobacco fields in the Alta Valle del Tevere.

5. Moroccan migrants refer to the Italian passport by its red color.

6. "[P]reservi l'eredità culturale, sociale ed economica che deriva dalla coltura e dalla lavorazione di questo prodotto . . . l'intento è invece quello di restituire dignità e valorizzare il lavoro di tutti coloro che hanno operato ed operano in questo importante settore."

7. The CISL (Confederazione Italiana Sindacati Lavoratori; Italian Confederation of Trade Unions) was founded on Roman Catholic principles, but with a secular organization, in 1948 after splitting from the communist-associated CGIL (Confederazione Generale Italiana del Lavoro; Italian General Confederation of Labor). ANOLF (Associazione Nazionale Oltre le Frontiere; National Association Beyond Borders) was created in 1989. It is promoted by CISL and constituted almost exclusively of migrants from different ethnic backgrounds and without any particular political affiliation.

8. "Fatemi capire bene il concetto secondo cui un immigrato in Italia 'ruba il lavoro' mentre un italiano all'estero 'lotta per il proprio futuro.'"

9. The celebration of the *tabacchine* needs to be framed in a historical construction of Umbria, where the antifascist and anti-sharecropping struggles figured prominently. Until the 1980s, in fact, Umbria's collective regional identity was forged around class struggle and the peasant movement (Covino and Gallo 1989).

10. Migrant workers constitute about 85 percent of the people working in the tobacco industry in the Alta Valle del Tevere. The rest are Italians who, however, are solely employed in administration and high-end jobs. Among migrant workers, aside from Moroccans, about 4 percent are Algerians and 4 percent are Tunisians. There is also an important presence of Nigerians, mostly women, and a small percentage of newly arrived Dominicans (Abdelilah Am., personal communication, 30 July 2019, Umbertide).

11. "Un po' perché sono sparsi in parecchi centri: molti sono a Perugia, un altro nucleo importante è nell'alta valle del Tevere, altri gruppi sono a Gualdo Tadino, a Bastia, nella zona del Lago. [. . .] Ma più che Perugia, sono nella periferia e nei paesi."

12. "[G]li immigrati sono separati dagli autoctoni per mezzo di una barriera invisibile di discriminazione, pregiudizi, diffidenza. Frequentando i quartieri popolari e le periferie della città è facile rendersi conto della condizione di subalternità e di esclusione della maggior parte dei migranti. Ormai radicati da tempo nello spazio cittadino, i migranti marocchini abitano negli stessi quartieri, vanno negli stessi posti, negli stessi bar, e i loro figli frequentano le stesse scuole e gli stessi giardini dei torinesi di classe operaia. [. . .] Eppure, nonostante le eccezioni, i rapporti sociali con i nativi sono ancora ridotti, segnati da pregiudizi e diffidenza. [. . .] Esclusi dalle relazioni sociali e quotidiane, i migranti conducono una vita sociale separata rispetto alla realtà sociale torinese, facendo affidamento prevalentemente a relazioni e rapporti intracomunitari."

13. "[N]on ci sta nessun caporeparto per esempio marocchino, e ce ne stanno tanti, perché è un'azienda abbastanza grande, [. . .] io ti parlo proprio a livello di campo lavorativo, poi all'esterno non è che li frequento."

14. *"Ciao babbo."*

"Ciao Marco, come va?"

"Ma insomma babbo . . . ho preso 4 a geografia."

"Dio buono! E come mai? Ma che t'hanno domandato?"

"E . . . m' hanno detto dov'era il Marocco babbo."

"E bene, tu non gl' hai saputo risponde?"

"E no babbo, io non lo so dov'è?"

"Madonna dai, che ti aiuto io. Pia l'atlante, ci guardiamo insieme, dai!"

Il figlio prende l'atlante e lo porta là . . . il padre lo apre.

"Allora, vediamo un po' . . . allora, di qui c'è Castello, di qui c'è Citerna, San Sepolcro, Pistrino . . . eh, fijo mio dovrà esse di qui vicino perché, eh . . . vengono a lavorà in bicicletta e ci mettono un quarto d'ora!"

15. For an interesting discussion about relatedness among Sicilians and Tunisians in Mazara del Vallo, see Ben-Yehoyada (2017).

16. In Italy, citizenship is acquired through *ius sanguinis*, having Italian parents or ancestors; *ius soli temperato*, for children of immigrants who are born in Italy and whose parents satisfy a number of requirements; by marriage; and through naturalization, for migrants who have legally resided in Italy for ten or more years, have no criminal record, have sufficient financial resources, and have a suitable place to live, and who have passed a language exam. While the *ius soli temperato* is a long and difficult process

for most migrants I have worked with and for their children—at least until they reach economic independence—the currently debated *ius culturae*, which would grant Italian citizenship to children born in Italy or who arrived in Italy before turning twelve, as long as they have regularly attended school in Italy for a minimum of five years, continues to stall. Despite its popularity among the second generation, it is important to recognize that *ius culturae* emphasizes the notion of integration as assimilation and consequently is modeled on the preoccupations of the European Union. This is particularly true in light of the creation of the position of a vice president responsible for "Protecting our European Way of Life" by the European Commission in 2019—a title that provoked outrage, with critics denouncing the phrasing as an echo of far-right rhetoric that identifies Europe as white and Christian, and migration from Africa and the Middle East as a threat to that identity.

17. Italians' perceptions of Sikh men working in agriculture in the southern Lazio region, for example, are radically different from perceptions of Moroccan men working in the tobacco in the Alta Valle del Tevere. Unlike Moroccans, Sikhs in Italy are perceived as a "silent and harmless presence, often identified as the 'good' and the 'hard-working' migrants" (Bertolani 2013, 76).

18. *Qui cara madre*
siamo più o meno tutti uguali,
lo sporco lava-vetri
il delinquente spacciatore
e il "vu cumprà" ignorante
siamo tutti in uno
e non siamo nessuno.

19. Jokes and proverbs on different characteristics of tribes are common and part of a rich popular lore in Morocco. According to this lore, members of the Mzab—an important tribal confederation in the Casablanca-Settat region in precolonial Morocco—are known to be quarrelsome, as the following proverb collected during my fieldwork demonstrates: *mzab ujuh lǝmharsha, la maʿun ibqa, la fattasha* (Mzab, a quarrelsome face, no plate remains intact, no small lamp remains lit).

20. A magazine article about Moroccan migration in Italy describes the town of Beni Mellal, in the Beni Mellal-Khenifra region of the Atlantic plains and plateaus, as the capital of the *vu' cumprà* (Cutuli 1992).

21. As recently as the summer of 2019, the operation *spiagge sicure* (safe beaches) saw the implementation of police patrolling the beaches, the main task of whom was to prohibit vendors without a permit to sell their merchandise and to fine anyone attempting to purchase any merchandise from them up to 7,000 euros.

22. Corrosacz examines the link between the use of the term *marucchen*—a dialectical variant of *marocchino* used in the region of Modena to indicate southern Italian migrants in the 1980s—and the contemporary use of the term *marocchino*, which refers to non-European migrants and particularly to Africans and North Africans (2008).

23. In Rosarno—a commune in a largely agricultural area of Calabria—there was a "game" called *andare per marocchini* (to go looking for Moroccans). In order to play the "game," young Italian men rode scooters while holding wooden ball bats in their hand; as they passed by non-European migrants walking back and forth from work, they would hit them, like baseball players hitting the ball (Costantino 2010).

24. In Italian, the pejorative suffix *-acci* (pl. masc.) can be appended to nouns, adjectives, and adverbs alike.

25. See http://www.gdli.it/pdf_viewer/Scripts/pdf.js/web/viewer.asp?file=/PDF /GDLI09/GDLI_09_ocr_837.pdf&parola=marano; Di Cesare 2018.

26. During World War II the French recruited women as prostitutes for Moroccan soldiers. During my fieldwork in Morocco, I met one of these women who had been sent to the former French Indochina to entertain Moroccan troops in the region from 1945 to 1954. Khalti Fatma (Aunt Fatma), who was once a famous professional singer-dancer in the region of Beni Mellal, was now old and destitute, living with one of her adopted sons in a bare two-room mud house with no electricity or running water, reduced to living off handouts. To my knowledge, she received no pension from the French government.

27. "Il 21 maggio arrivannu come diavoli dalle montagne. Veramente noi ci aspettavamo i liberatori e difatti a Mangiavacca, dove stavamo noi, la gente uscì con una bandiera bianca, credevamo che erano i liberatori. Invece, come 'ncummenzannu a venì, se purtannu le femmine a 'ncumenzannu a fa sfregi. A Lenola c'è stato nu massacro vero. Si diceva che sti marocchini erano venuti pe' sfrontà il fronte. I tedeschi tenevano tante fortezze e allora i marocchini rischiavano, non pensavano alla vita. [. . .] [I] marocchini a passà passannu, ma passò gnu focu. Llà non si è salvato nisciuno. A Lenola ne hanno ammazzate tre e pure una di cinquant'anni, la taglianno cu na forbice. Un signore ammazzò nu marocchino che aveva violentato tutte e tre le figlie, tre belle vagnone e vicino a isso. Insomma nu paese intero in ginocchio. Porelle, le ficinnu come la veste di Cristo, chelle vagnone."

28. Similar atrocities were committed by Moroccan troops who fought in the Spanish Civil War (1936–39). Unlike in Italy, in Spain the reputation of Moroccans as rapists was reinforced by the centuries-old Orientalist portrayal of the Moor (Calderwood 2018; Al Touma 2018). For the role played by the figure of the Moor in the responses to contemporary Moroccan migration in Spain, see Flesler (2008).

29. The first meaning of *marocchinare* is associated with early encounters between Arabs and Muslims during the Middle Ages, and later with encounters conjuring rhetoric about a time of peaceful coexistence, invoked in liberal discourses about migration and multiethnic Europe. The second and more recent meaning has to do with encounters that are used to challenge the idea of a peaceful coexistence, allowing far-right and neofascist parties to invoke the Crusades and supporting their anti-Arab and anti-Muslim propaganda.

30. "Violentare, violare, stuprare (con riferimento alle violenze compiute da truppe marocchine nell'Italia centrale e meridionale durante l'ultimo periodo della seconda guerra mondiale).—Anche: contagiare di sifilide."

31. Christelle Taraud discusses hypermasculinity in reference to a "virile colonization" (*colonisation virile*) aimed at undermining Arabs by assuring the superiority, including in terms of sexual potency, of the French (2008, 124). In this context, the construction of the colonized as hypermasculine went hand in hand with his hyperfeminization and emasculation.

32. See Escolar 2019, 124–25, for a summary of the literary and cinematic representations of the *goumiers*.

33. In Italy, any utterance thought to be incomprehensible is equated to Arabic, as indicated by a common way saying: *ma che parli arabo?* (but are you speaking Arabic?).

34. The poster can be viewed at https://www.corriere.it/politica/cards/polemica-manifesti-fascisti-forza-nuova/i-manifesti-fascisti_principale.shtml.

35. The cover of the book in question can be seen at https://books.google.com/books?id=dAtgDwAAQBAJ&printsec=frontcover#v=onepage&q&f=false.

36. "I goumiers traevano una sordida gratificazione nell'avere rapporti sessuali con donne bianche, le consideravano, secondo la loro tradizione-, assecondate e comunque non contrastate in questo dal Comando francese, prede di guerra o, anche una rivendicazione religiosa contro i cristiani, ricordando quello che avevano fatto i cavalieri templari contro i musulmani. [. . .] Curzio Malaparte nel suo libro 'La pelle' [. . .] li aveva studiati nei loro sguardi di cupidigia e di desiderio per le donne bianche."

37. For a discussion about the manhood of migrant men returning in Morocco see Elliot (2021, 123–45).

38. For Capello *muḍa* or *muda* (fashion) is the Arabic adaptation of the Italian term *moda* (2008, 101).

39. Literally, modern music; a genre inspired by twentieth-century Egyptian music.

40. *Raï* is a genre of North African popular music associated with western Algeria, particularly the city of Oran, and eastern Morocco.

41. The *rǝzza* is a turban made of a long white muslin strip wrapped around the head.

42. Albeit in a different context, Abdellah Hammoudi writes about the process of feminization that male disciples must undergo—showing submission and obedience to their masters, displaying modesty, and carrying out traditionally feminine activities—before accessing positions of dominance (1997, 138).

43. Thank you to Hicham Chami for discussing this particular moment in the performance. Musicians trained in *'aiṭa*, as in the case of Stati, view these types of cadential points as a modulation, even though there is no change in the *maqam* after this particular cadence (Ciucci 2012a).

44. "In generale, i familiari rimasti in Marocco distinguono gli emigrati in due categorie: gli uomini d'onore che ritornano *salim was ghanim* (sani e salvi dopo aver fatto fortuna) per fare il bene dei loro cari, e quelli che invece 'diventano italiani,' cioè dimenticano i parenti e tornano raramente nel paese d'origine, e perciò vengono chiamati *wuld al-haram* (bastardo, lett. figlio del peccato). [. . .] L'espressione 'diventare italiano' non significa solo, come nel caso specifico, venir meno agli obblighi parentali, ma, in generale, perdere l'insieme dei valori morali."

45. Although it seems like a good sum of money to receive for each performance, it is not enough to pay for an entire troupe. This is the reason musicians like Stati come to Italy alone: it is cheaper for someone who organizes these types of events to hire instrumentalists like Younes from among the Moroccans residing in Italy. With the exception of the airfare, it is also unclear what other expenses of the musicians are covered.

CHAPTER FOUR

1. A seaside town located between Rabat and Casablanca.

2. *Khǝima* refers to the traditional black Bedouin tent made of wool and goat or camel's hair, whose pyramidal structure is characterized by a triangle produced by the vertical bars at the center of the tent (*rkaiz*). *Khǝima*, however, is a term that Abdelilah Ab. employs to represent a household in which different people related by blood reside, and where each room (*ghurfa* or *bit*) is devoted to a member of the household and/or his family unit (see also Eickelman 1976, 42).

3. The name of the soccer stadium in Milan.

4. Although born and raised in Khouribga, here Abdelilah Ta. emphasizes his tribal affiliations with the Ouled Bouria, whose territory is nearby the town of Ben Ahmed.

5. Referring to the old way in which the regions were named in Morocco, the territory of the Chaouia included the Casablanca-Settat region as well as part of what nowadays—after the name changes of Moroccan regions—is referred to as the Beni Mellal-Kenifra region.

6. *Raḥim* (pl. *rḥəm*) is a term that denotes uterine relations and kinships highly valued by my interlocutors (see also Persichetti 2004).

7. Abdellatif's statement is not far from the truth. Casablanca has always been described as a city with a heterogeneous population coming from the nearby tribes of the Chaouia, Doukkala, and Tadla regions, nowadays the Casablanca-Settat and Beni Mellal-Khenifra regions (Mission Scientifique du Maroc 1915, 1:53–54).

8. Abdelilah Ab. refers to some of the major tribes that have historically inhabited the Casablanca-Settat region: A'chach, Beni Meskine, Mdakra, Mediouna, Mzab, Mza Mza, Ouled 'Ali, Ouled Bouziri, Ouled Hariz, Ouled Sa'id, Ouled Sidi Bendaoud, Ouled Ziane, Zenata, and Ziada (Mission Scientifique du Maroc 1915, 2:4).

9. The term used in northern Italian urban centers was considered pejorative. Similar to other terms such as *villano* (villain), *contadino* (peasant), *burino* (hick), and *cafone* (crass), *terrone* indicated an agricultural laborer and was used to refer to migrants from southern Italy—a region characterized by agriculture and considered particularly backward—regarded as underdeveloped peasants. *Terrone*, deriving from *terra* (soil), indicated someone who was intimately linked to the land, and a person whose dark complexion resembled the color of the soil (Battaglia 2002, XX, 962).

10. Although the slougi share some characteristics with the saluki in the Mashreq, they are considered to be a separate breed.

11. On the role of Moroccan theatrical tradition of performances as forms of resistance, see Amine and Carlson 2012; Hinda 2016.

12. The verb *sərrəḥ* (to set free, to release) that my interlocutors use to describe how one can let the eyes wander in the countryside has a strong resonance with the rural, if one considers that it also means to graze freely and to put cattle out to pasture.

13. This is one playlist that Mustapha Ma., originally from Souk Sebt, plays while in the car with his friends, one of the favorite and most common types of subterranean listening. Out of the mostly *sha'bi* selections, only two tracks are not connected to *l-'arubiya*: track 9 is inspired by the *sha'bi* of the Mashreq; track 10 is *sha'bi* in Amazigh. The list also contains two remakes of traditional songs (tracks 1 and 8) and five traditional performances (tracks 11, 12, 14, 15, and 16). The playlist, as one may notice, does not include any Italian music.

1. *sha'bi* remake of a traditional song, "L-'alwa"
2. *sha'bi-'abidat r-rma*
3. *sha'bi-'aiṭa*
4. *sha'bi-'aiṭa*
5. *sha'bi-'aiṭa*
6. *sha'bi-'aiṭa*
7. *sha'bi-'aita*
8. *'abidat r-rma* remake of a traditional song, "Lhədya"
9. *sha'bi* Mashreq
10. *sha'bi* Amazigh

11. *'aiṭa*
12. *'abidat r-rma*
13. *sha'bi-'aiṭa*
14. *'abidaṭ r-rma*
15. Traditional all-female troupe
16. *'abidat r-rma*

14. "L-ghaba" performed by Fatna Bent l-Houcine (audio ex. 4.2) and Abidat Rma Khouribga (audio ex. 4.3), and a *sha'bi* version (audio ex. 4.4).

15. Philip Schuyler has commented on how *rwais* musicians in southwestern Morocco describe having a good voice as having a good throat (1979, 105).

16. I have occasionally heard recordings of *bnat r-rma* (daughters of the hunters); however, the music they perform is indistinguishable from that performed by all-female troupes that, in Morocco, are indicated by various names based on region and repertory (see Ciucci 2005).

17. Schade-Poulsen remarks how a style of *raï* described as *trāb* (lit., "soil") was associated with the Algerian countryside (1999, 113).

18. The stage name of a legendary *shikha*, Fatima Zahafa, derives from being a person with such a disability.

19. According to an anecdote from *Kitāb al-Aghānī l-Kabir*, the best singer is said to be the one with the best voice (*ṣawt*), which is better than the voice of the *jinn*, humans (*ins*), wild animals (*waḥsh*), and birds (*ṭayr*) (Sawa 2019, 221).

20. The Moroccan scholar Driss Cherkaoui writes that many Moroccans believe animals have a soul (*ruḥ*, breath) (2004, 100 n. 13) and thus possess a spiritual essence.

21. In this verse *katti* (*kanti* is spelled in accordance with the assimilated sound of the vernacular), "if you were" is feminine although the bard is masculine. The verse illustrates the everyday manner of speaking of the countryside, where verbs are often conjugated in the feminine forms and used for both men and women in the second-person singular.

22. The population of the Atlantic plains and plateaus associates the town of Berrechid with the first psychiatric institution built by the French in 1920, clearly expressed by a verse from a poem of *'aiṭa*: *'la səttat isti a bərrəshid idawi 'la casa jmə' l-kwawi* (Settat blows your mind, Berrechid cures you, Casablanca burns you).

23. Blacksmiths are regarded with a certain ambiguity in Morocco, since they work with fire and glowing iron. Treated with fear and contempt, their activity is considered to be impure and is associated with magic, and they are traditionally in charge of rituals. Their metal products are said to have beneficial and protective effects to the point that, at marriage ceremonies, these objects are believed to dispel bad luck and bring fertility (Auclair, Hoarau, and Ewague 2015, 85–86).

24. Schade Poulsen discusses a *raï* song in which the forest indicates a milieu where there are men, women, and alcohol (1999, 114–15). "Milouda," a poem of *'aiṭa*, narrates the tale of a woman who goes to the forest with her newborn baby to meet her lover. The mother leaves the baby alone under a tree, where it ends up being killed by a wolf. In *Dance of Outlaws*, a documentary film by Mohamed El Aboudi (2012), a male musician tells a *shikha*, "I must penetrate you in this forest for your voice not to be bad" (*khəṣṣ ḥta nḍrəb lil shi khərṭa fi had l-ghaba, 'ad iulli ṣautək ma khaibsh*).

25. The former name of one of the regions of the Atlantic plains and plateaus.

26. In lieu of *nta*, Shikh Sharqi uses *tta* in accordance with the assimilated sound of the vernacular.

27. Referring to the gait of a person who is drunk, connecting this verse to the previous one in which the glass is a metaphor for alcohol.

28. In traditional households a son will never tell his father that he wants to get married. He will instead use such expressions as "I want to fill the house" or "I want to fulfill [the duties of] my religion" (*bghait nkəmməl dini*).

29. The woman here wishes to be saddled like a donkey so that she can be used to go and fetch water. The verse refers to the custom of people living in the countryside of going on a mule to fetch from a nearby source of water (such as a well or river). In the verse, the woman wants to use this ruse in hopes of running into her lover. The verb may also mean to copulate.

30. Iron here refers to a knife.

31. There are two places in which people can go seek Shikh Sharqi's advice or to hire his troupe: a café in Ben Slimane, the town where he resides, and at the nearby *suq* Ziaida.

32. The significance of "Hajti fi grini" across generations is clearly documented by the presence of a number of renditions of the poem interpreted by different performers on the web, including DJ remixes.

33. The absence of visual representations is also due to the fact that historically *shikhat* did not want their family to find out about their profession, which is why they often perform under stage names.

34. In Moroccan Arabic, *rasi rasək* (lit., my head your head), is used to describe closeness between two people, a situation in which something that is very personal or private can be revealed, shared, or experienced with someone. The term *ras* (head, upper part, apex, tip, top summit, peak, extremity) may also be used in discourses about sexuality, either to indicate the penis (*bu-ras*) or to indicate someone who has reached sexual climax (*jah rasu*, he has arrived at his head, at his peak).

35. Referring to an individual of the Ragraga tribe in the region near Essaouira.

36. The expression "the wings betrayed me" (*l-jnawəh khanuni*) refers to the condition of a lover whom passion has robbed of their strength or reason.

37. Ḥaṣba is the region associated with the port city of Safi and its province, which is where the members of the group in question were born or have resided. The name of the region also gives the name to the style of *'aiṭa* I discuss in these pages: *'aiṭa ḥaṣbawiya*.

38. Lit., "red on the foot," but the red here indicates a foot decorated with henna.

39. Lit., "a little word," but indicating an insult.

40. A reference to the Jbala mountains in northern Morocco.

41. A port city along the Atlantic Plains and more specifically in the Marrakesh-Safi region.

42. El Jadida is a coastal town in the Casablanca-Settat region.

43. A coastal town in the Casablanca-Settat region.

CONCLUSION

1. "Speak Softly, Love," the love theme from *The Godfather*.

2. For a discussion about the gender of sitting and its connotation for men see Elliot (2021, 9).

3. A 2009 video by Abidat Rma Khouribga opens up with a mise-en-scène of *l-'arubiya*, where the group is surrounded on stage by farm animals. As Redouane catches a hen by the legs, the cackling sound marks the space of *l-'arubiya* (video ex. 5.2).

Bibliography

Abbassi, Abdelaziz. 1977. "A Sociolinguistic Analysis of Multilingualism in Morocco." PhD diss., University of Texas at Austin.

Abdeljamil, Khadija. 1993. "L'énonciation dans la chanson populaire arabe de femmes au Maroc (chikhat)." PhD diss., Université Lumière–Lyon II.

El Aboudi, Mohamed, dir. 2012. "Dance of Outlaws." Copenhagen: Danish Broadcasting Corporation. DVD, 59 min.

Adam, André. 1968. *Casablanca, essai sur la transformation de la société marocaine au contact de l'Occident.* 2 vols. Paris: Centre national de la recherche scientifique.

Adidi, Abdelaziz. 2000. *Les villes minières marocaines face au défi du développement durable.* Rabat: Institut national d'aménagement et d'urbanisme.

Adonis. 1990. *An Introduction to Arabic Poetics.* London: Saqi.

Agrour, Rachid. 2012. "Contribution à l'étude d'un mot voyageur: Chleuh (Contribution to the Studies of a Traveler Word: Chleuh)." *Cahiers d'Études Africaines* 52 (208): 767–811.

Aguila, Jésus, and Mokhtar Zagzoule. 2000. "Guide pour l'écoute du CD." *Horizons Maghrébins: Le droit à la mémoire. Rihla/Traversée: Musiques du Maroc* 43: 173–97.

Ahmed, Sara. 2000. *Strange Encounters: Embodied Others in Post-Coloniality.* New York: Routledge.

Alaoui, Oum-Hani. 2009. "Migratory Trajectories: Moroccan Borderlands and Translocal Imaginaries." PhD diss., Princeton University.

Alunni, Lorenzo. 2017. "La soglia di tolleranza. Coltivazione del tabacco, tumori e gestione del rischio in Alta Valle del Tevere." *Antropologia* 4 (1): 155–77.

Álvarez, David. 2013. "Recording Daily Life in the Margins of History and the Nation: Rachid Nini's *Diary of a Clandestine Migrant.*" *Baleful Postcoloniality* 36 (1): 148–78.

Alzetta, Roberto. 2004. "Un approccio culturale allo studio della migrazione marocchina in Liguria: Il caso dei Beni Meskine." In *Primo rapporto sull' immigrazione a Genova,* edited by Maurizio Ambrosini, Deborah Erminio, and Andrea Ravecca, 233–61. Genoa: Fratelli Frilli Editori.

Amine, Khalid, and Marvin Carlson. 2012. *The Theatres of Morocco, Algeria and Tunisia: Performance Traditions of the Maghreb.* New York: Palgrave Macmillan.

Anderson, Lisa. 1986. *The State and Social Transformation in Tunisia and Libia, 1830–1980.* Princeton, NJ: Princeton University Press.

Ankouz, Mohamed, and Mohamed El Aïchouni. 1999. "La forêt: Un patrimoine, une loi et un régime." In *Le grand livre de la forêt marocaine,* edited by Philippe Blerot and Omar Mhirit, 31–37. Sprimont, Belgium: Mardaga.

ANPAL (Agenzia Nazionale Politiche Attive Lavoro). 2019. *La comunitá marocchina in Italia. Rapporto annuale sulla presenza dei migranti*. Rome: ANPAL. https://www.lavoro.gov.it/documenti-e-norme/studi-e-statistiche/Documents/Rapporti%20 annuali%20sulle%20comunità%20omigranti%20in%20Italia%20-%20anno%20 2019/Marocco-rapporto-2019.pdf.

Antonelli, Fulvia. 2010. "Le due età dell'emigrazione." *Mondi migranti* 3: 85–97.

Asad, Talal. 2009. "The Idea of an Anthropology of Islam." *Qui parle* 17 (2): 1–30.

Atouf, Elkbir. 2014. *Aux origines anticipatrices des migrations marocaines vers l'Algérie coloniale et la France colonisatrice (1830–1942)*. Agadir, Morocco: Faculté des Lettres et des Sciences Humaines, Université Ibn Zohr.

Aubin, Eugène. 1906. *Morocco of Today*. London: J. M. Dent.

Auclair, Laurent, Benoît Hoarau, and Abdelhadi Ewague. 2015. "Les chasseurs du Sahara atlantique ont-ils inventé la métallurgie? Les haches 'à tranchant en éventail' dans l'art rupestre du sud marocain." *L'anthropologie* 119 (1): 72–88.

Ayache, Germain. 1979. *Études d'histoire marocaine*. Rabat: Société marocaine des éditeurs réunis.

Aydoun, Ahmed. 2014. *Musiques du Maroc*. 2nd ed. Casablanca: La Croisée des Chemins.

Awad, Hassan. 1964. "Morocco's Expanding Towns." *Geographical Journal* 130 (1): 49–64.

Bachis, Francesco. 2009. "Il posto dei Marocchini: Confini simbolici e conflitto in un piccolo paese del centro Sardegna." *Lares* 75 (3): 551–74.

Badimon, Monserrat Emperador, and Koenraad Bogaert. 2014. "'The State Owes Us a Future': The Framing of 'Exclusion' by the Protest Movements of the Unemployed in Morocco." In *From Silence to Protest: International Perspectives on Weakly Resourced Groups*, edited by Didier Chabanet and Frédéric Royall, 175–92. Burlington, VT: Ashgate.

Bahrawi, Hasan. 2002. *Fann al-'aiṭa bi-al-Maghrib: Musahama fi al-Ta'rif*. Rabat, Morocco: Ittiḥad Kitab al-Maghrib.

Bakhtin, Mikhail. 1981. *The Dialogic Imagination: Four Essays*. Edited by Michael Holquist. Austin: University of Texas Press.

Battaglia, Salvatore. 2002. *Grande dizionario della lingua italiana*. Turin: UTET.

Baris, Tommaso. 2003. *Tra due fuochi: Esperienza e memoria della guerra lungo la linea Gustav*. Rome: Laterza.

Baroudi, Abdallah. 1989. *Maroc: Impérialisme et émigration*. Rotterdam: Editions Hiwar.

Barthes, Roland. 1978. *Image, Music, Text*. New York: Hill & Wang.

Basso, Keith. 1996. *Wisdom Sits in Place: Landscape and Language among the Western Apache*. Albuquerque: University of New Mexico.

Bauman, Richard, and Charles Briggs. 2003. *Voices of Modernity: Language Ideologies and the Politics of Inequality*. Cambridge: Cambridge University Press.

Ben Jelloun, Tahar. 2006. *Partir*. Paris: Gallimard.

Bentahar, Mekki. 1988. *Villes et campagnes au Maroc: Les problèmes sociaux de l'urbanisation*. Rabat, Morocco: Editell B. P. 97-R. P.

Ben-Yehoyada, Naor. 2017. *The Mediterranean Incarnate: Region Formation between Sicily and Tunisia since World War II*. Chicago: University of Chicago Press.

Berriane, Mohamed. 1989. "Holiday Migration of Moroccan Nationals." *Tourism Recreation Research* 14 (2): 23–26.

———, Hein de Haas, and Katharina Natter. 2015. "Introduction: Revisiting Moroccan Migrations." *Journal of North African Studies* 20 (4): 503–21.

Bertolani, Barbara. 2013. "The Sikhs in Italy: A Growing Heterogeneous and Plural Presence." In *Testing Pluralism: Globalizing Belief, Localizing Gods*, edited by Giuseppe Giordan and William H. Swatos, 75–93. Leiden: Brill.

Bianco, Luisa. 2015. *Emigrare dal Marocco: Squilibri socio-ambientali ed esodo da un polo minerario (Khouribga), 1921–2013*. Soveria Mannelli, Italy: Rubbettino.

Binebine, Mahi. [1999] 2012. *Welcome to Paradise*. Translated by Lulu Norman. Portland, OR: Tin House Books.

Blake, David. 2019. "Timbre." In *The Oxford Handbook of Critical Concepts in Music Theory*, edited by Alexander Rehding and Steven Rings, 136–59. Oxford and New York: Oxford University Press.

Bleuchot, Hervé. 1969. "Une ville minière marocaine: Khouribga." *Revue de l'Occident musulman et de la Méditerranée* 6: 29–51.

Blum, Stephen. 2015. "Afterword." In *Musical Exodus: Al-Andalus and Its Jewish Diasporas*, edited by Ruth Davis, 199–206. Lanham, MD: Rowman & Littlefield.

Bonsal, Stephen. 1893. *Morocco As It Is: With an Account of Sir Charles Euan Smith's Recent Mission to Fez*. London: W. H. Allen.

Boukous, Ahmed. 1995. *Société, langues et cultures au Maroc: Enjeux symboliques*. Rabat, Morocco: Publications de la Faculté des Lettres et des Sciences Humaines.

Bouderbala, Najib, Mohamed Chraïbi, and Paul Pascon. 1974. *La question agraire au Maroc*. Rabat: Société marocaines des éditeurs réunis.

Boussouf, Abdellah. 2019. "Le sentiment d'appartenance profond au Maroc est renforcé." *La vie éco*, 26 July, 90–91.

Bracalente, Bruno. 1989. "L'Umbria nel modello di industrializzazione diffusa." In Covino and Gallo, *L'Umbria*, 451–94.

Brăiloiu, Constantin. 1984. *Problems of Ethnomusicology*. Edited and translated by A. L. Lloyd. Cambridge and New York: Cambridge University Press.

Brera, Paolo. 2020. "Il nostro volo charter dal Marocco a Pescara per salvare i raccolti." *La Repubblica*, 21 May. https://www.repubblica.it/cronaca/2020/05/21/news /il_nostro_volo_charter_dal_marocco_a_pescara_per_salvare_i_raccolti _-301031007/.

Brett, Michael. 1995. "The Way of the Nomad." *Bulletin of the School of Oriental and African Studies* 58 (2): 251–69.

———. 1999. *Ibn Khaldun and the Medieval Maghrib*. Brookfield, VT: Ashgate.

Brunot, Louis. 1920. *La mer dans les traditions et les industries indigènes à Rabat & Salé*. Paris: Éditions Ernest Leroux.

———. 2013. *Au seuil de la vie marocaine*. Rabat: Centre Jacques-Berque. doi:10.4000/ books.cjb.406.

Bū Salām, Muḥammad ibn al-Bashīr. 1991. *Tārīkh qabīlat Banī Mallāl, 1854–1916: Jawānib min tārīkh Dayr al-Aṭlas al-Mutawassiṭ wa-minṭiqat Tādlā*. Rabat: Maṭbaʿat al-Maʿārif al-Jadīdah.

Buhmid, Muhammad. 1995. "Innahum Yuridun al-ʿAita ka-Dajij li-Jamiʾ al Hushud." *al-Ittihad al-Ishtiraki*, 15 April, 6.

Burke, Edmund III. 1976. *Prelude to Protectorate in Morocco: Precolonial Protest and Resistance, 1860–1912*. Chicago: University of Chicago Press.

———. 2014. *The Ethnographic State: France and the Invention of Moroccan Islam*. Oakland: University of California Press.

Calderwood, Eric. 2018. *Colonial al-Andalus: Spain and the Making of Modern Moroccan Culture*. Cambridge, MA: Belknap Press.

Callen, Jeffrey. 2006. "French Fries in the Tagine: Re-imagining Moroccan Popular Music." PhD diss., University of California, Los Angeles.

Campani, Giovanna. 2008. *Dalle minoranze agli immigrati: La questione del pluralismo culturale e religioso in Italia*. Milan: Unicopli.

Canova, Giovanni. 2010–11. "Cavalli e cavallieri nella poesia araba antica." *Quaderni di Studi Arabi* 5–6: 235–52.

Canetti, Elias. 1978. *The Voices of Marrakesh: A Record of a Visit*. Translated by J. A. Underwood. London: M. Boyars.

Capello, Carlo. 2008. *Le prigioni invisibili: Etnografia multisitata della migrazione marocchina*. Milan: FrancoAngeli.

Capitani, Loredana, Lucia Piras, and Vanda Scarpelli. 1983. *". . . È una storia lunga . . .": Lotte e coscienza delle tabacchine umbre negli anni '50*. Perugia: Grafica Salvi.

Caruso, Fulvia. 2019. "Faire de la musique ensemble: un programme de recherche-action avec des migrants à Crémone (Italie)." *Cahiers d'ethnomusicologie* 32: 161–78.

Caton, Steven. 1990. *"Peaks of Yemen I Summon": Poetry as Cultural Practice in a North Yemeni Tribe*. Berkeley and Los Angeles: University of California Press.

Cattedra, Raffaele. 2017. "Bidonville: Paradigme et réalité refoulée de la ville du xxᵉ siècle." In *Les mots de la stigmatisation urbaine*, edited by Jean-Charles Depaule. https://books.openedition.org/editionsmsh/9204.

Chakrabarty, Dipesh. 2000. *Provincializing Europe: Postcolonial Thought and Historical Difference*. Princeton, NJ: Princeton University Press.

Chambers, Iain. 2008. *Mediterranean Crossings: The Politics of an Interrupted Modernity*. Durham, NC: Duke University Press.

Ech-Charfi, Ahmed, and Lamyae Azzouzi. 2017. "Ethnic Stereotypes and Lexical Semantics: The Emergence of the Rural/Urban Opposition in Moroccan Arabic." In *Sociolinguistics in African Contexts: Perspectives and Challenges*, edited by Augustin Emmanuel Ebongue and Ellen Hurst, 147–70. Cham, Switzerland: Springer International.

Chávez, Alex. 2017. *Sounds of Crossings: Music, Migration, and the Aural Poetics of Huapango Arribeño*. Durham, NC: Duke University Press.

Cherkaoui, Driss. 2004. "The Story of the Human Being, the Woodcutter: The Anatomy of a Traditional Moroccan Oral Tale." *Journal of North African Studies* 9 (1): 78–103.

Chottin, Alexis. 1931. "'Les visages' de la musique marocaine." *Le Ménestrel* 93 (20): 217–19; (21): 230–31.

———.1939. *Tableau de la musique marocaine*. Paris: Paul Geuthner.

Chraïbi, Driss. 1956. *L'âne*. Paris: Denoël.

Chuse, Loren. 2003. *The Cantaoras: Music, Gender, and Identity in Flamenco Song*. New York: Routledge.

Ciotti, Emiliano. 2018. *"Le Marocchinate:" Cronaca di uno stupro di massa*. Tricase, Italy: Youcanprint.

Ciucci, Alessandra. 2005. "Les musiciennes professionnelles au Maroc." *Cahiers de musiques traditionnelles* 18: 183–200.

———. 2008. "Poems of Honor, Voices of Shame: The 'Aiṭa and the Moroccan Shikhat." PhD diss., Graduate Center of the City University of New York.

———. 2010. "De-orientalizing the 'Aita and Re-orienting the Shikhat." In *French Orientalism: Culture, Politics, and the Imagined Other*, edited by Desmond Hosford and Chong J. Wojtkowski, 71–96. Newcastle upon Tyne: Cambridge Scholars Press.

————. 2012a. "'The Text Must Remain the Same': History, Collective Memory and Sung Poetry in Morocco." *Ethnomusicology: The Journal of the Society for Ethnomusicology* 56 (3): 476–504.

————. 2012b. "Embodying the Countryside in 'Aita Hasbawiya (Morocco)." *Yearbook for Traditional Music* 44: 144–60.

————. 2017. "Performing 'L-'alwa': A Sacred and Erotic Journey in Morocco." *Ethnomusicology Forum* 26 (2): 151–70.

Cohen, Jeffrey. 2004. *The Culture of Migration in Southern Mexico*. Austin: University of Texas Press.

Colin, Georges. 1999. *Arabe marocain: Inédits de Georges S. Colin; Bicentenaire de l'Inalco, 1975–1995*, edited by Dominique Caubet and Zakia Iraqui-Sinaceur. Aix-en-Provence: Edisud.

Colucci, Michele. 2018. "Per una storia del governo dell'immigrazione straniera in Italia: Dagli anni sessanta alla crisi delle politiche." *Meridiana* 91: 9–36.

Combs-Schilling, M. E. 1989. *Sacred Performances: Islam, Sexuality, and Sacrifice*. New York: Columbia University Press.

Coplan, David. 1994. *In the Time of Cannibals: The Word Music of South Africa's Basotho Migrants*. Chicago: University of Chicago Press.

Corosacz, Valeria Ribeiro. 2008. "Da 'marruchen a marocchino': Il razzismo descritto da operai meridionali e stranieri a Modena." *Studi culturali* 5 (1): 51–74.

Cosentino, Alessandro. 2019. *Esengo: Pratiche musicali liturgiche nella chiesa congolese di Roma*. Rome: Neoclassica.

Costantino, Celeste. 2010. "A caccia di 'neri': Così si divertono i giovani di Rosarno." *Il Manifesto*, 9 January 9.

Covino, Renato, and Giampaolo Gallo, eds. 1989. *L'Umbria*. Turin: Giulio Einaudi Editore.

Crapanzano, Vincent. 2004. *Imaginative Horizons: An Essay in Literary-Philosophical Anthropology*. Chicago: University of Chicago Press.

Cruzzolin, Riccardo. 1997. "L'indagine sociologica." In Duca and Cruzzolin, *Sistema agro-alimentare e lavoro immigrato*, 128–61.

Cutuli, Maria Grazia. 1992. "Marocco-Italia: Sulle orme degli immigrati clandestini." *Epoca*, 4 November, 132–40.

Dakhlia, Jocelyne. 1988. "Dans la mouvance du prince: La symbolique du pouvoir itinérant au Maghreb." *Annales: Histoire, sciences sociales* 43 (3): 735–60.

D'Amico, Leonardo, ed. 2005. *Musica dei popoli: Un viaggio nella musica tradizionale del mondo*. Rome: Castelvecchi Editore.

d'Erlanger, Rodolphe. 1930–59. *La musique arabe*. 6 vols. Paris: Paul Geuthner.

Dal Lago, Alessandro. 1999. *Non-persone: L'esclusione dei migranti in una società globale*. Milano: Feltrinelli.

Danielson, Virginia. 1988. "The Arab Middle East." In *Popular Musics of the Non-Western World: An Introductory Survey*, by Peter Manuel, 141–60. Oxford and New York: Oxford University Press.

————. 1997. *The Voice of Egypt: Umm Kulthūm, Arabic Song, and Egyptian Society in the Twentieth Century*. Chicago: University of Chicago Press.

Daoud, Zakya, and Inea Engler. 1981. "Agrarian Capitalism and the Moroccan Crisis." *MERIP Reports* 99: 27–33.

Dari, Layla. 2017. "Orchestre multietniche e confronti interculturale nell'Europa Meridionale: Possibili processi di integrazione, ibridazione musicale e cittadinanza in Italia e Portogallo." PhD diss., Università degli Studi di Firenze.

Dave, Nomi. 2019. *The Revolution's Echoes: Music, Politics, and Pleasure in Guinea.* Chicago: University of Chicago Press.

Davila, Carl. 2013. *The Andalusian Music of Morocco: Al-Āla; History, Society and Text.* Wiesbaden: Reichert Verlag.

———. 2015. "The Andalusi Turn: The *Nūba* in Mediterranean History." *Mediterranean Studies* 23 (2): 149–69.

Davis, Diana K. 2007. *Resurrecting the Granary of Rome: Environmental History and French Colonial Expansion in North Africa.* Athens: Ohio University Press.

———, and Edmund Burke III, eds. 2011. *Environmental Imaginaries of the Middle East and North Africa.* Athens: Ohio University Press.

De Genova, Nicholas, ed. 2017. *The Borders of "Europe": Autonomy of Migration Tactics Of Bordering.* Durham, NC: Duke University Press.

de Haas, Hein. 2014. "Morocco: Setting the Stage for Becoming a Migration Transition Country?" *Migration Information Source*, 19 March. https://www.migrationpolicy .org/article/morocco-setting-stage-becoming-migration-transition-country.

de Prémare, Alfred-Louis, ed. 1993. *Dictionnaire arabe-français: Établi sur la base de fichiers, ouvrages, enquêtes, manuscrits, études et documents divers.* 12 vols. Paris: L'Harmattan.

De Sica, Vittorio. [1960] 2012. *La ciociara.* Milan: RCS MediaGroup. DVD, 110 min.

Del Prete, Rossella, ed. 2012. *Dentro e fuori la fabbrica: Il tabacco in Italia tra memoria e prospettiva.* Milan: FrancoAngeli.

Dent, Alexander. 2009. *River of Tears: Country Music, Memory, and Modernity in Brazil.* Durham, NC: Duke University Press.

Devitt, Camilla. 2013. "Circular Economic Migration between Italy and Morocco." In *Circular Migration between Europe and Its Neighbourhood: Choice or Necessity?*, edited by Anna Triandafyllidou. Oxford and New York: Oxford University Press. https://oxford.universitypressscholarship.com/view/10.1093/acprof:oso/978019 9674510.001.0001/acprof-9780199674510-chapter-5.

Di Cesare, Donatella. 2017. *Stranieri residenti: Una filosofia della migrazione.* Turin: Bollati Boringhieri.

———. 2018. *Marrani: L'altro dell'altro.* Turin: Giulio Einaudi Editore.

Di Giacomo, Carla, and Ginevra Demaio. 2019. "Pensioni, prestazioni assistenziali e ammortizzatori sociali erogati agli immigrati: Analisi dagli archive dell'Inps." In *Dossier Statistico Immigrazione 2019*, 275–79. Rome: IDOS.

Di Sciullo, Luca. 2019. "Tre modelli per una lettura trasversale dei territori." In *Dossier statistico immigrazione 2019*, 329–31. Rome: IDOS.

Dialmy, Abdessamad. 2008. "La masculinité au Maroc entre traditions, modernité et intégrisme." In *Masculinities in Contemporary Africa*, edited by Egodi Uchendu, 73–87. Dakar: Council for the Development of Social Science Research in Africa.

Duca, Luca. 1997. "Lavoro immigrato e agricoltura." In Duca and Cruzzolin, *Sistema agro-alimentare e lavoro immigrato*, 85–127

Duca, Luca, and Riccardo Cruzzolin, eds. 1997. *Sistema agro-alimentare e lavoro immigrato: Un'indagine in terra di lavoro e nell'Alta Valle del Tevere.* Perugia: CIDIS.

Duchac, René. 1970. "Propositions pour une recherche sur le développement de Khouribga." *Revue de l'Occident musulman et de la Méditerranée* 7: 49–69.

Eickelman, Dale F. 1976. *Moroccan Islam: Tradition and Society in a Pilgrimage Center.* Austin: University of Texas Press.

Eickelman, Dale F., and James Piscatori, eds. 1990. *Muslim Travellers: Pilgrimage, Migration, and the Religious Imagination*. London: Routledge.

Eisenstein, Herbert. 2014. "Animals." In *Encyclopaedia of Islam Three*, edited by Kate Fleet, Gudrum Krämer, Denis Matringe, John Nawas, Everett Rowson. Leiden: Brill. https://referenceworks.brillonline.com/entries/encyclopaedia-of-islam-3/animals-COM_24225?s.num=418&s.start=400.

Elalamy, Youssouf Amine. 2000. *Les clandestins*. Casablanca: Eddif.

Elliot, Alice. 2016. "Paused Subjects: Waiting for Migration in North Africa." *Time & Society* 25 (2): 102–16.

———. 2021. *The Outside: Migration as Life in Morocco*. Bloomington: Indiana University Press.

Essafi, Ali. 2006. *Dumūʿ al-Shaykhāt/Le blues des Shikhates*. Seattle: Arab Film Distribution. DVD. 52 min.

Escolar, Marisa. 2019. *Allied Encounters: The Gendered Redemption of World War II Italy*. New York: Fordham University Press.

Ewing, Katherine Pratt. 2008. *Stolen Honor: Stigmatizing Muslim Men in Berlin*. Stanford, CA: Stanford University Press.

Facci, Serena. 2017. "La gioia nel cantare, la bellezza nel pregare: Canto e liturgia nelle chiese di rito orientale a Roma." In *Musica ed esperienza religiosa: Un'ipotesi di ricerca tra musicologia e pedagogia*, edited by Mauro Casadei Turroni Monti and Cesarino Ruini, 72–86. Rome: Franco Angeli.

El Fad, Hassan. 2018. "Kabur yʿaud ila al-badiya." *Assabah*, 2 May.

Fāḍil, Yūsuf. 2000. *Ḥashīsh: riwāyah*. Al-Dār al-Bayḍā, Morocco: Nashr al-Fanak.

Fales, Cornelia. 2002. "The Paradox of Timbre." *Ethnomusicology* 46 (1): 56–95.

Faloppa, Federico. 2011. *Razzisti a parole (per tacere dei fatti)*. Rome: Laterza.

Fanon, Frantz. 1963. *The Wretched of the Earth*. New York: Grove Press.

Al-Fārābī, 1934. *Al-Fārābī's Arabic-Latin Writings on music in the Iḥṣā' al'ulūm*. Translated and with commentary by Henry George Farmer. Glasgow: Civic Press.

Feld, Steven. 1984. "Communication, Music, and Speech about Music." *Yearbook for Traditional Music* 16 (1): 1–18.

———. 1996. "Waterfall of Song: An Acoustemology of Place Resounding in Bosavi, Papua New Guinea." In Feld and Basso, *Senses of Place*, 91–136.

Feld, Steven, and Keith H. Basso, eds. 1996. *Senses of Place*. Santa Fe, NM: School of American Research Press.

Fellezs, Kevin. 2019. *Listen but Don't Ask Question: Hawaiian Slack Guitar across the Transpacific*. Durham, NC: Duke University Press.

Flesler, Daniela. 2008. *The Return of the Moor: Spanish Responses to Contemporary Moroccan Immigration*. West Lafayette, IN: Purdue University Press.

Fox, Aaron. 2004. *Real Country: Music and Language in Working-Class Culture*. Durham, NC: Duke University Press.

Gaffuri, Luigi. 2019. "Le politiche di ingresso e i visti rilasciati nel 2018." In *Dossier statistico immigrazione 2019*, 126–29. Rome: IDOS.

Genini, Izza. 1987. *Morocco, Body and Soul*. 11 vols. New York: Icarus Films. DVD.

Gershovich, Moshe. 2016. "Memory and Representation of War and Violence: Moroccan Combatants in French Uniforms during the Second World War." In *Colonial Soldiers in Europe, 1914–1945*, edited by Eric Storm and Ali Al Tuma, 77–96. New York: Routledge.

Geertz, Clifford. 1987. "*Toutes Directions*: Reading the Signs in an Urban Sprawl." *International Journal of Middle East Studies* 21 (3): 291–306.

Giacalone, Fiorella. 2003. "Vivere da Marocchini in Umbria." *Risonanze: Luoghi, movimenti, culture in prima persona* 5. http://www.leolink.it/risonanze2000 /pag%2014n5.htm.

Giacchè, Luciano. 1989. "L'Umbria in posa." In Covino and Gallo, *L'Umbria*, 495–504.

Gilman, Sander L. 1985. *Difference and Pathology: Stereotypes of Sexuality, Race, and Madness*. Ithaca, NY: Cornell University Press.

Glasser, Jonathan. 2016. *The Lost Paradise: Andalusi Music in Urban North Africa*. Chicago: University of Chicago Press.

Grasselli, Pierluigi, Francesco Musotti, and Tommaso Sediari, eds. 2006. *L'industrializzazione leggera dell'Alto Tevere: Territorio e trasformazioni economiche*. Città di Castello: Petruzzi Editore.

Greene, Paul D. 2005. "Introduction." In *Wired for Sound: Engineering and Technologies in Sonic Cultures*, edited by Paul D. Greene and Thomas Porcello. Middletown, CT: Wesleyan University Press.

Gribaudi, Gabriella. 2005. *Guerra totale: Tra bombe alleate e violenze naziste; Napoli e il fronte meridionale, 1940–44*. Turin: Bollati Boringhieri.

Hachimi, Atiqa. 2012. "The Urban and the Urbane: Identities, Language Ideologies, and Arab Dialects in Morocco." *Language in Society* 41 (3): 321–41.

Hammoudi, Abdellah. 1997. *Master and Disciple: The Cultural Foundations of Moroccan Authoritarianism*. Chicago: University of Chicago Press.

Hannoum, Abdelmajid. 2003. "Translation and the Colonial Imaginary: Ibn Khaldûn Orientalist." *History and Theory* 42: 61–81.

Harrami, Noureddine, and Mohamed Mahdi. 2006. "Mobilité internationale et dynamique de changement dans les sociétés de départ: À propos de la migration des 'Fkih Ben Salah' (Maroc) en Italie." In *Mediterraneo e migrazioni oggi. In memoria di Ottavia Schmidt di Friedberg*, edited by Emanuela Trevisan Semi, 35–50. Venice: Il Ponte.

Hanks, William F. 2000. *Intertexts: Writings on Language, Utterance, and Context*. New York: Rowman & Littlefield.

Harvey, David. 1973. *Social Justice and the City*. London: Edward Arnold.

Hassan, Scheherazade Qassim, and Philippe Vigreux, eds. 1992. *Musique arabe: Le congrès du Caire de 1932*. Cairo: CEDEJ.

Heath, Jeffrey. 2002. *Jewish and Muslim Dialects of Moroccan Arabic*. New York: Routledge.

Herzfeld, Michael. 1985. *The Poetics of Manhood: Contest and Identity in a Cretan Mountain Village*. Princeton, NJ: Princeton University Press.

Hinda, Abdeladim. 2016. "Tayeb Saddiki: Bridging the Colonial and Post-Colonial in Moroccan Theatre." *Arab Journal of Performance Studies* 2: 50–61.

Hirschkind, Charles. 2006. *The Ethical Soundscape: Cassette Sermons and Islamic Counterpublics*. New York: Columbia University Press.

Hoffman, Katherine H. 2008. *We Share Walls: Language, Land, and Gender in Berber Morocco*. Malden, MA: Blackwell.

Holst-Warhaft, Gail. 1983. *Road to Rembetika: Music of a Greek Sub-Culture; Songs of Love, Sorrow and Hashish*. Athens: Denise Harvey.

HuffPost Maroc. 2014. "Tu sais que tu es aroubi quand. . . ." 14 December.

Ibn Khaldun. 1958. *The Muqaddimah: An Introduction to History*. 3 vols. Translated by Franz Rosenthal. London: Routledge & Kegan Paul.

IDOS (Centro Studi e Ricerche). 2013. *La comunità marocchina in Italia: Un ponte sul Mediterraneo.* Rome: IDOS.

———. 2019. *Dossier statistico immigrazione.* Rome: IDOS.

Inhorn, Marcia, and Konstantina Isidoros. 2018. "Introduction." *Men and Masculinities* 21 (3): 219–27.

Al-Jabri, Mohamed Abed. 1999. *Arab-Islamic Philosophy: A Contemporary Critique.* Translated by Aziz Abbassi. Austin: University of Texas Press.

Jacobs, Jennifer. 2007. "'Unintelligibles' in Vocal Performances at Middle Eastern Marriage Celebrations." *Text & Talk* 27 (4): 483–507.

Jacquement, Marco. 1996. "From the Atlas to the Alps: Chronicle of a Moroccan Migration." *Public Culture* 8: 377–88.

Jansen, M. Angela. 2016. "Defining Moroccanness: The Aesthetics and Politics of Contemporary Moroccan Fashion." *Journal of North African Studies* 21 (1): 132–47.

Juntunen, Marko. 2015. "Jeunes hommes des classes populaires à Larache: Affirmer sa virilité et se construire un avenir dans une communauté frontalière marocaine." *Ateliers d'anthropologie* 42. https://journals.openedition.org/ateliers/9996.

Kapchan, Deborah. 1996. *Gender on the Market: Moroccan Women and the Revoicing of Tradition.* Philadelphia: University of Pennsylvania Press.

———. 2003. "Nashaṭ: The Gender of Musical Celebration in Morococco." In Magrini, *Music and Gender,* 251–64.

Karl, Brian. 2012. "Across a Divide: Mediations of Contemporary Popular Music in Morocco and Spain." PhD diss., Columbia University.

Al-Kātib, al-Ḥasan Ibn Aḥmad Ali. 1972. *La perfection des connaissances musicales.* Translated by Amnon Shiloah. Paris: Paul Geuthner.

Khalid Masud, Muhammad. 1990. "The Obligation to Migrate: The Doctrine of *Hijra* in Islamic Law." In Eickelman and Piscatori, *Muslim Travellers,* 29–49.

Kharoufi, Mostafa. 1983. "Sociétés pastorales en crise au Maroc: Le cas des 'moutonniers' Béni Meskine d'El Borouj après la sécheresse." *Méditerranée* 49 (3): 69–77.

———. 2004. "Effets de l'émigration vers l'Italie des Beni Meskine (Maroc occidental)." In *Maghreb, dimensions de la complexité: Études choisies de l'IRMC (1992–2003),* edited by Anne-Marie Planel. Tunis: Institut de recherche sur le Maghreb contemporain. https://books.openedition.org/irmc/1589?lang=en.

Khatibi, Abdelkebir. 2019. *Plural Maghreb: Writings on Postcolonialism.* London: Bloomsbury Academic.

Kosansky, Oren. 2016. "When Jews Speak Arabic: Dialectology and Difference in Colonial Morocco." *Comparative Studies in Society and History* 58 (1): 5–39.

Kuipers, Joel. 1999. "Ululations from the Weyewa Highlands (Sumba): Simultaneity, Audience Response, and Models of Cooperation." *Ethnomusicology* 43 (3): 490–507.

Laabi, Abdellatif. 1967. "Le gâchis." *Souffles* 7–8: 1–14.

Lalami, Leila. 2005. *Hope and Other Dangerous Pursuits.* Orlando, FL: Harvest Books, Harcourt.

Larkin, Brian. 2008. *Signal and Noise: Media, Infrastructure, and Urban Culture in Nigeria.* Durham, NC: Duke University Press.

Laroui, Abdellah. 1977. *The History of the Maghrib: An Interpretative Essay.* Princeton, NJ: Princeton University Press.

Le Chatelier, Alfred. 1902. *Notes sur les villes et tribus du Maroc en 1890.* 2 vols. Angers: Imprimerie A. Burdin.

Légey, Françoise. 1926. *Contes & légendes populaires du Maroc: Recueillis à Marrakech.* Paris: E. Leroux.

Levin, Theodore, and Valentina Süzükei. 2018. "Timbre-Centered Listening in the Soundscape of Tuva." In *The Oxford Handbook of Timbre,* edited by Alexander Rehding and Emily I. Dolan. Oxford and New York: Oxford University Press. https://www.oxfordhandbooks.com/view/10.1093/oxfordhb/9780190637224 .001.0001/oxfordhb-9780190637224-e-15.

Loti, Pierre. 1890. *Into Morocco.* Translated by E. P. Robins. New York: Welch, Fracker.

Mahdi, Mohamed. 2014. "Devenir du foncier agricole au Maroc: Un cas d'accaparement des terres." *New Medit* 13 (4): 2–10.

Mack, Mehammed Amadeus. 2017. *Sexagon: Muslims, France, and the Sexualization of National Culture.* New York: Fordham University Press.

MacMaster, Neil. 2020. *War in the Mountains: Peasant Society and Counterinsurgency in Algeria, 1918–1958.* Oxford and New York: Oxford University Press.

Maghraoui, Driss, ed. 2013. *Revisiting the Colonial Past in Morocco.* New York: Routledge.

———. 2014. "The *goumiers* in the Second World War: History and Colonial Representation." *Journal of North African Studies* 19 (4): 571–86.

Magrini, Romano. 2019. "I lavoratori stranieri nel settore agricolo." In *Dossier Statistico Immigrazione 2019,* 283–88. Rome: IDOS.

Magrini, Tullia, ed. 2003. *Music and Gender: Perspectives from the Mediterranean.* Chicago: University of Chicago Press.

Makaremi, Chowra. 2011. "The Waiting Zone." In *Memory and Migration: Multidisciplinary Approaches to Memory Studies,* edited by Julia Creet and Andreas Kitzman, 68–92. Toronto: University of Toronto Press.

Mansouri, Driss. 2014. "Au prisme d'Ibn Khaldūn: Nation et communauté au Maroc." In *Pratiquer les sciences sociales au Maghreb: Textes pour Driss Mansouri avec un choix de ses articles,* edited by Mohamed Almoubaker and François Pouillon, 452–72. Casablanca: Centre Jacques-Berque.

Maraini, Toni. 2017. "Qualche precisazione a proposito dei *Goumiers.*" *Poliscritture: Laboratorio di cultura critica,* 28 July. http://www.poliscritture.it/2017/07/28/la -memoria-dei-goumiers/.

Massad, Joseph. 2007. *Desiring Arabs.* Chicago: University of Chicago Press.

Matar, Nabil. 2019. "The 'Mediterranean' through Arab Eyes in the Early Modern Period: From Rūmī to 'White In-Between Sea.'" In *The Making of the Modern Mediterranean: Views from the South,* edited by Judith Tucker, 16–35. Oakland: University of California Press.

Mazzīn, Muḥammad. 1986. *Fās wa-bādiyatuhā: Musāhamah fī tārīkh al-Maghrib al-Sa'dī, 1549M–1637M.* Rabat: al-Mamlakah al-Maghribīyah, Jāmi'at Muḥammas al-Khāmis, Kullīyat al-Ādāb wa-al-'Ilium al-Insānīyah.

———.1992. *Fès médiévale: Entre légende et histoire; Un carrefour de l'Orient à l'apogée d'un rêve.* Paris: Éditions Autrement.

McMurray, David. 2001. *In and Out of Morocco: Smuggling and Migration in a Frontier Boomtown.* Minneapolis: University of Minnesota Press.

Mellino, Miguel. 2012. "De-Provincializing Italy: Notes on Race, Racialization, and Italy's Coloniality." In *Postcolonial Italy: Challenging National Homogeneity,* edited by Cristina Lombardi-Diop and Caterina Romero, 83–100. New York: Palgrave Macmillan.

Meintjes, Louise. 2017. *Dust of the Zulu: Ngoma Aesthetics after Apartheid.* Durham, NC: Duke University Press.

Menin, Laura. 2016. "'Men Do Not Get Scared! (*rjjala mā tāy-khāfūsh*)': Luck, Destiny and the Gendered Vocabularies of Clandestine Migration in Central Morocco." *Archivio antropologico mediterraneo* 18 (1): 25–36.

Mescoli, Elsa. 2014. "Towards the Elsewhere: Discourses on Migration and Mobility Practices between Morocco and Italy." *Identities: Global Studies in Power and Culture* 21 (3–4): 290–304.

Miller, Flagg. 2005. "Of Songs and Signs: Audiocassette Poetry, Moral Character, and the Culture of Circulation in Yemen." *American Ethnologist* 32 (1): 82–99.

Miller, Jeannie. 2017. "Man Is Not the Only Speaking Animal: Thresholds and Idiom in al-Jāḥiẓ." In *Arabic Humanities, Islamic Thought: Essays in Honor of Everett K. Rowson*, edited by Joseph E. Lowry and Shawkat M. Toorawa, 94–121. Boston: Brill.

Minca, Claudio. 2004. *Orizzonte mediterraneo*. Padua: CEDAM.

Mission Scientifique du Maroc. 1915–. *Villes et tribus du Maroc: Documents et renseignements; Casablanca et les Châouïa*. Paris: Ernest Leroux Éditeur.

Mitchell, Timothy. 2000. "The Stage of Modernity." In *Questions of Modernity*, edited by Timothy Mitchell, 1–34. Minneapolis: University of Minnesota Press.

Mokhiber, James. 2013. "'Le protectorat dans la peau': Prosper Ricard and the 'Native Arts' in French Colonial Morocco, 1899–1952." In Maghraoui, *Revisiting the Colonial Past in Morocco*, 257–84.

Moravia, Alberto. 1957. *La ciociara*. Milan: Bompiani.

El Moudden, Abderrahmane. 1990. "The Ambivalence of *Rihla*: Community Integration and Self-Definition in Moroccan Travel Accounts, 1300–1800." In Eickelman and Piscatori, *Muslim Travellers*, 69–84.

Moual, Karima. 2020. "I musulmani d'Italia: 'Dateci un posto per i nostri defunti.'" 31 May. https://www.repubblica.it/cronaca/2020/05/31/news/i_musulmani_d _italia_dateci_un_posto_per_i_nostri_defunti_-301068417/.

Muzi, Luca, and Lorenzo Tondo. 2019. "I migranti sfruttati per il tabacco." *Internazionale*, 7 June, 38–41.

Nabti, Mahdi. 2010. *Les Aïssawa: Soufisme, musique et rituels de transe au Maroc*. Paris: Harmattan.

Najmi, Hasan. 2007. *Ghina' al-'iṭa: al-Sh'ir al-Shafawi wa-l-Musiqa al-Taqlidiyah fī al-Maghrib*. 2 vols. Casablanca: Dar Tubqal li-l-Nashr.

Nassiry, El Habib. 2013. *'Abidat r-Rma*. Khouribga: Imprimerie Beni Snassen.

Nelson, Kristina. 1985. *The Art of Reciting the Qur'an*. Austin: University of Texas Press.

Nieuwkerk, Karin van. 2019. *Manhood Is not Easy: Egyptian Masculinities through the Life of Sayyid Henkish*. Cairo: American University Press.

Ochoa Gautier, Ana María. 2014. *Aurality: Listening and Knowledge in Nineteenth-Century Colombia*. Durham, NC: Duke University Press.

Olwage, Grant. 2006. "The Class and Colour of Tone: An Essay on the Social History of Vocal Timbre." *Ethnomusicology Forum* 13 (2): 203–26.

Ossman, Susan. 1994. *Picturing Casablanca: Portraits of Power in a Modern City*. Berkeley and Los Angeles: University of California Press.

Ouachene, Nadia. 2020. "L'animal, figure fascinante du conte: Quelle symbolique pour quelle culture?" *Faits de langue et société* 6: 92–105.

Pandolfo, Stefania. 2007. "'The Burning': Finitude and the Politico-Theological Imagination of Illegal Migration." *Anthropological Theory* 7 (3): 329–63.

———. 2018. *Knot of the Soul: Madness, Psychoanalysis, Islam*. Chicago: University of Chicago Press.

Papandreu, Dimitri. 2005. "Peasant Culture and Modernization in Twentieth Century Umbria." PhD diss., University of California, Santa Cruz.

Parla, Ayşe. 2020. "Revisiting 'Honor' through Migrant Vulnerabilities in Turkey." *History and Anthropology* 31 (1): 84–104.

Pasler, Jann. 2012–13. "Musical Hybridity in Flux: Representing Race, Colonial Policy, and Modernity in French North Africa, 1860s–1930s." *Afrika Zamani* 20–21: 21–68.

———. 2015. "The Racial and Colonial Implications of Music Ethnographies in the French Empire, 1860s–1930s." In *Critical Music Historiography: Probing Canons, Ideologies, and Institutions*, edited by Vesa Kurkela and Markus Mantere, 17–44. New York: Routledge.

Persichetti, Alessandra. 2003a. *Tra Marocco e Italia: Solidarietà agnatica ed emigrazione*. Rome: CISU.

———. 2003b. "Emigrazione, Islam, e onore: I Marocchini di Ben Ahmed in Italia." In *Un' immigrazione normale*, edited by Giuseppe Sciortino and Asher Colombo, 223–52. Bologna: Il Mulino.

———. 2004. "La parenté 'Rahim.'" *L'Homme* 169: 89–126.

Plastino, Goffredo, ed. 2013. *Mediterranean Mosaic: Popular Music and Global Sounds*. New York: Routledge.

Porcello, Thomas, Louise Meintjes, Ana María Ochoa Gautier, and David W. Samuels. 2010. "The Reorganization of the Sensory World." *Annual Review of Anthropology* 39: 51–66.

Portelli, Alessandro. 2014. *Memorie urbane: Musiche migranti in Italia*. Rome: Guaraldi.

Puig, Nicolas. 2006. "Sha'abî, 'populaire': Usages et significations d'une notion ambiguë dans le monde de la musique en Égypte." *Civilisations* 53 (1/2): 23–44.

Rabinow, Paul. 1995. *French Modern: Norms and Forms of the Social Environment*. Chicago: University of Chicago Press.

Rachik, Abderrahmane. 1995. *Ville et pouvoirs au Maroc*. Casablanca: Afrique Orient.

Rachik, Hassan. 2003. *Symboliser la nation: Essai sur l'usage des identités collectives au Maroc*. Casablanca: Le Fennec.

———. 2016a. "Les 'Marocains': Construction d'une catégorie." In *L'esprit du terrain: Études anthropologiques au Maroc*. Rabat, Morocco: Centre Jacques-Berque. https:// books.openedition.org/cjb/830.

———. 2016b. "Roumi et beldi: Réflexions sur la perception de l'Occidental à travers une dichotomie locale." In *L'esprit du terrain: Études anthropologiques au Maroc*. Rabat, Morocco: Centre Jacques-Berque. https://books.openedition.org/cjb/823.

———. 2019. *Socio-anthropologie rurale: structure, organisation et changement au Maghreb*. Casablanca: La Croisée des Chemins.

———. 2020. "Understanding Colonial Anthropology: On the Ethnographic Situation Approach." *Hespéris-Tamuda* 55 (2): 41–60.

Racy, Ali Jihad. 2003. *Making Music in the Arab World: The Culture and Artistry of Ṭarab*. Cambridge and New York: Cambridge University Press.

Rakuk, Allal. 2000a. *al-Ghina' al-Sha'bi al-Maghribi: Anmaṭ wa-Tajalliyat*. Rabat: Maktabat al-Ṭalib.

———. 2000b. "al-'Ayta: Chant du Maroc profond entre musique et histoire." *Horizons maghrébins* 43: 16–21.

————. 2001. *al-Muqawamah wa-aḥdath min al-tarikh al-ijtimaʿi fi al-adab al-shafawa al-Maghribi (1890–1956)*. Rabat: al-Mandubiyah al-Samiyah li-Qudamaʾ al-Muqawimin wa-Aʿḍaʾ Jaysh al-Taḥrir.

————. 2008. *La chanson populaire marocaine: Une géographie culturelle diversifiée*. Rabat: Rabat Net Maroc.

Reyes, Adelaida. Forthcoming. "Migration: Ethnomusicological Terra (In)cognita?" In *Music of the Twenty-First Century Diasporas: Research and Methods*, edited by Serena Facci and Giovanni Giuriati. Venice: Fondazione Luigi Cini.

Reynolds, Dwight. 2020. *The Musical Heritage of Al-Andalus*. London: Routledge.

Riccio, Antonio. 2008. *Etnografia della memoria: Storie e testimonianze del secondo conflitto mondiale nei Monti Aurunci*. Rome: Kappa.

Rosen, Lawrence. 1984. *Bargaining for Reality: The Construction of Social Relations in a Muslim Community*. Chicago: University of Chicago Press.

Rosenberg, Ruth. 2015. *Music, Travel, and Imperial Encounter in 19th-Century France: Musical Apprehensions*. New York: Routledge.

Sabelli, Sonia. 2006. "Vibrazioni da altrove: Un'inchiesta sulla musica dei migranti in Italia." In *Nuovo planetario italiano: Geografia e antologia della migrazione in Italia e in Europa*, edited by Armando Gnisci, 519–37. Turin: Città Aperta.

Sabry, Tarik. 2005. "Emigration as Popular Culture: The Case of Morocco." *European Journal of Cultural Studies* 8 (1): 5–22.

————. 2010. *Cultural Encounters in the Arab World: On Media, the Modern and the Everyday*. London: I. B. Taurus.

Saccia, Cristina. 2012. "I luoghi del tabacco in Umbria, sommersi o salvati? Il caso del Museo Storico e Scientifico del Tabacco di San Giustino." In Del Prete, *Dentro e fuori la fabbrica*, 59–82.

Sadiqi, Fatima, and Moha Ennaji. 2004. "The Impact of Male Migration from Morocco to Europe on Women: A Gender Approach." *Finisterra* 39 (77): 59–76.

Sahnoun, Chouaib. 2012. "Khouribga, la cité aux mille maux." *Libération*, 22 March. https://www.libe.ma/Khouribga-la-cite-aux-mille-maux_a26240.html.

Salih, Ruba. 2000. "Identità, modelli di consumo e costruzione di sé tra il Marocco e l'Italia. Una critica di genere alla migrazione transnazionale." *Afriche e Orienti: Rivista di studi ai confini tra africa mediterraneo e medio oriente* 3–4: 26–32.

Salzbrunn, Monika, Farida Souiah, and Simon Mastrangelo. 2015. "Les 'brûleurs' de frontières dans la musique populaire tunisienne: La migration non documentée au prisme de chanson de rap et de mezoued." *Afrique contemporaine* 254: 37–56.

Al-Samaany, Nasser. 2000. "Travel Literature of Moroccan Pilgrims during the 11–12th/17–18th Centuries: Thematic and Artistic Study." PhD diss., University of Leeds.

Sayad, Abdelmalek. 2000. "El Ghorba: From Original Sin to Collective Lie." *Ethnography* 1 (2): 147–71.

————. 2004. *The Suffering of the Immigrant*. Cambridge: Polity Press.

Sawa, George Dimitri. 2004. *Music Performance Practice in the Early ʿAbbasid Era 132–320 AH/750–932 AD*. 2nd ed. Ottawa: Institute of Medieval Music.

————, ed. 2019. *Musical and Socio-Cultural Anecdotes from Kitāb al-Aghānī al-Kabīr*. Leiden: Brill.

Sbihi, Ahmed. 1932. *Proverbes inédits des vieilles femmes marocaines: recueillis par Si Ahmed Sbhi*. Translated and with commentary by Abdelkader Benchehida. Fez: M. Debyeux.

Schade-Poulsen, Marc. 1999. *Men and Popular Music in Algeria: The Social Significance of Raï*. Austin: University of Texas Press.

Schuyler, Philip D. 1979. "A Repertory of Ideas: The Music of the Western 'Rwais,' Berber Professional Musicians from Southwestern Morocco." PhD diss., University of Washington.

———. 1984. "Berber Professional Musicians in Performance." In *Performance Practice: Ethnomusicological Perspectives*, edited by Gerard Béhague, 91–148. Westport, CT: Greenwood Press.

———. 1990–91. "Music and Tradition in Yemen." *Asian Music* 22 (1): 51–71.

Sebti, Abdelahad. 2001. "Variations marocaines autour du moment colonial." In *Les usages politiques du passé*, edited by François Hartod and Jacques Revel, 187–97. Paris: Éditions de l'École des Hautes Etudes en Sciences Sociales.

———. 2013. "Colonial Experiences and Territorial Practices." In Maghraoui, *Revisiting the Colonial Past in Morocco*, 38–65.

Seremetakis, Nadia, ed. 1994. *The Senses Still: Perception and Memory as Material Culture in Modernity*. Boulder, CO: Westview Press.

Sereni, Paolo. 2010. "Il lavoro degli immigrati." In *Primo rapporto sull'immigrazione in Umbria*. Perugia: Agenzia Umbria Ricerche.

Shannon, Jonathan Holt. 2006. *Among the Jasmine Trees: Music and Modernity in Contemporary Syria*. Middletown, CT: Wesleayan University Press.

———. 2015. *Performing al-Andalus: Music and Nostalgia across the Mediterranean*. Bloomington: Indiana University Press.

Shehadi, Fadlou. 1995. *Philosophies of Music in Medieval Islam*. New York: Brill.

Shepard, Todd. 2017. *Sex, France, and Arab Men, 1962–1979*. Chicago: University of Chicago Press.

Shiloah, Amnon. 1963. *Caractéristiques de l'art vocal arabe au Moyen-âge*. Tel-Aviv: Israel Music Institute.

———. 1991. "La voix et les techniques vocales chez les Arabes." *Cahiers d'ethnomusicologie* 4: 85–101.

Simour, Lhoussain. 2016. *Larbi Batma, Nass el-Ghiwan and Postcolonial Music in Morocco*. Jefferson, NC: McFarland.

Sonevytsky, Maria. 2019. *Wild Music: Sound and Sovereignty in Ukraine*. Middletown, CT: Wesleyan University Press.

Stokes, Martin. 2011. "Migrant/Migrating Music and the Mediterranean." In *Migrating Music*, edited by Jason Toynbee and Byron Dueck, 28–37. New York: Routledge.

Soum-Pouyalet, Fanny. 2007. *Le corps, la voix, le voile: Cheikhat marocaines*. Paris: CNRS.

Stetkevych, Jaroslav. 2016. *The Hunt in Arabic Poetry: From Heroic to Lyric to Metapoetic*. Notre Dame, IN: Notre Dame University Press.

Suárez-Navaz, Liliana. 2004. *Rebordering the Mediterranean: Boundaries and Citizenship in Southern Europe*. New York: Berghahn Books.

Swearingen, Will Davis. 1987. *Moroccan Mirages: Agrarian Dreams and Deceptions, 1912–1986*. Princeton, NJ: Princeton University Press.

Talley, Gwyneth. 2020. "Exceptional Horsewomen: Navigating the Moroccan Equestrian Sport of *tbourida*." *Journal of North African Studies*, https://doi.org/10.1080/13629387.2020.1833324.

Taraud, Christelle. 2008. "Genre, sexualité et colonisation: La colonisation française au Maghreb." In "Colonialismes," edited by Amandine Lauro, special issue, *Sextant* 25: 117–27.

————. 2016. "Virility in the Colonial Context: From the Late Eighteenth to the Twentieth Century." In *A History of Virility*, edited by Alain Corbin, Jean-Jacques Courtine, and Georges Vigarello, 325–45. New York: Columbia University Press.

Tazi, Nadia. 2018. *Le genre intraitable: Politique de la virilité dans le monde musulman.* Arles: Actes Sud.

Tenzon, Michele. 2019. "*Mise en valeur* and Repopulation in Colonial Rural Development in French Morocco." In *Routledge Handbook of Urban Planning in Africa*, edited by Carlos Nunes Silva, 44–60. London: Routledge.

Al Touma, Ali. 2018. *Guns, Culture and Moors: Racial Perceptions, Cultural Impacts and the Moroccan Participation in the Spanish Civil War (1936–1939).* London: Taylor & Francis.

Tozy, Mohamed. 2020. "Social Services Establish the Relationship between the Government and Those Who Are Governed." Interviewed by Moussa Matrouf. *Telquel*, 16 April. http://ar.telquel.ma/ع‏‎اجتمال‏‎ا-تامدخل‏‎ا-يزوطل‏‎ا-انوروك-سورد/.

Triki, Hamid, Thami Ouazzani, and Brigitte Barberi Daum. 1993. *La colline des potiers: Histoire d'une ville et de sa poterie.* Casablanca: Edition Lak International.

Valensi, Lucette. 1985. *Tunisian Peasants in the Eighteenth and Nineteenth Centuries.* Cambridge: Cambridge University Press.

Vacchiano, Francesco. 2013. "Fencing In the South: The Strait of Gibraltar as a Paradigm of the New Border Regime in the Mediterranean." *Journal of Mediterranean Studies* 22 (2): 337–64.

————. 2018. "Du *kariān* au *ħreg* et retour. Spatialité subalterne et désir d'émigration au Maroc." In *Citadinités subalterns en Afrique*, edited by Thomas Fouquet and Odile Goerg, 157–76. Paris: Éditions Karthala.

Wallach, Jeremy. 2008. *Modern Noise, Fluid Genres: Popular Music in Indonesia 1997–2001.* Madison: University of Wisconsin Press.

Waterbury, John. 1970. *The Commander and the Faithful: The Moroccan Political Elite; A Study in Segmented Politics.* New York: Columbia University Press.

————. 1991. "Peasants Defy Categorization (as Well as Landlords and the State)." In *Peasants and Politics in the Middle East*, edited by Farhad Kazemi and John Waterbury, 1–23. Miami: Florida International University Press.

Webb, Peter. 2016. *Imagining the Arabs: Arab Identity and the Rise of Islam.* Edinburgh: Edinburgh University Press.

Weidman, Amanda. 2014. "Anthropology and Voice." *Annual Review of Anthropology* 43: 37–51.

————. 2015. "Voice." In *Keywords in Sound*, edited by David Novak and Matt Sakakeeny, 232–45. Durham, NC: Duke University Press.

Williams, Raymond. 1973. *The Country and the City.* Oxford and New York: Oxford University Press.

Willoughby, Heather. 2012. "The Sound of Han: P'ansori, Timbre and a Korean Ethos of Pain and Suffering." *Yearbook for Traditional Music* 32: 17–30.

Wyrtzen, Jonathan. 2015. *Making Morocco: Colonial Intervention and the Politics of Identity.* Ithaca, NY: Cornell University Press.

Zartman, William. 1963. *Government and Politics in Northern Africa.* New York: Praeger.

Zika, Lamia. 2008. "Transforming the City from Below." In *Subaltern and Social Protest: History from Below in the Middle East and North Africa*, edited by Stephanie Cronin, 116–37. New York: Routledge.

Index

Abdelilah Ab.: map of migration route, 56, 78; personal narrative (*see under* personal narratives)

Abdelilah Am., 89–90, 116

Abdelilah Ry., 134

Abdelilah Ta., 80, 91, 115

Abdellah, Mulay, 163

Abdellah (first name), 1–2, 13

Abdellatif (first name), 116

Abderrahim (first name), 152

'abidat r-rma, 5, 7, 11–12, 28, 34, 63–64, 108, 113, 119, 121, 124, 129, 134; adaptation of genre, 64; analysis of rhythmic performance, 131–32; animal and human sounds, relationships between, 132–33; animal movements, mimicry of, 7, 119; animal sounds, mimicry of, 7, 119, 131–33, 136; audio formats of, 64; broadcasts of, 52; circulation of, 64–65; as clandestine communication, 119; cries, 131; dancing, 119; at festivals, 52; and *L-ḥarraga* (see *ḥarraga, L-*); instrumentation of, 7, 64–65, 76, 134 (*see also* musical instruments); origins in hunting, 131; Ouled Brahim (*'abidat r-rma* troupe), song text in Arabic and English, 76–78; poetic form of, 7; and poetry, 11; and *qaṣa'id* (odes, sing. *qaṣida*), 7 (see also *qaṣida*); *rami*, definition, 147–48; reclamation of, 34; recording techniques and technologies for, 64–65; recordings of, 52, 64–65; revalorization of, 52–53; saints and holy shrines in, 138;

silencing of, in colonial writing on music, 47. See also *ghaba, L-*

acrobatics and acrobats, 7, 31

agnatic solidarity, 18, 21. *See also* migrants, Moroccan: family-based migration

agribusiness. *See* Umbria: economy of; Umbria: farming in

Ahmed (first name), 60, 151–53

air travel, 9, 20, 57

Aissawa (religious order), 109

'aiṭa, 5–7, 11–12, 34, 47, 67, 94, 105–6, 113, 121, 123, 124, 129, 149, 151, 154–57, 158–71, 178; advocates for reforming the genre, 50; *brawǝl*, as light repertoire, 6; broadcasts of, 52; Chottin's description of, 49; as complex genre, 6; and dancing, 6, 168; definition of genre, 6–7; and festivals, 52, 122; as folklore at festivals, 122; instrumentation of, 6 (*see also* musical instruments); *klam* (text), 6; *naṣṣ* (text), 6; and *qaṣa'id* (odes, sing. *qaṣida*), 6; reclamation of, 34; recordings of, 52; revalorization of, 52–53; saints and holy shrines in, 138; in writing about music during the French Protectorate, 47–51. See also *Ḥajti fi grini; shikhat*

Akrout (first name), 129

aksak ("limping" rhythm), 131

al-Akbar, Mulay Idriss (778–921 CE), 137–38

al-ala (Andalusian musical tradition), 46, 107, 125

al-Andalus, 2, 78. See also *al-āla*

Al-Fārābī, 48